THE CONTROVERSY
OVER CAPITALISM

The Controversy over Capitalism

STUDIES IN THE
SOCIAL PHILOSOPHY
OF THE
RUSSIAN POPULISTS

BY

A. WALICKI

OXFORD
AT THE CLARENDON PRESS
1969

Oxford University Press, Ely House, London W. 1

GLASGOW NEW YORK TORONTO MELBOURNE WELLINGTON
CAPE TOWN SALISBURY IBADAN NAIROBI LUSAKA ADDIS ABABA
BOMBAY CALCUTTA MADRAS KARACHI LAHORE DACCA
KUALA LUMPUR SINGAPORE HONG KONG TOKYO

PRINTED IN GREAT BRITAIN

CONTENTS

ACKNOWLEDGEMENTS

THIS book was written in Oxford and owes much to a number of people. First of all, I am greatly indebted to the Warden and Fellows of All Souls College among whom I was privileged to work—as a visiting Fellow—in the academic year 1966/7. I can hardly exaggerate the debt I owe to Professor Sir Isaiah Berlin who has discussed with me the ideas contained in the book and who has helped me in many other ways. I deeply appreciate the painstaking efforts of my English friends—Mr. Harry Willetts, Mrs. Ellen de Kadt, and Mr. and Mrs. Arlene and Anthony Polonsky—who corrected the style of the book. I also wish to thank Mr. J. S. G. Simmons who helped me to find everything that I needed in the libraries of Oxford. Finally, I owe a real debt of gratitude to all those who contributed to the stimulating and friendly atmosphere which surrounded me during my stay in England.

ANDRZEJ WALICKI

Warsaw
April 1968

I

THE CONCEPT OF POPULISM

THIS book was not intended to be a comprehensive study of Russian Populism, its historical genesis, development, and decay. We confined ourselves to some aspects of the ideology of the *classical* Russian Populism and even within these limits our approach is not the strictly historical one. However, we are convinced that we have selected those aspects of Populism which are the most helpful for the proper understanding of what it really was. The most essential characteristic features of the full-fledged Russian Populism were revealed, we think, in its attitude towards capitalism and towards Marxism; towards capitalism and towards 'Capital'.

Such an approach, however, needs a justification. First of all, we must avoid terminological confusion. The term 'Populism' (*narodnichestvo*) has become associated with so many different meanings that it seems necessary to begin with the semantic question.

The need of a semantic inquiry into the history of the term 'Populism' has been realized both in the Soviet Union and in the West. It is significant that Boris Koz'min—the scholar whose works have played the leading part in the recent revival of the studies of Populism in the USSR—thought it necessary to dwell upon the semantic problems (although he had confined his inquiry to the word 'Populism' as used in the works of Lenin).[1] In the West this problem has been tackled by Richard Pipes who has given a systematic and useful study of the history of the word

[1] Cf. B. P. Koz'min, 'Narodnichestvo na burzhuazno-demokraticheskom étape osvoboditel'nogo dvizheniya v Rossii', *Istoricheskie zapiski*, vol. lxv, 1959. Reprinted in B. P. Koz'min, *Iz istorii revolutsionnoĭ mÿsli v Rossii*, Moscow 1961.

'Populism' and who has derived from it an interesting, though disputable, conclusion concerning the proper usage of this term.[1] This conclusion says, in short, that the concept of Populism, as presented, among others, by Koz'min, is in fact 'a polemical device created and popularized by Marxist publicists in the early nineties' and, as such, has 'no historical justification'.[2]

The present author is fully aware that his own usage of the term is closely bound up with precisely this concept of Populism which Pipes has dismissed as being 'historically unjustified'. Nevertheless, Pipes's article provides a useful point of departure from which to clarify the conception of Populism which we wish to present, and to justify, in this book.

On the face of it, wrote Pipes, the meaning of the term 'Populism' is obvious:

it describes an agrarian socialism of the second half of the nineteenth century, which upheld the proposition that Russia could by-pass the capitalist stage of development and proceed through the *artel'* and peasant commune directly to socialism. Its inspiration came from Herzen and Chernýshevskiĭ, and its strategy from Lavrov, Bakunin, and Tkachëv. It first manifested itself overtly in the 'going to the people' movement, and reached its zenith with the terror of the People's Will, after which it quickly lost ground to Marxism. This, as it were, classic conception of *narodnichestvo* constitutes, for example, the framework of the most recent and most extensive treatment of the subject, Professor Venturi's *Populismo russo*, originally published in 1952.[3]

It is to Pipes's merit that he called in question this 'classic' or, rather, current conception of Populism. He has established that the word 'Populism' has had two distinct and to some extent contradictory meanings—the narrow *historical* meaning and the broad Marxist one. The first of them he accepts, the second he, apparently, wants to eliminate as having been historically unjustified and 'rejected by those

---

[1] R. Pipes, 'Narodnichestvo: A Semantic Inquiry', *Slavic Review*, vol. xxiii, no. 3, September 1964.
[2] Ibid., p. 458.   [3] Ibid., pp. 441–2.

on whom it was pinned'.[1] We disagree with this conclusion but we accept the distinction and we think that a conscious choice between the two meanings of the word is a precondition of a consistent conception of Populism. In the first sense the term Populism denotes 'a theory advocating the hegemony of the masses over the educated elite',[2] in the second sense it denotes a theory of the non-capitalist development of Russia; in the first case it was opposed to the 'abstract intellectualism' of those revolutionaries who tried to teach the peasants, to impose on them the ideals of Western socialism, instead of learning what were their real needs and acting in the name of such interests and ideals of which the peasants had already become aware; in the second case it was opposed to sociological and economic theories which claimed that capitalism was an unavoidable stage of development and that Russia was no exception to this general law of evolution.

In the first sense, Populism, strictly speaking, was only a short episode in the Russian revolutionary movement: it emerged in the middle of the seventies and soon either gave way to new attitudes, represented by the revolutionary terrorists, or, having undergone an appropriate transformation, adopted the theoretical standpoint of Marxism. We may add to this that later, in the eighties and nineties, the view that the ideas of the intelligentsia should give way to the opinions of the people was upheld, and brought to dangerous extremes, by the followers of I. Kablits (Yuzov) who, in his fervent anti-intellectualism, came very close to reactionary obscurantism. We may also—abandoning the strictly 'historical' point of view—look for the 'Populist' attitude towards the peasant masses in the earlier years and find it among the 'Bakuninists' of the beginning of the seventies. It would be wholly unjustified, however, to apply the name 'Populists' (in its first sense) to the followers of Lavrov, to the Russian Jacobins or to the members of the

[1] Ibid., p. 458. [2] Ibid.

'Will of the People'; if we wish to use the word 'Populism' in its narrow, historical sense we must agree with Plekhanov that 'Will of the People' was a 'complete and universal rejection of Populism'.[1] It is evident, therefore, that the current conception of Populism, as described by Pipes and as presented in Venturi's otherwise excellent book is, from this point of view, too broad, since it comprises all the currents of the Russian revolutionary movement of the sixties and seventies, including the *Will of the People* in which, quite rightly, it sees the culmination of the Populist *revolutionary movement*.

In the second sense, Populism was not an organized movement but an ideology, a broad current of thought, differentiated within itself, having its representatives not only among revolutionaries but also among non-revolutionary publicists who advocated legal reforms in the interests of the peasantry. All the Russian revolutionaries of the seventies, irrespective of the differences in their views on revolutionary strategy and on the proper relation between the intelligentsia and the people, represented, in this sense, different variants of Populism. In this respect the current conception of Populism is more justified, but otherwise it lacks precision and tends to be too vague. On the other hand, it tends sometimes to be too narrow since it shifts the emphasis from Populist *ideology* to the Populist *revolutionary movement* and, especially, neglects non-revolutionary Populist thinkers, whose contribution to the Populist ideology was often greater than that of the revolutionaries; Mikhaĭlovskiĭ, for instance, who was in many respects the most representative and in-fluential theoretician of Populism, is hardly mentioned in Venturi's book and his theories are not discussed in it at all.[2] In a word: the conception of Populism which assumes that

---

[1] G. V. Plekhanov, *Izbrannȳe filosofskie proizvedeniya*, Moscow 1956, vol. i, p. 66 (quoted by Pipes, p. 453).

[2] It should be noted, however, that an English edition of Venturi's book appeared under the title: *Roots of Revolution. A History of the Populist and Socialist Movements in Nineteenth Century Russia*, London 1960. This title is much better

Populism 'reached its zenith with the terror of the People's Will' makes no clear distinction between Populism as such (i.e. Populism as a current of thought) and the Populist revolutionary movement—a distinction which *should* be made if we wish to avoid confusion.

Strictly speaking, it seems to us that Russian Populism in the broad sense of this word cannot be defined as a political *movement*. When we say 'the Populist revolutionary movement', we mean the revolutionary movement which had espoused the Populist *ideology*; the word 'Populist', therefore, defines not the movement but only some aspects of the *ideology* of the movement. The 'movement to the people' and the revolutionary terrorism represented very different, if not opposite, types of revolutionary movements; Tkachëv, the revolutionary 'Jacobin', and Vorontsov, the 'apolitical' reformist, had very little in common in terms of *political* attitudes. What united these very different men and very different movements was a certain body of ideas, certain attitudes towards capitalism, as opposed to the archaic structures of Russian social life.

The argument, put forward by Pipes against the second concept of Populism, consists in indicating that it was a relatively new usage of the word, introduced and popularized by Marxist publicists in the nineties; its main creator, we are told, was Struve, who, obviously disregarding the differences among the various adversaries of capitalist development in Russia, arbitrarily put them together under one label and modelled their controversies with Russian Marxists on the disputes between the Slavophiles and the Westernizers of the forties. This argument, however, is not convincing. Firstly, even in Struve's usage the new concept of Populism was not so abstract and arbitrary as to be applied 'to anyone who believed in the ability of Russia to by-pass capitalism';[1] it

than *Populismo russo* since it clearly indicates that the book deals not with Populism as a current of thought but with the Populist period in Russian revolutionary movement.

[1] R. Pipes, op. cit., p. 458.

was never applied, for instance, to Constantine Leont'ev although he was certainly a most resolute adversary of the bourgeois development of Russia. People to whom the label was applied represented different, sometimes mutually exclusive, variants of a really existing, though unnamed, broad current of thought; most of them were, at least partially, aware of it, and the name 'narodnichestvo' was not badly chosen since the belief in the 'principles of the people' (*narodnye nachala*), as opposed to capitalism, was bound up with almost all historically registered meanings of this word, even the most loose and imprecise ones. Secondly, though the role of Struve should not be overlooked, the new concept of Populism owes incomparably more to Lenin. It was Lenin who gave it a more concrete historical and sociological connotation by pointing out that Populism was a protest against capitalism from the point of view of the small immediate producers who, being ruined by capitalist development, saw in it only a retrogression but, at the same time, demanded the abolition of the older, feudal forms of exploitation. It was Lenin, and not Struve, who laid the foundation of the Soviet scholarly achievements in this field; the prejudiced, unfair treatment of Populism and the scarcity, if not virtual absence, of works on it, so characteristic, unfortunately, of a long period in the development of social sciences in the USSR, was connected with an obvious deviation from the position of Lenin.[1] Koz'min, therefore, was quite right in calling for a return to Lenin in order to eliminate these prejudices and to undo the harm which had been brought about by them.

This does not mean, of course, that it is either possible or desirable to look at Russian Populism from the perspective of the 1890s. Too many things have changed since that time.

---

[1] Koz'min wrote about this: 'Only Lenin's criticism of Populism was reproduced and Lenin's recognition of the great historical significance of this current of revolutionary thought was passed over in silence. This practice amounted sometimes to an open falsification.' (B. P. Koz'min, *Iz istorii revolutsionnoǐ mysli v Rossii*, p. 640.)

Plekhanov's scheme of the development of Russia has been invalidated by the fact that the Russian socialist revolution almost coincided in time with the overthrow of absolutism and that socialist production has been organized there despite the relative backwardness and isolation of the country. The very applicability of universal patterns of development must be called in question in view of the new problems which have been posed by the new, ex-colonial nations; the idea of the non-capitalist development of backward peasant countries has become a reality—although a hard and difficult reality—in many parts of our world. All these factors seriously undermined the position of classical evolutionism in the social sciences against which Russian Populists had so strongly protested already at the time of its indisputable domination of sociology. Its theory of unilinear social development has been attacked from many quarters: by the functionalists, by the diffusionists who advanced the thesis that a civilization might skip a stage of development because of the borrowing and diffusion of cultural items, and, finally and most radically, by the cultural relativists. The Marxist theory of economic development has also undergone a considerable change, and different schools have emerged within it. We are convinced that these new historical data and corresponding shifts in theoretical thinking should be taken into account and utilized as a new vantage point for the study of Russian Populism. Nevertheless Lenin's conception of Populism seems to us to be still the best point of departure. His position in relation to Populism reminds us in some respects of the position of Marx in relation to the Left-Hegelians. And although Marx was often too severe, or even unjust, in his criticism of 'the German ideology' there can be little doubt that he knew it perfectly and that his view of it should not be disregarded by the students of the German thought.

Koz'min has rightly noticed that Lenin, like everybody in his time, used the word *narodnichestvo* in many senses, including the narrow historical sense. The most important of these different usages of the term was, according to him, the broadest one. In this sense Populism was, as Lenin put it, 'a whole vision of the world whose history begins with Herzen and ends with Danielson';[1] it was 'a theoretical doctrine that gives a particular solution to highly important sociological and economic problems',[2] 'a major trend' in Russian social thought,[3] 'an immense area of social thinking'.[4] It was the common term for all democratic ideologies in Russia—both revolutionary and non-revolutionary—which expressed the standpoint of small producers (particularly peasants) and looked for ways of non-capitalist economic development; a term which could be applied not only to the revolutionaries of the seventies and to the so-called 'liberal Populists' of the eighties–nineties but also to Chernȳshevskiĭ and, to some extent, to the peasant parties of the beginning of the twentieth century. We agree with Koz'min that this broad meaning of the word 'Populism' is very important for the correct understanding of Lenin's view on the subject. It seems worth while to notice that in some of Lenin's articles the term 'Populism' is applied—as a certain typological category—to some non-Russian ideologies: thus, for instance, in the article 'Democracy and Populism in China' (1912) the ideology of Sun Yat-sen has been classified as 'Populist': 'the Chinese democrat', writes Lenin, 'argues exactly like a Russian. His similarity to a Russian Populist is so great that it goes as far as a complete identity of fundamental ideas and of many individual expressions.'[5] This broad comparative perspective seems to us very attractive

[1] *Leninskii sbornik*, vol. xix, p. 237 (quoted by Koz'min, op. cit., pp. 645–6).
[2] V. I. Lenin, *Collected Works*, Moscow–London (since 1960), vol. i, p. 337.
[3] Ibid., p. 338.
[4] *Leninskii sbornik*, vol. xix, p. 237.
[5] V. I. Lenin, *Collected Works*, vol. xviii, p. 163. (In this edition of Lenin's works the word 'narodnichestvo' is rendered 'narodism'; we think, however, that it is appropriate to replace this awkward neologism with the generally accepted term 'Populism'.)

and valuable. It enables us to see Russian Populism as a particular variant of an ideological pattern which emerges in different backward societies in periods of transition and reflects the characteristic class position of the peasantry. It does not mean, of course, that Populism can be regarded as a *direct* expression of peasant ideology; it is an ideology formulated by a democratic intelligentsia who in backward countries, lacking a strong bourgeois class structure, enjoy as a rule greater social authority and play a more important part in national life than intellectuals in the economically more developed states.

In the Soviet Union Koz'min's reconstruction of Lenin's conception of Populism amounted to a revision and rejection of the prevailing canon of interpretation: a canon which artificially opposed the 'revolutionary democrats' of the sixties to the Populists of the seventies, separated Chernȳshevskiĭ from the later ideologists of Populism, in whom only a 'lowering of thought' was seen, and depreciated the historical significance of both Populist thought and the Populist revolutionary movement. To reject this canon meant to remove a great obstacle which had for a long time stood in the way of an unprejudiced and sympathetic approach to the subject.

The recognition that Chernȳshevskiĭ must not be separated from, let alone opposed to, Populism, should not lead, however, to the obliteration of differences which distinguished him from the full-fledged Populism of the seventies. We think that Koz'min went too far in his attempt to put the emphasis on Chernȳshevskiĭ's Populism, and that he was wrong in rejecting the long-established view that Populism in its *classical* form had emerged only at the end of the sixties.[1] His reconstruction of Lenin's conception of Populism is one-sided, since it obviously tends to disregard Lenin's distinction

---

[1] As to Venturi, he has acknowledged that 'strictly speaking' before 1870 there was only pre-Populism in Russia but he gave up this discrimination in order to avoid pedantry (cf. *Roots of Revolution*, preface, p. xxxiii).

between the 'heritage' of the sixties (i.e. the heritage of Chernyshevskiĭ), and the Populist 'addition' to it. He was right when he emphasized that, according to Lenin, the history of the Populist socialism can and should be traced back to the 'Russian socialism' of Herzen. He was wrong, however, when he suggested that Lenin's acknowledgement of Herzen's contribution to the Populist theories amounted to ranking him among the Populists. It seems proper to remind that Lenin, after all, was quite unequivocal in classifying Herzen as a 'gentry revolutionary', that is, a representative of an earlier, pre-Populist phase in the development of Russian revolutionary thought.[1]

An examination of the views of the early Populists and all those thinkers who had contributed to the Populist doctrine lies outside the scope of this study. However, if we wish to make clearer our conception of Populism (and our interpretation of Lenin's conception of it), we cannot avoid a short discussion of the relationship between the classical Populism and the ideas of its 'fathers'.

Let us dwell first on the 'Populism' of Herzen. Like the Populists, he opposed the bourgeois development of Russia and hoped for her direct transition to socialism through the peasant commune. It is striking, however, how different was his image of capitalism and the viewpoint from which he criticized it. He did not think of capitalism in terms of political economy; the standpoint of the small producer, being divorced from his means of production by the development of the large-scale capitalist industry, was completely absent in his criticism of the capitalist West. Strictly speaking, he criticized not capitalism as an economic formation (of which he had no clear notion) but bourgeois society as a socio-cultural phenomenon, interpreting it in 'historiosophical' terms as a symptom of the final decay of the decrepit 'old world'. He was repelled by *bourgeoisie* whom he treated, with a somewhat aristocratic contempt, as a class of vulgar and

[1] Cf. Lenin, *Collected Works*, vol. xviii (In Memory of Herzen).

depraved upstarts. For the Populists, who, as we shall see, were in this respect disciples of Marx, capitalism was tantamount with the expropriation, proletarianization, and utter misery of the masses. For Herzen, on the contrary, capitalism was a stage of final stabilization and growing welfare; he did not hesitate to state that even the problem of proletariat has subsided, that the worker in all European countries is a future bourgeois.[1] In contrast with the Populists's (and Marx's) concern about the growing pauperization of the masses, he saw capitalism as an epoch of the social advance of the masses, and attributed this advance to *bourgeoisie*:

With the coming of bourgeoisie individual characters are effaced, but these effaced persons are better fed (. . .) the beauty of the race is effaced, but its prosperity increases. . . . It is for this reason that bourgeoisie is triumphing and is bound to triumph. It is useless to tell a hungry man: 'It suits you better to be hungry, don't look for food.'[2]

This is, certainly, the opposite of the Populist view of capitalism. It would be fair to say that Herzen criticized capitalism not from the Populist but, rather, from the aristocratic standpoint. It is difficult to imagine a more aristocratic attitude towards 'the crowd' than this:

I had grown to hate the crowding and crush of civilization . . . I looked with horror mixed with disgust at the continually moving, swarming crowd, foreseeing how it would rob me of half of my seat at the theatre and in the diligence, how it would dash like a wild beast into the railway carriages, how it would heat and pervade the air.[3]

It is really amazing how little was Herzen interested in, and acquainted with, the painful contradictions of capitalist development, how little was he worried by the prospect of the proletarianization of artisans and peasants; this whole

[1] A. Herzen, 'Ends and Beginning', in *My Past and Thoughts*, vol. vi, London 1927 (transl. by C. Garnett), pp. 11–12.
[2] Ibid., p. 12. [3] Ibid., p. 14.

set of problems, which had been posed by the 'petty-bourgeois socialists' (Sismondi) and, later, reinterpreted by Marx, was almost completely alien to his image of the 'final stage' of the 'old world'. He looked at capitalism from the other end—not from the point of view of the high price of industrialization but from the point of view of its major result—the cheap and standardized consumption. And in this respect his observations (like the similar observations of Tocqueville) were sometimes very far-sighted, not pre-Marxian but rather post-Marxian, anticipating the criticism of what we now call 'mass society' and 'mass culture'. He wrote:

Everything—the theatre, holiday making, books, pictures, clothes—everything has gone down in quality and gone up terribly in numbers. The crowd of which I was speaking is the best proof of success, of strength, of growth; it is bursting through all the dams, overflowing and flooding everything; it is content with anything and can never have enough.

Everywhere the hundred-thousand-headed hydra lies in wait to listen to everything, to look at everything indiscriminately, to be dressed in anything, to be fed on anything—this is the all-powerful crowd of 'conglomerated mediocrity' (to use Stuart Mill's expression) which purchases everything and so dominates everything.[1]

There is nothing—absolutely nothing—Populist in *this* kind of criticism of the bourgeois society. Populism was a broad current of Russian democratic thought which reflected the class standpoint of small producers (mainly peasants), willing to get rid of the remnants of serfdom, but, at the same time, endangered by the development of capitalism. If this definition (given by Lenin) is to be accepted and taken seriously, we must conclude that Herzen cannot be described as a Populist. It is justified to begin the history of the Populist theories with his 'Russian socialism'; it is unjustified, however, to present Herzen as an ideologist of small producers. He was

---

[1] A. Herzen, 'Ends and Beginning', in *My Past and Thoughts*, vol. vi, London 1927 (transl. by C. Garnett), pp. 15-16.

THE CONCEPT OF POPULISM

not a 'petty-bourgeois socialist'; he was a 'gentry revolutionary' and a 'gentry socialist', a disappointed aristocratic liberal, a disillusioned Westernizer, who, having
despaired about the West, looked for consolation in the
thought that his own country had not yet reached its 'final
form'. There is nothing accidental in the fact that he had
great difficulty in finding a common language with the
democratic 'raznochintsy̆' of the sixties; that he sharply
polemized with Chernȳshevskiĭ and Dobrolyubov, defending
the spiritual heritage of the 'superfluous men' of the gentry;
that the revolutionaries of the so-called 'young emigration'
accused him of lordliness and liberalism and, finally, broke
off even their personal relations with him.[1] It is understandable that he, on his part, was repelled by their
plebeian roughness and in his splendid memoirs *My Past and
Thoughts* emphasized with pride that he belonged to a better
generation—to 'the men of the forties'. The great historical
significance of his 'Russian socialism' consists, among
others, in the fact that it was the most important and direct
link between the Slavophilism and Westernism of the
forties and the Populist ideologies of the second half of the
century.[2]

---

[1] Cf. Koz'min's study 'Gertsen, Ogarëv i "molodaya émigratsiya"' (in his
Iz istorii revolyutsionnoĭ mȳsli v Rossii, pp. 483–578).

[2] Herzen's doctrine of the 'Russian Socialism' can be described as an attempt
at a kind of synthesis of the conflicting views of Russia's past and future, which
had emerged in the epoch of Nicholas I. Like Chaadaev—an aristocratic
Westernizer, a strange and lonely religious thinker whose splendid intellectual
portrait is painted in Herzen's memoirs—Herzen asserted that Russia was 'a
country without history', a country where no 'burden of the past' would
hinder the introduction of a new and better social order. With the Slavophiles
he shared the belief in the peasant commune as the germ of social regeneration
and the conviction that collectivism (identified by him with socialism or even
communism) was inherent in the character of the Russian people; at the beginning of the fifties he went so far as to proclaim that socialism was a bridge on
which he and the Slavophiles could meet and join hands. (A. I. Gersten,
Sobranie sochineniĭ, vol. vii, Moscow 1957, p. 118). And, finally, he remained true
to the idea of free, autonomous personality which constituted the core of the
Weltanschauung of the classical Westernism of the forties. The peasant commune, he thought, should be permeated by the 'idea of personality', which had
been introduced to Russia from the West and which was represented by the

Chernȳshevskiĭ's case was very different from Herzen's. In view of its crucial importance for the systematization and interpretation of Lenin's conception of Populism, it seems proper to examine it within the framework of Lenin's general views on the development of the Russian social thought. To do this we must begin with Lenin's category of 'Enlightenment' (*prosvestitel'stvo*) which was, and still is, a source of many misunderstandings.

The category of 'Enlightenment' in its application to the Russian 'heritage of the sixties' was introduced first by Plekhanov who was struck by the similarity between the philosophical views of the Russian radical democrats of the sixties and the eighteenth-century French enlighteners. Indeed, the materialism and common-sense rationalism of the Russian radicals of the period of reforms was bound up with the eighteenth-century concept of an essentially unchangeable and rational 'human nature'. This concept, looming behind Chernȳshevskiĭ's 'anthropological principle', served them as powerful means in their passionate struggle against the institutions, traditions, and prejudices of a semi-feudal society, which was similar to the struggle once waged by the thinkers of the French Enlightenment. Unhistorical and dogmatic eighteenth-century rationalism was especially strong in Dobrolyubov who saw the very essence of progress in the eternal fight of 'natural' tendencies of development against 'unnatural' ones. The philosophical views of Chernȳshevskiĭ, set forth mainly in his *Anthropological Principle in Philosophy* (1860),[1] were more complicated, for he tried to combine the naturalism and rationalism of the Enlightenment with some elements of historicism and Hegelian dialectics.

Russian intelligentsia, especially by the educated Russian gentry. The task of 'Russian socialism' was thus to reconcile the values of the Westernized Russian intelligentsia with the 'communism' of the Russian peasantry: 'to preserve the commune and to render the individual free' (Gertsen, *Sobranie sochinenii*, vol. xii, p. 156). For a detailed analysis of the relationship between Herzen's 'Russian socialism' and the Slavophiles–Westernizers controversy of the forties, see A. Walicki, *W kręgu konserwatywnej utopii*, Warsaw 1964, chap. 16.

[1] Cf. N. G. Chern˜shevskiĭ, *Selected Philosophical Essays*, Moscow 1953.

He considered himself a disciple of Feuerbach and indeed there were some characteristically Feuerbachian motifs in his anthropocentrism, in his staunch defence of the human individual against the usurpations of the Hegelian hypostases of 'the General'.[1] On the whole, however, his 'anthropological principle', together with his theory of 'rational egoism' (very similar to the theory of Helvetius), coincided in essentials with the cruder Dobrolyubov's concept of 'human nature'; its inseparable moral ingredient, its emphasis upon anthropocentrism and upon the liberation of the individual, made it consonant with the true spirit of the European Enlightenment.

From Plekhanov's point of view the most essential was the fact that both the French and the Russian 'enlighteners' (including Chernȳshevskiĭ) were historical idealists, seeing the progresses of human intellect and the spread of enlightenment as prime movers of historical development of society. Lenin, having accepted the concept of the 'Russian Enlightenment' of the 1860s, gave it a different cast: from his point of view the most important was not the theoretical but the socio-historical content of the views of the 'enlighteners'. For him the essential analogy between the ideology of the eighteenth-century Enlightenment and the Russian radicalism of the sixties consisted, first of all, in their anti-feudal, bourgeois-democratic quality: both, according to him, represented bourgeois democracy in the climax of its ascending phase, in which it was still honest, courageous, unequivocally progressive, and bound up with a sincere concern about the general happiness of mankind.

The characterization of the Russian 'Enlightenment' was given by Lenin in his article 'The Heritage We Renounce'.

[1] We may find these motifs even in his aesthetics, in his early dissertation *The Aesthetic Relation Between Art and Reality* (1853), in which he proclaimed that the highest and most authentic beauty is to be found not in the realm of Platonic ideals or the Hegelian Spirit but among men of flesh and blood, among real and individual human beings. (The conclusion of his argument was that art is merely a substitute for nature and that beauty is identical with the fullness of life.)

He enumerated the following features of it: (1) 'violent hostility to serfdom and *all its* economic, social and legal products', (2) 'ardent advocacy of education, self-government, liberty, European forms of life and all-round Europeanization of Russia generally', (3) 'defence of the interests of the masses, chiefly of the peasants (who, in the days of the enlighteners, were not yet fully emancipated or only in the process of being emancipated), the sincere belief that abolition of serfdom and its survivals would be followed by universal well-being, and a sincere desire to help bring this about'.[1] 'These three features', concluded Lenin, 'constitute the essence of what in our country is called "the heritage of the sixties", and it is important to emphasize that *there is nothing whatsoever of Populism in this heritage*'.[2] For an example of what he meant by 'Russian enlightener' Lenin chose Skaldin who had been a rather mediocre and second-class writer. One of the reasons for this decision was simply Russian censorship, which would not permit an open reference to the heritage of Chernȳshevskiĭ. There can be no doubt, however, that according to Lenin not Skaldin but Chernȳshevskiĭ was the central figure among the 'enlighteners' of the sixties. The article 'The Heritage We Renounce' is thus a serious argument for the thesis that in Lenin's conception Chernȳshevskiĭ and the Populists represented two different currents of thought.

---

[1] Lenin, *Collected Works*, vol. ii, p. 504.

[2] Ibid., pp. 504–5. Populism, as opposed to the 'heritage', was characterized by Lenin as 'a system of views which comprises the following three features': (1) 'Belief that capitalism in Russia represents a deterioration, a retrogression', (2) 'Belief in the exceptional character of the Russian economic system in general, and of the peasantry, with its village community, *artel'*, etc., in particular', (3) 'Disregard of the connection between the "intelligentsia" and the country's legal and political institutions, on the one hand, and the material interests of definite social classes on the other' (ibid., pp. 513–14. The last point referred to the so-called 'subjective sociology'). In a later article ('Democracy and Populism in China') Lenin took the view that Populism 'in the specific sense of that term, i.e. as distinct from democracy, as a supplement to democracy', consisted in a combination of advocacy of radical agrarian reform with 'socialist dreams, with hopes of avoiding the capitalist path' (ibid., vol. xviii, pp. 165–6).

Koz'min who was, of course, aware of it, set against this argument a thesis that in Lenin's conception the opposition between 'enlighteners' and Populists was not absolute: an 'enlightener' could be at the same time a Populist. This is perfectly true, and there is no doubt that it was so in the case of Chernÿshevskiĭ. Koz'min had rightly noticed that Lenin's characterization of Skaldin as a typical 'enlightener' could be applied to Chernÿshevskiĭ only partially. Let us try to develop this thought. Like Skaldin, Chernÿshevskiĭ was an ardent Westernizer, a propagator of the 'all-round Europeanization of Russia', at the same time, however, in contrast with Skaldin, he defended with great energy the peasant commune in which the liberal economists saw the greatest drag on the European development of Russia. Skaldin sharply criticized Russian serfdom but (in contra-distinction to the Populists) was not aware of the painful contradictions of capitalist progress; this could not be said about Chernÿshevskiĭ, who wanted to protect the Russian peasantry from the sufferings bound up with the classical English type of capitalist development. Skaldin propagated the ideas of Adam Smith and of the liberal political economy; Chernÿshevskiĭ criticized these ideas from the point of view of an 'economy of the working masses', denounced the apolo-gists of bourgeois industrialism whom he accused of making an idol of 'national wealth' and neglecting the welfare of the people (but—it should be stressed—he did not share the view that capitalism as such was but 'a deterioration, a retrogression'). It is justified to conclude from this that Russian censorship was not *the only* reason for Lenin's decision to choose Skaldin, and not Chernÿshevskiĭ, as an example of a typical 'enlightener': he wished to present an 'enlightener' who had *not* been a Populist, who could exemplify the *pure form* of the antifeudal ideology of the radical bourgeois democracy. The democratism of Skaldin could not stand the comparison with the democratism of Chernÿshevskiĭ but it had, from this point of view, the important advantage of

C

being free from any Populist 'addition'. Lenin himself wrote: 'We have taken Skaldin as an example precisely because, while he was *undoubtedly* a representative of the "heritage", he was at the same time a confirmed enemy of those ancient institutions which the Populists have taken under their protection.'[1]

As we know, Chernȳshevskiĭ, in contrast with Skaldin, was himself a convinced protector of the 'ancient institution' of the peasant commune. He even proposed to the Slavophiles a kind of alliance for the joint defence of the commune against liberal economists, who demanded that it be abolished together with feudal bondage (this alliance, however, could not be concluded, because the motives of the two partners were entirely different).[2] In his *Criticism of Philosophical Prejudices Against the Communal Ownership of the Land* (1859) he argued that Russia, and backward countries in general, could benefit from the experience and scientific achievements of the West and, thanks to this, skip the 'intermediate stages of development' or at least enormously reduce their length. His main argument for the commune was a dialectical conception of progress, claiming that the first stage of any development is, as a rule, similar in form to the third; thus, primitive communal collectivism is similar in form to the developed collectivism of a socialist society and can make easier a direct transition to it. The Populists, who, as we shall see, reinterpreted this argumentation in terms of the dialectical triad which they had found in Marx's *Capital*,[3] made it the main theoretical foundation of their views. And it may be added that they were quite right in considering themselves to be the continuators of Chernȳshevskiĭ's

---

[1] Lenin, *Collected Works*, vol. ii, p. 505.

[2] Cf. the following statement of Chernȳshevskiĭ: 'There are in Slavophilism some healthy elements which deserve to be supported. And, if we were to choose, Slavophilism is much better than this intellectual torpor, this denial of modern ideas which so often appears among us under the aegis of fidelity to the Western civilization.' (Chernȳshevskiĭ, *Polnoe sobranie sochineniĭ*, vol. iv, Moscow 1948, p. 760.)

[3] See p. 60.

thought: in both cases the defence of the peasant commune was motivated by a deep concern for the welfare of the peasantry whom they wished to protect against expropriation and proletarianization. There was a true Populist sentiment in Chernȳshevskiï's words:

... let us not dare touch on the sacred and saving custom that we have inherited from our past, all the misery of which is redeemed by one invaluable legacy—let us not dare assault the common use of land—the great bounty on the introduction of which depends now the welfare of land-tilling classes in Western Europe. May their example be a lesson to us.[1]

And yet, there was a lot of quite conspicuous and significant differences between Chernȳshevskiï and the full-fledged, classical Populism of the seventies. Chernȳshevskiï did not think that the preservation of the commune was incompatible with the capitalist development and, on the whole, was by no means an adversary of the bourgeois progress in Russia. Like the other 'enlighteners' of the sixties he was a convinced Westernizer and, as such, resolutely rejected Herzen's image of the 'decrepit Europe';[2] the Russians, he thought, should still learn from the West and humbly recognize the superiority of Western achievements.[3] He wished for Russia a shortened, more rapid, and more humane progress, but he never opposed Russia to the West and rejected the view that the Russian peasant commune represented a germ of a different and higher type of social development. He was aware of the painful contradictions of capitalism but he still thought it to represent a great progress in comparison with the pre-capitalist forms of society; he bitterly criticized the epigones of the liberal political economy but, in sharp contrast with Mikhaïlovskiï, Eliseev, Tkachëv,

[1] Chernȳshevskiï, *Izbrannȳe ékonomicheskie proizvedeniya*, Moscow 1948, vol. i, p. 108 (quoted in the translation by A. Gerschenkron, *Economic Backwardness in Historical Perspective*, New York–London 1962, p. 172).
[2] See Chernȳshevskiï's article 'O prichinakh padeniya Rima' ['On the causes of the fall of the ancient Rome'], in *Polnoe sobranie sochineniï*, vol. vii, Moscow 1950, pp. 643–69.
[3] Ibid., p. 663.

and other Populists of the seventies, highly appreciated the
merits of its classics. In short, his 'enemy number 1' was not
capitalism but Russian backwardness—'asiatic conditions
of life, asiatic social structure, asiatic order'.[1]

It is very significant that after the abolition of serfdom
the Populist traits of Chernȳshevskiǐ's ideology began to
give way to the 'bourgeois democratic' political radicalism.
Before the reform he emphasized that the democrats were
sworn enemies only of the aristocratic party and thus hinted
that they could be reconciled with absolutism on condition
that it would carry out progressive social policy.[2] After the
reform, bitterly disappointed with its results and with the
'bureaucratic' (read: autocratic) way in which it had been
prepared, he came to the conclusion that no social question
could be successfuly resolved in Russia without political
change, i.e. without breaking the chains of autocracy.[3]
In the seventies, in his Siberian exile, he clung to this conviction so firmly that he even refused to read books on the
peasant question and on the peasant commune. In one of his
letters he wrote: 'I am sick of such things . . . I nauseate at
"peasants" and "peasant landholding".'[4] The meaning of
this harsh judgement is quite clear: in contrast with the
Populists, who, as we shall see, proclaimed a peculiar 'apoliticism', Chernȳshevskiǐ thought that in Russian conditions
it was utterly meaningless to approach social problems in
abstraction from the urgent need of a political change.

The difference between the 'heritage' and classical
Populism—that is, by the same token, between Chernȳshevskiǐ and his Populist disciples—will be even clearer if we
confront the category of 'Enlightenment' with the category
of 'economic romanticism'—a category which has been
applied by Lenin in his analyses of the economic and social

[1] *Polnoe sobranie sochineniǐ*, vol. v, p. 698.
[2] Cf. ibid., p. 216.
[3] See p. 84.
[4] Quoted in Yu. Steklov, *N. G. Chernȳshevskiǐ, ego zhizn' i deyatel'nost'*, Moscow–
Leningrad 1928, vol. i, p. 450.

content of Populism.[1] It will not be a great simplification to say that the representatives of the 'heritage of the sixties' were seen by Lenin predominantly as 'enlighteners' whereas the Populists were seen by him predominantly as 'romanticists'. 'Romanticism' means in this context a criticism of capitalism from the point of view of a backward-looking petty-bourgeois utopia, an idealization of a pre-capitalist type of economic and social relations. The 'enlighteners', in Lenin's view, were the ideologists of radical bourgeois democracy, fighting against the remnants of feudalism, with confidence in capitalist progress but not seeing or underestimating its negative sides (Chernȳshevskiĭ, who saw them clearly, was in this respect not a typical 'enlightener'). The Populists, as opposed to the 'enlighteners', were the ideologists of democracy who, having realized the tragic contradictions inherent in capitalist development, made a step forward in comparison with the 'enlighteners':

> Populism [wrote Lenin] made a big *step forward* compared with the heritage *by posing* for the attention of society problems which the guardians of the heritage were partly (in their time) not yet able to pose, or partly did not, and do not, pose because of their inherent narrowness of outlook. In *posing* these problems the Populists performed a great *historical* service, and it is quite natural and understandable, that, having offered a solution (whatever it may be worth) for these problems, Populism, *thereby* occupied a foremost place among the progressive trends of Russian social thought.[2]

At the same time, however, it was a step backward since the Populists, having lost all confidence in the bourgeois, 'European' progress, adopted the standpoint of 'economic romanticism'. The ideology of 'Enlightenment' was dominant in the Russian democratic movement in the sixties, i.e. when the attention of all progressive Russians was focused on the struggle for the abolition of serfdom; Populism was

---

[1] Cf. especially 'A Characterisation of Economic Romanticism', Lenin, *Collected Works*, vol. ii.   [2] Ibid., pp. 515–16.

an ideological reflection of the new problems which emerged in Russia after the reform. Both the 'enlighteners' and the Populists defended the interests of 'the people' (i.e. first of all, the interests of peasantry); the Populists, however, in contradistinction to the 'enlighteners', combined in their ideology an anti-feudal bourgeois democratism with a petty-bourgeois conservative reaction against bourgeois progress. That is why the 'heritage of the sixties' was un-equivocally progressive while the heritage of Populism was in this respect rather ambiguous. In Lenin's words: 'That is why the Populist, in matters of theory, is just as much a Janus, looking with one face to the past and the other to the future.'[1]

The 'reactionary' face of the Populist Janus was seen by Lenin in Populist socialism. In the 'general democratic points' of their programmes the Populists were progressive but their socialist theories were—according to Lenin— petty-bourgeois, utopian, and permeated by reactionary 'economic romanticism'.

To many of us this judgement may appear too severe. But we must not forget the sense in which Lenin applied to Populism the term 'reactionary'.

This term [he explained] is employed in its historico-philosophical sense, describing only the *error* of the theoreticians who take models for their theories from *obsolete* forms of society. It does not apply at all to the personal qualities of these theoreticians or to their programmes. Everybody knows that neither Sismondi nor Proudhon were reactionaries in the ordinary sense of the term.[2]

We think that two other qualifications should be added to this. Firstly, it seems to us that in approaching populist socialism from the perspective of our times, it is difficult to deny that not only the 'backward-looking' but also the 'forward-looking' face of Janus can be discovered in it. Secondly, we think that some 'reactionary' ideologies should not be easily dismissed, that a 'reactionary' standpoint in

---

[1] Lenin, *Collected Works*, vol. i, p. 503.
[2] Ibid., vol. ii, p. 217.

social theory ('reactionary' in the 'historico-philosophical' sense) can sometimes be not an obstacle but a vantage point. It was the 'reactionary' character of their social ideals which enabled the Western petty-bourgeois socialists to discover aspects of capitalism which remained unnoticed by the liberal apologists of bourgeois progress.[1] In his treatise *A Characterisation of Economic Romanticism* Lenin drew an impressive parallel between the economic views of the Populists and the views of Sismondi. The parallel is, on the whole, convincing, but it would be a great simplification to conclude from it that the Populists were merely epigones of Sismondi. Populism emerged in a backward country but, nevertheless, the populist economists of the eighties and nineties could not be 'pure' followers of Sismondi. They knew that the 'socialization of labour' and a large-scale industrialization was necessary for the development and independence of their country; after all, they had read Marx and learned a great deal from him. 'The social process of development does not consist in a mechanical repetition of the sequence of phases through which the more advanced societies have already passed.'[2] This generalization, we think, may also be applied to the history of ideas, and Russian Populism provides a good illustration of it.

To sum up. We agree with Pipes that the 'broad and objective' definition of Populism has been introduced by

---

[1] 'This school of Socialism dissected with great acuteness the contradictions in the condition of modern production. It laid bare the hypocritical apologies of economists. It proved, inconvertibly, the disastrous effects of machinery and division of labour; the concentration of capital and land in a few hands; over-production and crisis; it pointed out the inevitable ruin of the petty bourgeois and peasant, the misery of the proletariat, the anarchy in production, the crying inequalities in the distribution of wealth, the industrial war of extermination between nations, the dissolution of old moral bonds, of the old family relations, of the old nationalities.' (K. Marx and F. Engels, *Communist Manifesto: Socialist Landmark*. With an Introduction by Harold J. Laski, London 1948, pp. 156–7.)

[2] W. Kula, *Problemy i metody historii gospodarczej* [*Problems and Methods of Economic History*], Warsaw 1963, p. 715.

Marxists, we think, however, that it is by no means as 'broad' as to be applied 'to anyone who believed in the ability of Russia to by-pass capitalism'.[1] It is in fact—in any case in Lenin's usage—much more precise, and cannot be dismissed as a mere 'polemical device'. It is rather a *methodological device*, and a very good one. It delineates an important set of problems, enables us to prescind from mere political or doctrinal divisions and to see the essential unity of a socially determined *Weltanschauung*; it is precise enough as a means of classification and can be made even more precise, since it gives good reasons for making a useful distinction between 'classical Populism' of the post-reform period and 'early Populism', or 'pre-Populism' of the sixties. This distinction, it should be stressed, does not amount to saying that the 'early Populists' were not 'true Populists'; it indicates only that 'Populism' is a dynamic, and not a static, concept.

We agree with Koz'min that the history of Populism began with Herzen and Chernȳshevskiĭ; we think, however, that *classical* Populism emerged only at the turn of the sixties to the seventies. There is no doubt that the 'Russian socialism' of Herzen was an immediate predecessor of Populist socialism but, nevertheless, it would be an oversimplification to call Herzen simply a Populist: he belonged to a different generation, was the product of a different intellectual formation, and deserves a separate chapter in the history of Russian social thought. Chernȳshevskiĭ too, although much more a Populist than Herzen, cannot be called a *full-fledged* Populist. In many respects he *was* a Populist but his significance in Russian intellectual history should not be reduced to his Populism. He was first of all an 'enlightener' and his Populism was, as it were, a Populism *in statu nascendi*, emerging *within* the ideological framework of the Russian 'Enlightenment' of the sixties. Among his legitimate continuators and

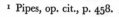

---

[1] Pipes, op. cit., p. 458.

disciples are found not only Populists but also Pisarev whose ideology was decidedly anti-Populist.[1]

Lenin's conception of Populism is for us a kind of 'historical justification' of our usage of the term and a point of departure for our interpretation of Populist thought. The main emphasis, however, is put in this book on such aspects of Russian Populism which had not come to the fore in Lenin's view of it but which are clearly visible today.

Lenin interpreted Populism in terms of its relation to the development of capitalism in Russia. There is, however,

[1] After Chernyshevskiĭ's imprisonment and the death of Dobrolyubov (1861), Dmitriĭ Pisarev (1840–68) became the most influential publicist of the democratic camp. His main concern was the emancipation of the individual from traditional beliefs and rules of behaviour; the main role in liberating men from prejudices and irrational social bonds he ascribed to the development and popularization of the natural sciences. There was no place in his ideology for the romantic idealization of the common people. In his articles he advocated the attitude of 'thinking realists' whose literary prototype he saw in Bazarov, the 'nihilistic' hero of Turgenev's novel *Fathers and Sons*; defying the generation of 'the fathers', he agreed to call himself a 'nihilist', in the sense that he rejected everything which could not be justified from a 'realistic', utilitarian point of view (with the passage of years, mainly under the influence of reactionary publicists who used the word as a term of abuse, the label 'nihilist' also stuck to the Populist revolutionaries, without, however, being accepted by them). He was by no means an adversary of capitalist development; on the contrary, enlightened capitalists were in his eyes 'thinking realists', greatly contributing to the general welfare of society. The main enemy of 'realism' he saw in 'aesthetics', by which he meant the aesthetic and idealistic attitude towards life, characteristic of the intellectuals from the gentry. In his obsessive fight against 'aesthetics' he went so far as to proclaim that the creation and consumption of 'merely artistic' values contradicts the principle of 'the economy of material and intellectual forces' and that music and plastic arts are wholly superfluous for mankind. In a review of Chernyshevskiĭ's aesthetic theory (*Destruction of Aesthetics*, 1865) he interpreted it as amounting to a total liquidation of aesthetics and in his articles 'Pushkin and Belinskiĭ' he ridiculed the poetry of Pushkin and criticized its evaluation by Belinskiĭ, in whom he recognized only a 'semi-realist'. This aggressive iconoclasm and puritan radicalism in the domain of art was a kind of compensation for the moderation of his social programme, which was reduced to peaceful, patient work for material and intellectual progress.

The emergence of the classical Populism was accompanied by a conscious rejection of 'Pisarevism'. 'Realism' was replaced by a romantic idealization of the common people and the spirit of revolutionary self-sacrifice; the cult of natural sciences gave way to another extreme—to the conviction (characteristic especially of the Bakuninists) that higher education contributes only to the further increase of inequality.

another aspect of the problem, bound up with the belated
character of the Russian economic development. Russian
Populism was not only an ideological reaction to the development of capitalism *inside Russia*—it was also a reaction to
the capitalist economy and socialist thought of the West. It
reflected *not only* the problems of small producers in confrontation with large-scale capitalist production; it reflected
also specific problems of a backward peasant country in
confrontation with the highly developed capitalist states. It
was a Russian reaction to Western capitalism and, also, a Russian response to Western socialism—a reaction to Western
capitalism and Western socialism by democratic intelligentsia
in a backward peasant country at an early stage of capitalist
development. And it is quite understandable that the classical Russian Populism was, first of all, a reaction to Marxism—
after all, Marx was by then the leading figure of European
socialism and, at the same time, the author of the most
authoritative book on the development of capitalism. It is
by no means an accident that the beginning of the full-fledged,
classical Populism coincided in time with the first wave of
the diffusion of Marxist ideas in Russia. This is why we have
paid so much attention to the relationship between Populism and Marxism. It is not an exaggeration to say that the
encounter with Marx was of paramount importance for the
formation of the Populist ideology, that without Marx it
would have been different from what it was.

As a conventional date marking the emergence of the
ideology of *classical* Populism we propose the year 1869.
Three classical documents of Populism were published
then: Lavrov's *Historical Letters*, Mikhaïlovskiĭ's treatise
What is Progress?, and Flerovskiĭ's book *The Situation of the
Working Class in Russia*. The first two called into question
the optimistic belief in progress, so characteristic of the
'enlighteners', emphasized the painful contradictoriness of
historical processes, and, finally, undermined and rejected
naturalistic evolutionism with its conception of a unilinear

developmental path; by the same token they removed the theoretical foundation for the view that Russia had to follow the general pattern of the capitalist development of the West. Flerovskiĭ, in his turn, made these historico-philosophical questions cruelly concrete and down-to-earth. His vivid description of the growing destitution of the Russian peasantry and of the new capitalist forms of exploitation emerging in Russian villages was followed by the conclusion that everything should be done to *prevent* further travelling along capitalist paths and to utilize, instead, the possibilities of development inherent in the peasant commune.

One more qualification should be made in order to avoid misunderstanding. The adjective 'classical' is applied in this book to Populist *thought* after 1869, and not to any individual Populist *thinker*. Populism was a broad current of thought, differentiated within itself; it was a supra-individual ideological structure within which many positions were possible, sometimes complementary and sometimes symmetrically opposed to each other. It is clear, therefore, that it is hardly possible to find in an individual thinker all the aspects and all the constitutive elements of such a structure; in each individual case the proportions are different and in some cases the complete lack of an important element can even be established. Thus, for instance, Lavrov was hardly an 'economic romanticist'; 'economic romanticism' was undoubtedly an important feature of Populism, Lavrov, however, represented within the Populist ideology the rationalistic and individualistic tradition of the 'enlighteners', and this tradition was also a constituent part of Populism. Tkachëv, taken separately, was a quite unique and atypical figure but, nevertheless, it is justified to interpret his ideas as the most extreme expression of a particular aspect of classical Populism. Both Lavrov and Tkachëv thus gave a classical expression of some aspects of Populism, and not a faithful reflection of the whole structure of Populism. The difference between them and Chernȳshevskiĭ, whose ideology, after all, also contained some important elements of Populism, consisted in the fact that they opposed each other within the *classical Populist framework of thought*. And it is this general framework, together with the characteristic pattern of possible standpoints within it, that constitutes the distinctiveness and the unity—the structure—of Populist thought.

II

CLASSICAL POPULISM AND ITS PREDICAMENTS

1. *The Controversy about Progress*

THE popularity of Lavrov's *Historical Letters* among the democratic youth was enormous indeed. It was due mainly to one chapter of this book, entitled 'The Cost of Progress'. 'Mankind', wrote Lavrov, 'has paid dearly so that a few thinkers sitting in their studies could discuss its progress.'[1] The personal development of 'critically thinking individuals' from among the privileged 'cultivated minority' has been purchased with the hard labour and terrible sufferings of many generations of heavily exploited people; each thought, each idea, 'has been bought with the blood, sufferings, or toil of millions'.[2] The civilized minority should never forget about it but should make every effort to discharge this debt. Each ethical and critically thinking individual should say to himself: 'I shall relieve myself of responsibility for the bloody cost of my own development if I utilize this same development to diminish evil in the present and in the future.'[3]

We find in these words an excellent expression of the state of mind of the educated, progressive youth which was tormented by a feeling of social guilt and wished to sacrifice itself for the sake of the people's welfare. First of all it was the state of mind of the 'conscience-stricken gentry' (a term introduced by N. K. Mikhaĭlovskiĭ) which, along with the

---

[1] P. L. Lavrov, *Filosofiya i sotsiologiya*, vol. ii, Moscow 1965, p. 81. Quoted in the translation by J. P. Scanlan in *Russian Philosophy*, edited by James M. Edie, James P. Scanlan, and Mary-Barbara Zeldin, with the collaboration of George L. Kline, Chicago, Quadrangle Books, 1965, vol. ii, p. 138.

[2] Ibid., p. 86. Cf. *Russian Philosophy*, vol. ii, p. 143.

[3] Ibid., p. 86. Cf. *Russian Philosophy*, p. 143.

more sober 'raznochintsȳ', then played an important part in the Russian democratic movement. Lavrov's book formulated their problems and gave an answer to their questions. And the most important of these questions was: What is progress? What is to be done by an individual who wishes to discharge his social debt?

The strong feeling that the 'debt to the people' *must* be paid off led young Populists to the indignant rejection of all the theories which claimed that progress was an inevitable, 'objective', and 'natural' process. In the Russian conditions such theories were but a convenient tool of the apologists of capitalism, i.e. of the people who used to explain away and justify the sufferings of the masses in the name of the 'objective laws of history' or the 'iron laws of political economy'. Against such 'objectivism' Lavrov set his vindication of 'subjectivism' and he was supported in this by Nicholas Mikhaïlovskiï. The common features of their views have been labelled (rather unfortunately) 'subjective sociology' or the 'subjective method'. This Populist 'subjectivism' has been ridiculed by Plekhanov but it certainly deserves to be taken seriously and to be examined more 'objectively'.

The controversy between 'objectivism' and 'subjectivism' had a long history in Russia. Its origins should be traced back to the Russian Hegelianism of the thirties and forties. Bakunin, who himself belonged to the 'generation of the forties', wrote about it in 1870:

In the thirties, under the oppressive rule of Nicholas I, there first emerged in Russia the theory of the objectivists who explained all historical facts by reference to their logical necessity, denied any significance to individual deeds and recognized but one real, invincible and omnipotent force in history—the force of its immanent reason. It is a very useful theory for those who, being afraid of action, wish to put themselves right with themselves and with others by presenting an excuse for their shameful inactivity. This theory is still demoralizing a large part of our educated youth of gentry origin.[1]

[1] M. Bakunin, *Nauka i nasushchnoe revolyutsionnoe delo*, Geneva 1870, p. 32.

Writing about the 'objectivists' of the thirties Bakunin meant his own and Belinskiĭ's 'reconciliation with reality'.[1] This highly philosophical 'reconciliation', drawing its arguments from a one-sided interpretation of Hegelianism, consisted in a recognition that the existing social and political reality was sanctioned by the objective Reason of History and that one *had* to accept it, to look at it from the point of view of 'the whole' and not from the distorting perspective of one's 'subjective individuality'. The practical conclusion was that instead of attempting to change reality to suit one's 'subjective' postulates one had to adjust oneself to the demands of reality. It should be added that at the very beginning of the forties Bakunin and Belinskiĭ renounced their 'reconciliation' and rehabilitated Schillerian 'subjectivism' which they had so severely condemned before. 'Subjectivism', thus, meant in their language the individual's protest against the inhuman laws of the Hegelian *Weltgeist*. Later, in the fifties and sixties, the same attitude could be found in Herzen's denunciation of the liberal political economy with its theory of uncontrolled, 'natural' development, and in Chernȳshevskiĭ's criticism of the epigones of Westernism, especially Boris Chicherin, who combined liberal economy with the Hegelian doctrine of historical necessity.[2] Still later, in the seventies, the struggle against the positivistic naturalism of the bourgeois theories of progress, especially against the theory of Spencer and, also, social Darwinism, became most important.

The basic assumptions of 'subjective sociology' can be embraced in three points. First, it was *a defence of ethicism—*

---

[1] It was proclaimed in Bakunin's article 'Foreword to Hegel's Gymnasial Speeches', published in 1838 and generally accepted as the first manifesto of Russian Hegelianism. Its philosophical justification was Hegel's famous pronouncement: 'What is real is rational, what is rational is real.'

[2] Cf. Chernȳshevskiĭ, *Polnoe sobranie sochineniĭ*, vol. v, Moscow 1950, pp. 650–1. Chicherin clung to the Hegelian concept of society as a supra-individual whole, subject to the 'iron rule' of historical necessity; in contrast with this, Chernȳshevskiĭ conceived society as 'a sum of individual lives' (ibid., p. 385), subject to rational manipulation in the interests of majority.

a strong conviction that moral values can be neither eliminated nor derived from facts, that moral evil cannot be
'scientifically' explained away and that moral protest
against suffering is valuable and obligatory irrespective of
any 'objective' conditions. Secondly, it was *an epistemological
and methodological standpoint* which denied or disputed the
possibility of the 'objective' approach in the social sciences;
'subjectivism', in this sense, consisted in the assertion that
historical and sociological knowledge can never be really
'objective' because it always depends upon the unconscious
emotions or (much better) on the consciously chosen ideals
of scholars. Thirdly, it was a *philosophy of history* which
claimed that the 'subjective factor'—human thought and
will—can effectively oppose the so-called 'laws' of development and play a decisive part in the historical process.
Lavrov based upon it his 'practical philosophy' which proclaimed that 'critically thinking individuals', having united
in a party, could become a social force and change the existing state of affairs in the direction indicated by their 'subjective' aims.

Progress—maintained the author of *Historical Letters*—is
not at all a necessary, 'objective', and automatically functioning law of development. Such laws do not exist, historical
events are always unique and unrepeatable (this assertion
of Lavrov's was, to some extent, an anticipation of the
theses of Windelband and Rickert). The main problem,
therefore, is the problem of selection, the problem of finding
a criterion which would enable us to pick out 'what is
important and meaningful' from the amorphous mass of
historical data. Such a criterion must be subjective because
it always depends on the choice of the social ideal. Thus,
every classification of historical data is based upon the relationship of the facts to the ideal of the scholar and every
survey of historical events consists, essentially, in arranging
the whole of history around the events which paved the way
for realization of this ideal. Lavrov wrote: 'In the historical

perspective set by our moral ideal, we stand at the end of the historical process; the entire past is related to our ideal as a series of preparatory steps which lead inevitably to a definite end.'[1] In this manner the historian arrives at the notion of 'progress'—a category which brings order into the raw historical material and imparts a meaning to the chaotic mass of 'facts'. In itself history has no meaning; there are many meanings to be found in it, but all of them are imparted to it by men. And a meaning presupposes an ideal.

This approach of historical facts to a real or ideal 'best' of which we are conscious, this evolution of our moral ideal in the past life of mankind, is for everyone the *only* meaning of history, the only *law* of the historical ordering of events, the law of *progress*—whether we consider the progress to be in fact continuous or subject to fluctuation, whether we believe in its actual realization or only its realization in consciousness.[2]

The same philosophical premises underlie Lavrov's theory of meaningful action. The precondition of truly human and truly historical activity was, according to him, an act of appraisal and a conscious choice of the ideal. Human history began, thus, with the emergence of 'critically thinking individuals', trying to shape the destiny of men by means of criticism and 'idealization'. Criticism destroys the old society, idealization enables men to build a new and better one; the first presupposes a highly developed ability of rationalistic and sceptical analysis, the second presupposes an ardent and dogmatic faith, but the combination of both is necessary for those who wish to change the world. We should add to this that Lavrov distinguished between a 'false' and a 'legitimate and truly human idealization'. By the 'false idealization' he meant something very similar to 'rationalization' in the Freudian sense or to 'ideology' in Karl Mannheim's usage of this word:[3] 'idealization' in this

---

[1] Lavrov, op. cit., p. 44. Cf. *Russian Philosophy*, p. 131.
[2] Lavrov, op. cit., pp. 44–5. Cf. *Russian Philosophy*, p. 132.
[3] C. K. Mannheim, *Ideology and Utopia*, New York–London 1952.

sense meant simply man's effort, usually unconscious, to hide the real motives of his behaviour and to interpret his aspirations in terms of noble and disinterested aims. The other kind of 'idealization'—the 'truly human' one—was, in turn, something similar to Mannheim's 'utopia'. Its essence was described by Lavrov as setting one's ideal in opposition to the existing social order and to the vested interests of its supporters who try to conceal their class egoism under the mask of various 'false idealizations'.

His own ideal Lavrov embraced in the following formula: 'The physical, intellectual, and moral development of the individual; the incorporation of truth and justice in social institutions.'[1] Or: 'Progress consists in the development of consciousness and in the incorporation of truth and justice in social institutions; it is a process which is being accomplished by means of the critical thought of individuals who aim at the transformation of their culture.'[2] By 'culture' Lavrov meant a stationary social structure, based upon religion, tradition, and folkways. The emergence of 'critically think-ing individuals' brings about a gradual transformation of 'culture' into 'civilization', i.e. into a dynamic society in which religion is being replaced by science and the rule of customs by the rule of rational law. The development of civilization is no longer 'organic', spontaneous, and uncon-scious, but determined increasingly by the conscious activity of individuals.[3] This theory of the author of *Historical Letters* was certainly one of the typical examples of the rationalistic over-estimation of the role of intellectual factors in human history. Its great attractiveness in Russia was due to the fact that the Populist youth felt themselves to be the 'critic-ally thinking individuals', an identification which Lavrov

---

[1] Lavrov, op. cit., p. 54. Cf. *Russian Philosophy*, p. 134.

[2] Lavrov, *Formula progressa N. K. Mikhaïlovskogo. Protivniki istorii. Nauchnye osnovy istorii civilizacii*, Spb. 1906, p. 41.

[3] This theory was further developed by Lavrov in his later sociological works. Cf. P. Sorokin, 'Osnovnye problemy sociologii P. L. Lavrova', in P. L. Lavrov, *Stat'i, vospominaniya, materialy*, published by 'Kolos', Petersburg 1922.

himself consciously intended. On the other hand, however, it did not harmonize with the Populist idealization of the archaic peasant community, which, irrespective of its possible role in shortening the transition to socialism, had to be recognized as belonging rather to the stationary 'culture'. We shall see that the followers of Lavrov, who participated in the 'go to the people' movement, realized this and, unlike the 'Bakuninists', did not appeal to the inherited 'instincts' of the Russian peasant but tried to enlighten him, to awaken him to critical thought. Their ideal of rational 'civilization' was the main cause of their failure to merge with orthodox Populism (in the narrow 'historical' sense) and, finally (disregarding the example of their teacher), of their abandonment of the Populist movement.

It is significant that Lavrov's theory was very close in some respects to the philosophy of history of the Russian Westernizers of the forties—to Belinskiĭ's thoughts about the increasing role of the individual and of the rational consciousness in history, to the reflections of Herzen on the progressive process of individualization, and to the conception of the liberal historian, T. Granovskiĭ, who saw the essence of progress in the 'individualization, of the masses by means of thought'.[1] The close connection of Lavrov's thought with the philosophical problems of the forties is evident in his early works: in his articles on Hegel and in his *Outlines of the Problems of a Philosophy of Practice* (1860).[2] Lavrov's 'subjectivism'—like Belinskiĭ's revolt against the cruelty of the *Weltgeist* and Herzen's 'philosophy of action'[3]—was directed, in the beginning, not so much against positivistic naturalism but, rather, against the fetishism of 'rational necessity' and against the absolutization of 'the General' in the Hegelian philosophy of history. His own philosophy of history drew its inspiration from Kant (the ideal of

---

[1] Cf. T. N. Granovskiĭ, *Sochineniya*, Moscow 1900, p. 445.

[2] Cf. P. L. Lavrov, *Filosofiya i sociologiya*, vol. i.

[3] Cf. A. Walicki, 'Hegel, Feuerbach and the Russian "Philosophical Left"', in *Annali dell' Instituto Giangiacomo Feltrinelli*, Anno Sesto, Milano 1963.

progress conceived as a 'regulative idea', as a postulate of the 'practical reason'), from the left-Hegelians, especially from B. Bauer ('critical thought' as the prime mover of progress) and from the 'anthropologism' of Feuerbach (anthropocentricity as opposed to 'objectivism' and to the Hegelian 'absolute spirit'). There existed also an evident affinity between the theory of *Historical Letters* and the views of the Russian 'enlighteners' of the sixties, who, like Lavrov, over-estimated the progressive role of science and of the intellectual élite. Chernȳshevskiĭ, for instance, saw the main vehicle of progress in the enlightened and emancipated individuals whose achievements were being adopted, through imitation, by common people who, left to themselves, would have remained steeped in the conservative 'routine' of life.[1] Pisarev with his theory of 'thinking realists' went still further in this direction, much further than Lavrov. But there was also a difference. Lavrov's 'subjectivism' was bound up with a certain relativism (although Lavrov himself tried to avoid it) whereas the 'enlighteners' appealed to a rational and essentially unchangeable 'human nature' and would not have agreed to call their ideals 'subjective'. They shared Lavrov's rationalistic individualism but, believing in a natural and universal scale of values, could be accused rather of unhistorical dogmatism than of historical relativism.

It is justified to say that Lavrov was the most extreme Westernizer and 'enlightener' within the Populist movement.

---

[1] Both Chernȳshevskiĭ and Lavrov agreed, however, that the intellectual development of 'critically thinking individuals' had already reached the point at which it has become possible to diminish the gulf between the intellectual élite and the masses. Chernȳshevskiĭ wrote: 'At the beginning, people of high intellectual development spring up from the ranks of the masses and, owing to their rapid advance, leave the masses farther and farther behind. But, on reaching very high degrees of development, the intellectual life of the advanced people assumes a character that becomes more and more intelligible to the common people, that corresponds more and more to the simple requirements of the masses. And in its relation to the intellectual life of the common people, the second, higher, half of historical intellectual life consists in a gradual reversion to that unity of national life which had existed at the very beginning, and had been destroyed during the first half of the movement.' (*Selected Philosophical Essays*, Moscow 1953, p. 190.)

His *Historical Letters* have, indeed, very little in common with Populism in the narrowest sense of this word, i.e. with theory advocating the hegemony of the common people over the educated élite. This little book, which had so well expresssed the moral conflicts of the Populist youth and, also, their feeling of self-importance and belief in their historical mission, left, strictly speaking, no place for the backward-looking utopianism, so characteristic of full-fledged Populism. Lavrov's connection with the great progressive traditions of modern Europe, particularly with individualistic and rationalistic humanism, was too strong. The central value of this humanism—freedom and development of individuality—had been challenged by him in his piercing words about the cost of progress, but in his subsequent reasonings it was fully reinstated and given new foundations. In the last analysis Lavrov's theory sanctioned the bloody process of historical development in the past: if critical thought is a prime mover of social progress, the price of 'blood, sufferings and toil of the millions', which has been paid for its development, has not been wasted; if the development of individuality, along with the incorporation of truth and justice in social institutions, is the main criterion of progress, one must conclude that European history has been, in spite of everything, a history of progress, and that the final result of the long process of the ever-increasing oppression and exploitation of the masses deserves, notwithstanding, a positive appreciation. With the qualification, of course, that now it is high time to discharge the debt.

In his subsequent sociological works Lavrov, under the influence of Marx, paid more attention to the economic aspect of social processes. The basic ideas of *Historical Letters* remained unchanged but, nevertheless, they lost some of their original significance. Most striking, perhaps, is the fact that in his later and more elaborated sociological works Lavrov treated the historical process as an *objective* process of social evolution, consisting in passing from the stage of 'culture' to the stage of 'civilization', from the 'unconscious solidarity of customs', to the conscious solidarity of emancipated individuals. The 'subjective method' was reduced, in these works, to the defence of value-judgements and to an emphasis on the 'subjective factor' in history; the very core of 'subjectivism', i.e. the denial of the possibility of an objective knowledge in the social sciences has, in fact, disappeared, the Kantian motifs have given way to the prevailing spirit of positivism. It was, however, rather a modification than a radical change in the structure of his thought. Already in *Historical Letters* there was a distinction between history, which deals with what is unique and unrepeatable, and sociology, which, in contradistinction to history, aims at discovering some general regularities of social development. A few years later, in his article 'On Method in Sociology' (1874), Lavrov did not hesitate to assert that in sociology both methods—the 'subjective' and the 'objective'—were justified and applicable. With the passage of time he even began to look for the 'objective' justification of social revolution and to speak about its 'historical inevitability'.[1] But it was not a concession to 'objectivism' in the sense of the Hegelian idolization of History or the liberal apologia for 'natural', uncontrolled development. It has been rightly noticed (by J. Hecker) that the 'subjective method' of Lavrov was very close in this respect to the 'anthropoteleological method' of L. F. Ward, who considered artificial teleological processes superior to the 'natural' ones but did not deny the existence of some general laws of social evolution.[2]

In the revolutionary milieu the theories of Lavrov met strong opposition on the part of the romantic 'Bakuninists'

[1] One of the chapters of Lavrov's work 'Sotsiyal'naya revolyutsiya i zadachi nravstvennosti' (in *Vestnik Narodnoi Voli*, 3, 1884 and 4, 1885) has the title: 'The inevitability of social revolution'.

[2] Cf. J. F. Hecker, *Russian Sociology. A Contribution to the History of Sociological Thought and Theory*, New York 1915, p. 118.

who criticized his intellectualism, his emphasis on enlightenment and his obvious lack of belief in the spontaneous
potential for revolt of the Russian peasant. The most serious
challenge to Lavrov's theory of progress was provided, however, not by the 'Bakuninists' but by Peter Tkachëv, the
ideologist of the 'Jacobin' current within the Populist revolutionary movement. His criticism, developed most fully in
the treatise 'What is the Party of Progress?' (1870),[1] struck
upon the most sensitive points of the doctrine of *Historical
Letters*. It showed clearly and forcefully the predicament of
Populist thinkers who tried to provide a solution to the
problem of individuality and social progress.

According to Tkachëv, the author of *Historical Letters* has
replaced the 'real' notion of progress with a 'formal' notion
which is completely useless as a criterion of classification:
if all ideals are necessarily 'subjective', all ideologies, even
the most reactionary ones, have an equal right to call themselves 'progressive'. The thesis that everything is important
or unimportant, good or bad, only with regard to man,
provides no good argument; it is true that we cannot know
a 'thing in itself' but it would be absurd to conclude from
this that the natural sciences are merely 'subjective'. The
same holds true for the theory of progress. It can attain to
objectivity because there are some universally valid, elemen-
tary, and 'self-evident' truths which may serve as an absolute yardstick for the measuring of 'progressiveness'. 'There
exists', wrote Tkachëv, 'an absolute criterion against which

---

[1] The manuscript of this article, dated 16 September 1870, was confiscated
by the Russian police (it was printed for the first time in: P. N. Tkachëv,
Izbrann̈ye sochineniya na sotsiyal'no-politicheskiye tem̈y, ed. B. P. Koz'min, vol. ii,
Moscow 1932, pp. 166–224). This does not mean that Tkachëv's criticism of
Lavrov remained unknown to their contemporaries. Tkachëv attacked Lavrov
in many of his other articles which were published during his lifetime (for instance, 'The Role of Thought in History', *Delo*, 9–12, 1875, 'The People and the
Revolution', *Nabat*, 4, 1876, 'Revolutionaries-reactionaries', *Nabat*, 5, 1876 and
others). We have chosen to present Tkachëv's ideas as developed in *What is the
Party of Progress?* because this treatise is both the first and most systematic
attempt to square accounts with the author of *Historical Letters* and, at the same
time, the best outline of the general premisses of Tkachëv's ideology.

to check the validity of ideologies; there is, therefore, the possibility of an infallible ideology, i.e. of an absolute, universally valid and obligatory formula of progress.'[1]

Tkachëv's rejection of the 'subjective method' was, however, by no means consistent and thoroughgoing. He had rejected relativism as an attitude dissolving faith in the absolute rightness of the chosen aim, but he did not intend to give up normativism and did not try to derive his ideal from any 'objective laws' of historical development. The notion of progress—he asserted—presupposes three elements: a movement, its direction, and its end. But to evoke in the human mind a clear notion of progress, only two of these elements are necessary. There is a progress in nature because in the organic world there is a movement going on in a definite direction; the end, in this case, is identical with the direction of the movement. In history such a steady, definite direction of movement cannot be found; contrary to the opinion of Spencer, the 'historical process should not be treated as an organic process because there is no steady one-way direction in it and *in itself* it is neither progressive nor retrogressive'.[2] Thus, the definition of social progress should contain only two elements: movement and end; looking for a steady, objective direction in the movement of society is as nonsensical as looking for ends in the organic world. The final and the only end of society (for Tkachëv this was an axiom) is the happiness of all its members. The absolute formula of progress presupposes, therefore, a scientific and objective definition of happiness.

Looking for such a definition Tkachëv based it on the 'excellent and universal', 'scientific and objective' definition of life, which he had found in Spencer's *Principles of Biology*. His conclusion was that happiness consisted in the satisfaction of needs, i.e. in a perfect balance between man's needs and the means to meet them which are at his disposal.

[1] P. N. Tkachëv, *Izbrannye sochineniya*, vol. ii, Moscow 1932, p. 174.
[2] Ibid., p. 194.

Human needs, however, are very diverse and some of them can be satisfied only at the cost of others. The artificial needs of the 'developed individualities' of the privileged minority are being satisfied at the cost of the working masses who are denied even the bare necessities. This was a good position from which to attack Lavrov. According to Tkachëv, the fact that the 'development of individuality' was placed in the foreground of Lavrov's formula of progress bore witness that the author of *Historical Letters* was essentially a spokesman of the privileged class of people who, being the producers of ideas, the 'critically thinking individuals', became accustomed to treating themselves as 'the salt of earth, the lever of history, the creators of human happiness' and to whom their very existence appeared a sufficient proof of historical progress.[1] From this point of view—continued Tkachëv—there was indeed a progress in history: the 'salt of earth' has been growing up and perfecting itself, its progress is evident. This kind of progress, however, has nothing in common with the progress of society. The personal development of 'critically thinking individuals', as Lavrov himself has pointed out, has been achieved at the cost of the masses; their constant progress paralleled a constant retrogression in the history of the common people. At last the situation of the people became so horrible that the privileged minority found itself threatened by it. This feeling of imminent danger gave rise to many pseudoprogressive theories which— like that of Lavrov—proclaimed the necessity of a more equal division of material and cultural riches. But all these theories 'openly and perseveringly defend the view that human individuality should retain the high level of development, which has been attained by the privileged minority, and even more: they wish to develop it further in the same direction'.[2] By the same token they reveal their reactionary essence. The so-called 'development of individuality' is a reactionary postulate, because the precondition of social

[1] Ibid., p. 218.　　　　[2] Ibid., p. 219.

happiness consists in the intellectual and moral levelling of individualities. The main task of the party of progress is, therefore, 'to stop the chaotic process of differentiation, which has been caused by retrogressive historical movement, to reduce the existing plurality of different individuals to a common denominator, to one level'.[1]

Thus, against the formula of progress, which had been set forth in *Historical Letters*, Tkachëv put forward his own formula which reads as follows:

To establish the fullest possible equality of individuals (one must not confuse this equality with the so-called political, juridical or even economic equality—it should be an *organic, physiological equality*, an equality stemming from the same education and from identical conditions of life) and to harmonize the needs of all individuals with the means which are available to satisfy these needs—that is the final and the only possible end of human society, that's the supreme criterion of historical progress. Everything which brings us nearer to this end, is progressive; everything which pushes us in another direction, is reactionary.[2]

In Tkachëv's eyes this formula was a simple deduction from his definition of happiness. The satisfaction of everybody's needs presupposes the adjustment of these needs to 'the existing level of the productivity of labour'. To achieve this, society should control and regulate the development of needs and deliberately suppress such individual needs as, at the existing level of economic development, could be satisfied only at the cost of other people. A complete levelling of needs is a fundamental condition of social happiness and the liquidation of the highly developed culture of the élite is the necessary price to be paid for it. Every differentiating process destroys the harmony between human needs and the existing level of production, increasing, thereby, the

---

[1] P. N. Tkachëv, *Izbrannÿe sochineniya*, vol. ii, Moscow 1932, p. 205.
[2] Ibid., pp. 206–7.

number of unhappy individuals in society. Under the conditions of compulsory egalitarianism, which is the aim of true progressives, individuals with greater needs, having no possibility of satisfying these additional needs at the cost of others, would be unhappy, so their own happiness requires the equation of their intellectual and moral development with that of the other, less-developed members of society. Any increase in needs should be collective and planned, harmonized with an increase in production. The political conceptions of Tkachëv (to which we shall return elsewhere in this book) clearly indicate that the task of the 'levelling of individuals' was to be taken up by the revolutionary vanguard who, having seized state power, would organize a centralized system of child-rearing and education, restraining the development of outstanding individualities and thus preserving intellectual and moral equality in society. The revolution—proclaimed Tkachëv—will not end with the seizure of power; it will be only the beginning of a total revolutionary transformation of society.

Tkachëv's polemic with Lavrov concerned not only the means of action; the final ends, the main values were also involved. In sharp contrast to Lavrov, cutting himself off from the tradition of Herzen and Chernÿshevskiĭ, Tkachëv flatly rejected 'the principle of individuality'. In the theory of 'critically thinking individuals', in the ideal of the all-round development of personality he saw the quintessence of individualism, which was in his eyes a bourgeois ideology, deeply inimical and alien to the people. In one of his articles he asserts that the principles of individualism had been formulated already by Protagoras and by the Sophists, who were the ideologists of the urban, bourgeois civilization of Athens; anti-individualism, however, has an equally old and a much more impressive genealogy—it had been formulated by Plato who, in his idealized image of ancient Sparta, forcefully expressed the principle of the total subordination of the individual to the social whole.[1] These ideas of Tkachëv separated him from the other Populist thinkers no less sharply than his 'Jacobin', 'Blanquist' conceptions of revolutionary struggle. His ideology did not fall within the framework of 'bourgeois democratism', even in the broadest sense of this phrase. A belated disciple of Morelly, Babeuf, and Buonarroti, he was in Russia—and perhaps in the whole of Europe in his time—the most consistent and extreme spokesman of that 'crude communism' which (to use the words of young Marx) 'negates the personality of man in every sphere'.[2] Koz'min was probably right when he suggested that the ominous vision of 'Shigalevism' in Dostoevskiĭ's novel *The Possessed* had been in point of fact an allusion to Tkachëv's ideas of the 'levelling of individuals'.[3]

The denial of the 'principle of individuality' was a specific solution of the characteristic dilemma of Populist thought. The inner logic and the contradictions inherent in Populist ideology very often led its representatives to ask the question: how could one reconcile the high appraisal of the archaic collectivism of the peasant commune with the postulate of individual freedom, the welfare of the people, which (according to Populist doctrine) demanded a stop to the process of Westernization, with the welfare of intelligentsia, who were a product of Westernization and who were vitally interested in its further progress. This dilemma, conceived as a theoretical problem and as a practical task, emerged for the first time in the 'Russian socialism' of Herzen. He wished to combine the 'communism' of the Russian peasant with the 'principle of individuality', represented by the Russian intelligentsia, and this task was tantamount in his eyes to a

---

[1] Cf. Tkachëv's article 'Utopicheskoe gosudarstvo burzhuazii', 1869 (P. N. Tkachëv, *Izbrannÿe sochineniya*, vol. ii, Moscow 1932).

[2] K. Marx, *Early Writings*, translated and edited by T. B. Bottomore, London 1963, p. 153 (Economic and Philosophical Manuscripts, Third Manuscript).

[3] Cf. B. P. Koz'min, *P. N. Tkachëv i revolyutsionnoe dvizhenie 1860-kh godov*, Moscow 1922, p. 193. Dostoevskiĭ could have become acquainted with Tkachëv's conception of the 'levelling of individuals' from the latter's article 'The People of the Future', published in *Delo*, 1868.

synthesis of the indigenous 'Russian principles' with European progress: the Russian people, in his conception, looked to the national values of the Russian past, whereas the Russian intelligentsia was conceived as that part of the Russian nation which had passed through the 'European school' and repeated intellectually—in an epitomized form—the whole development of the Western world. The solution of such a task was, however, very difficult, even in pure theory. The creator of 'Russian Socialism' demanded the maximizing of individual autonomy and freedom, but according to his own view the Russian commune, in its actual form, excluded any possibility of individual autonomy for its members. On the other hand, he saw the opposite situation in England: 'The Anglo-Saxon nations have liberated the individual at the cost of a complete loss of the communal principle, making men isolated and lonely; the Russian nation, on the contrary, preserved its commune at the cost of the total absorption of the individual by the social whole.'[1] It followed from this that the emancipation of the individual has been realized most fully in the most developed capitalist country, that individual freedom was bound up with the type of social and economic development which the Populists (including Herzen) used to treat as the most harmful for the people.

Awareness of this put before the Populist thinkers the inevitable question: is it true that the values represented by the 'principle of individuality' on the one hand, and by the 'communal principle' on the other, are complementary and can be harmonized? Perhaps they exclude each other? Tkachëv's answer to this question was unequivocal and devoid of any hesitation: yes, he proclaimed, these values are antagonistic, at least at present, and they cannot be reconciled until the full 'levelling of individuals' has been achieved.

A different answer is contained in the sociological and

[1] A. I. Gertsen, *Sobranie sochineniĭ*, vol. xii, Moscow 1957, p. 156.

historiosophical conceptions of N. K. Mikhaĭlovskiĭ. It consists in an attempt to show that the historical process has been, essentially, a retrogression not only (as Tkachëv thought) from the point of view of the 'people's welfare' but also, and even more, from the point of view of the development of individuality. The development of individuality—argued Mikhaĭlovskiĭ—is not at all a result of the Western type of social evolution; on the contrary, it is incompatible with this type of social evolution and being destroyed by so-called 'social progress'.

Mikhaĭlovskiĭ's conception of the mutual relationship between individuality and social progress is worthy of a detailed examination. The *Historical Letters* of Lavrov gave an unsurpassed formula of Populism as an ideology of the intelligentsia, as an expression of the aspirations and moral conflicts of 'critically thinking individuals'; the sociological doctrine of Mikhaĭlovskiĭ did not renounce the values of the enlightened and spiritually emancipated élite but, at the same time, represented Populism in its 'peasant' aspect, as a retrospective utopia, reflecting and expressing the point of view of small producers who were endangered by capitalist progress. The double-face of the Populist Janus is mirrored in it with a particular clearness and distinctness.

Mikhaĭlovskiĭ's article 'What is Progress?' is the first outline of the sociological interpretation of history which in its essentials was defended by him to the end of his life. Its negative frame of reference was provided by the sociological and historical conceptions of Spencer, first of all his theory of progress. Spencer, according to the Populist thinker, overlooked the fact that there are two types of progress— the progress of society and the progress of man—and that 'these two types of progress do not always perfectly coincide'.[1]

Following Spencer, Mikhaĭlovskiĭ took as a starting-point the so-called 'law of Baer' which had defined progress

---

[1] N. K. Mikhaĭlovskiĭ, *Polnoe sobranie sochineniĭ*, 5th edition, vol. i, Spb. 1911, p. 32. Cf. *Russian Philosophy*, vol. ii, p. 177.

in the organic world as a process of transition from inco-
herent homogeneity to coherent heterogeneity, from the
simple to the complex. His conclusions, however, were different from those of the English philosopher: in the 'law of
Baer' he saw a decisive argument for the view that there
existed an unavoidable antagonism between the 'organic
progress of society' and the many-sided development of
man. The organic type of social development, presupposing
a differentiation of society through the division of labour,
deprives men of their individual universality and wholeness,
reduces them to specialized, 'organs', entirely subordinated
to an allegedly higher organic whole; the differentiation
(heterogenization) and cohesion of society stands, thus, in
inverse ratio to the inner differentiation (heterogeneity,
many-sidedness) and integrality of individuals. Primitive
society is a homogeneous mass but each of its members,
taken separately, is quite heterogeneous; he 'combines in
himself all the powers and capacities which can develop,
given the cultural level and the local physical conditions of
the time'.[1] The division of labour with a corresponding social
differentiation destroys this primitive fullness and wholeness
of life, transforms the individual into a mere 'organ' of
the social organism. The development of this organism is
incompatible with the development of men because the
differentiation of every organism is necessarily bound up
with the retrogressive process of 'homogenization' of its
organs, i.e. of reducing their independence and wholeness
by means of one-sided specialization.[2] As the human organism

---

[1] N. K. Mikhaĭlovskiĭ, *Polnoe sobranie sochineniĭ*, 5th edition, vol. i, Spb.
1911, p. 32. Cf. *Russian Philosophy*, p. 177.

[2] In Mikhaĭlovskiĭ's terminology the 'integral' personality (*tsel'naya, tselost-
naya lichnost'*) was the opposite of the 'integrated' personality, i.e. a personality
which has undergone the process of its adjustment (integration) to the social
whole. 'Integration', in Mikhaĭlovskiĭ's usage of the word, was the opposite of
'differentiation', and his ideal of 'integral personality' presupposed that it
must be differentiated within itself, i.e. many-sided and all-round. In short,
'integrality' (in the context of Mikhaĭlovskiĭ's theory) means 'all-roundness'
whereas 'integration' means 'specialization'.

develops (differentiates itself) at the cost of its organs, so the social organism develops at the cost of men. The social organism, however, is an abstraction: only man is a *real* organism, only *his* pleasures and sufferings are real, and, therefore, only *his* welfare should be the measure of progress. And from this anthropocentric point of view, Spencer's formula of progress turns out to be, in point of fact, the formula of regression. The reason is simple: 'individual progress and social evolution (on the model of organic evolution) are mutually exclusive, just as the evolution of organs and the evolution of the whole organism are mutually exclusive'.[1]

An illustration of this was given in Mikhaĭlovskiĭ's philosophy of history, explaining the intellectual evolution of mankind by the evolution of the forms of labour. The general outline of this conception bears much resemblance to Lavrov's scheme of the phases of thought,[2] its content, however, is richer because 'the fate of human thought' was connected by Mikhaĭlovskiĭ with the problem of the division of labour and its impact on human individuality.

The first great epoch of history was called by Mikhaĭlovskiĭ the *objectively anthropocentric period*. Man at that time took himself for the real, objective, absolute centre of nature and explained all natural phenomena by referring them to himself—hence the animistic and anthropomorphic character of his religious representations. At the beginning of this period social co-operation was almost completely unknown.

[1] Mikhaĭlovskiĭ, op. cit., p. 41. Cf. *Russian Philosophy*, p. 180.

[2] Lavrov divided intellectual history of mankind into three epochs: the epoch of naïve subjectivism, the epoch of 'the study of the unchanging laws of the external world *in its objectivity*', and the epoch in which 'man again became the centre of the entire world, but this time the centre of the world not as it exists in itself, but as it is comprehended by man, conquered by his thought, and turned towards his aims'. 'At this point', commented Lavrov, 'the great law divined by Hegel, which seems to apply in very many spheres of human consciousness, was borne out: a third step, apparently a return to the first, in fact resolved the contradiction between the first and the second.' (*Russian Philosophy*, vol. ii, p. 125.)

The similarity between Lavrov's historical triad and Mikhaĭlovskiĭ's philosophy of history is obvious, but we should stress that this conception was barely adumbrated in Lavrov's *Historical Letters*.

Later, when the instinct of self-preservation forced people to join together, there appeared two forms of co-operation: the simple and the complex. The prototype of the first was the 'free group of hunters', the prototype of the second—the patriarchal family where the division into 'man's labour' and 'woman's labour' had been established and where women had become subordinated to men. Simple co-operation is not bound up with social differentiation and the specialization of functions—individuals preserve in it their inner 'differentiation' and the group preserves its homogeneity. In the case of complex co-operation, the reverse is true: 'In the first case [simple co-operation] we have a homogeneous society whose members are differentiated, equal, independent, and free; in the second case—a differentiated society whose members are unequal, unfree, one-sidedly specialized and hierarchically subordinated to each other.'[1] Simple co-operation enabled the progressive development of man, both physical and spiritual; complex co-operation set in motion *social* progress, the reverse side of which was a retrogression in the evolution of individuals. Thus, for instance, the division of labour in the family, increasing the differences between man and woman, deprived both sexes of a part of their human wholeness.

In the objectively anthropocentric period simple co-operation prevailed. By the time when complex co-operation had achieved the dominant position a new epoch—the *eccentric period*—had begun. By choosing such a strange name Mikhaïlovskiï wanted to indicate the peculiar quality of the vision of the world which he thought to be characteristic of that period. By 'eccentrism' he meant the lack of centre, resulting in the fractionizing and fragmentation of the whole. The division of labour brought about the fragmentation of the human personality and this, in turn, entailed a similar change in the apprehension of the world: reality disintegrated into a multitude of autonomous spheres, claiming to exist

Mikhaïlovskiï, op. cit., pp. 82–3.

'in themselves' and 'for their own sake'; anthropocentrism (although nominally preserved in the religious sphere) gave way to policentrism; the natural and social forces began to appear to man as something alien to him, external and 'objective'.

The source of this 'eccentrism' was seen by the Populist thinker in the increasing complication of human relationships. In simple co-operation, the aim of common efforts is clear to everybody; this brings about a feeling of solidarity and a mutual understanding among the members of the group; in the conditions of complex co-operation, the common aim becomes more and more elusive and, finally, breaks up into a multitude of separate, autonomous aims; theory becomes divorced from practice, science, art, and economy become autonomous 'ends in themselves'; men 'cease to understand each other although they are bound together as tightly as possible'.[1] It results in the emergence of isolated and antagonistic groups and in the growing annihilation of the conscious, moral solidarity of men. An analogy to this destructive process is provided by the development of science which, on the one hand, breaks up into different, narrow fields of specialization and, on the other hand, becomes a metaphysic, i.e. an abstract knowledge, separated from man and dehumanized in its 'absoluteness' and 'objectivity'. The forces and functions which had belonged once to the all-round, complete, and total individual became divorced from man, living their own life and indifferent, if not hostile, to each other.

Primitive man thought, poor fellow, that everything was created for him. And now it turns out that man himself is created for everything else but for his own sake. He exists for the sake of Justice, Morality, Science, Art. And each of these abstract beings demands of him an exclusive, absolute homage, all of them being openly at outs: Art has no need of Justice, Morality is opposed to Science, Wealth ignores Justice, formal Justice has

[1] Mikhaĭlovskiĭ, op. cit., p. 91.

nothing in common with Morality. But—a significant circumstance!—all these abstract categories, born in the process of social differentiation and constantly fighting each other, are unanimous in supporting the social order which has called them into being.[1]

It is justified to say that what Mikhaĭlovskiĭ tried to define and describe was in substance—to use the terminology of young Marx—the phenomenon of 'alienation'. Marx wrote:

The nature of alienation implies that each sphere applies a different and contradictory norm, that morality does not apply the same norm as political economy, etc., because each of them is a particular alienation of man; each is concentrated upon a specific area of alienated activity and is itself alienated from the other.[2]

The resemblance of this quotation to Mikhaĭlovskiĭ's concept of 'eccentrism' is striking; the works of young Marx, however, were long unknown and the Marxist adversaries of Mikhaĭlovskiĭ (especially Plekhanov whose necessitarian interpretation of Marxism left no place for something like alienation) were unable to appreciate this interesting aspect of his thought.

Mikhaĭlovskiĭ did not deny the great achievements of the 'eccentric' period in the domain of science, art, and industry,

[1] Ibid., pp. 98–9.
[2] K. Marx, *Early Writings* (Economic and Philosophical Manuscripts, Third Manuscript), p. 173. It may be added that young Marx, like Mikhaĭlovskiĭ, postulated the overcoming of the division of labour (for the sake of man's 'totality') and, also, opposed 'objectivism', seeing in it a corollary of 'reification'. 'Objectification', he wrote, 'is the practice of alienation.' (Ibid., p. 39. 'On the Jewish Question'.) His anti-utopianism did not refrain him from hoping for a radical overcoming of the division of labour in the future. He wrote: '. . . In communist society, where nobody has one exclusive sphere of activity but each can become accomplished in any branch he wishes, society regulates the general production and thus makes it possible to do one thing today and another tomorrow, to hunt in the morning, fish in the afternoon, rear cattle in the evening, criticise after dinner, just as I have a mind, without becoming hunter, fisherman, shepherd or critic.' (K. Marx and F. Engels, *The German Ideology*, London 1965, pp. 44–5.) Despite the jocose manner of writing, the ideal expressed by the young Marx in this passage seemed to be taken by him quite seriously. (Cf. R. Tucker, *Philosophy and Myth in Karl Marx*, Cambridge 1964, pp. 195–8.)

he thought only that the price which had been paid for them was too high and, secondly, that not all of them were due to the division of labour. Apart from the 'divided labour' there remained also some enclaves of 'undivided labour', simple co-operation with its corresponding type of human relations managed to escape from final destruction, and that was the reason why people still preserved an ability to struggle for their individuality against the alienated, objectified forces. The indestructibility of simple co-operation was, for Mikhaïlovskiĭ, a proof that there existed the possibility of its full renaissance which would inaugurate a new epoch of history, the long-awaited epoch of universal regeneration. This third epoch, prophesied by many of the greatest minds of humanity, was called by him the *subjectively anthropocentric period*. Man of that period will know that 'objectively' he is not at all the centre of the universe but he will also recognize his 'subjective' right to take himself for such a centre and to judge everything from the point of view of the living and indivisible human individuality. In the field of knowledge the first sign of this new attitude towards the world was seen by Mikhaïlovskiĭ in the philosophy of Comte, especially in the works of the second period of his activity: in his criticism of metaphysical abstractions, on the one hand, and of narrow specialization, on the other, in his thesis that every truth was a truth for man and not an 'absolute' truth in itself, in his justification of the 'subjective method' combined with the postulate of the 'subjective synthesis' of knowledge, and, at last, in his idea of the harmony and unity of individual existence as a fundamental condition of human happiness.[1] It is significant, however, that Mikhaïlovskiĭ felt himself closer to the 'orthodox' Comtians, who clung to the romantic elements of their master's thought, than to the scientific positivism of the Comtian 'revisionists', led by Littré. Comte himself, he argued, was, in spite of everything, too much in bondage to 'objectivism', and unable to emancipate

[1] Mikhaïlovskiĭ, op. cit., p. 90.

himself from the tremendous influence of the still prevailing, 'eccentric' vision of the world.[1]

A recapitulation of Mikhaïlovskiĭs' article was given in his famous 'formula of progress'. It reads as follows:

> Progress is the gradual approach to the integral individual, to the fullest possible and the most diversified division of labour among man's organs and the least possible division of labour among men. Everything that impedes this advance is immoral, unjust, pernicious, and unreasonable. Everything that diminishes the heterogeneity of society and thereby increases the heterogeneity of its members is moral, just, reasonable, and beneficial.[2]

From the sociological point of view this 'formula' is very interesting indeed. It expressed the very essence of the backward-looking Populist utopia, a utopia which idealized the primitive peasant economy by setting a high value on its autarky, on its independence of the capitalist market. Mikhaïlovskiĭ constantly repeated that the interests of individuality coincided with the interests of 'undivided', non-specialized labour, i.e. with the interests of the Russian peasantry. The Russian peasant, like primitive man, lives a life which is poor but full; being economically self-sufficient he is, therefore, an independent, 'all-round', and 'total' man. He satisfies all his needs by his own work, making use of all his capacities—he is a tiller and an artisan, a shepherd and an artist in one person. The peasant community is egalitarian, homogeneous, but its members have differentiated, many-sided individualities. The lack or weak development of complex co-operation enables them to preserve their in-dependence and simple co-operation unites them in mutual sympathy and understanding. This moral unity underlies the common ownership of land and the self-government of the Russian 'mir'.

Mikhaïlovskiĭ was quite aware that the actually existing peasant commune was in fact very far from his ideal. How-ever, he felt the cause of this lay not in the commune itself

[1] Ibid., p. 105.　　[2] Ibid., p. 150. Cf. *Russian Philosophy*, vol. ii, p. 187.

but in destructive influences from the outside and in the low level of the development of simple co-operation. This last explanation was based upon a distinction between *types* and *levels* of development. From the point of view of the *level* of development, the peasant commune cannot match a capitalist factory but, at the same time, it represents a higher *type* of development; Russia, being a peasant country, is still much less developed than Western capitalist countries, but in spite of that, is much superior to them as a type of development. The same holds true in the case of the corresponding levels and types of development of man's individuality. The 'principle of individuality', therefore, is not something which should be introduced to the Russian commune from outside, as it was thought by Herzen; the defence of the old 'principles of the people' is, thus, equivalent to the struggle for the higher type of individuality. The very notion of 'individuality' changed its content. 'Individuality' was seen by Mikhaĭlovskiĭ in man's indivisibility, in his 'wholeness', and not at all in the peculiar features and abilities distinguishing an individual from other people.[1] It followed from this that the individuality of great scholars and thinkers, i.e. the individuality of one-sided 'specialists', represented a lower type of development: 'The "I" of a Hegel', wrote Mikhaĭlovskiĭ, 'is, strictly speaking, but a meagre fraction of the human "I".'[2]

After this manner the theoretician of Populism who considered 'the principle individuality' to be the central value and the cornerstone of his world outlook came very close to Tkachëv, who violently rejected this principle, seeing in it the quintessence of bourgeois values. Mikhaĭlovskiĭ, of course, would never accept Tkachëv's idea of the forced

---

[1] 'By the word "individuality"', he wrote, 'people mean usually a complex of those qualities which distinguish the given individual from the other men. The adjective "individual" means (in this usage) "one's own", "peculiar". As to us, we give this word a completely different meaning: by "individuality" we mean the complex of *all the qualities* of the human organism *in general*.'

[2] Mikhaĭlovskiĭ, op. cit., p. 463.

'levelling of individuals'; nevertheless, it should be noticed that both Tkachëv and Mikhaĭlovskiĭ espoused the ideal of a homogeneous society and expressed in theoretical formula the spirit of a truly peasant primitive egalitarianism. It is understandable that Mikhaĭlovskiĭ's theory of progress provoked the author of *Historical Letters* to polemize against it. In a long article entitled 'The Formula of Progress of N. K. Mikhaĭlovskiĭ (1870) Lavrov set against this theory a whole series of grave objections. The liquidation of the division of labour—he asserted—would obstruct the development of technology and science; the complete 'homogeneity' of society excludes the emergence of 'critically thinking individuals' who are the carriers of new ideas and who, by the same token, distinguish themselves from the rest of the people; to fulfil the postulates of Mikhaĭlovskiĭ's 'formula of progress' means in fact to transform a dynamic society into a stationary, non-progressive one; finally, the acceptance of this formula is tantamount to proclaiming that the historical process consisted hitherto in a constant regression. Lavrov did not even hesitate to formulate the thesis which was so vehemently rejected by Tkachëv: the division of a primitive, homogeneous society into a hard-working majority and a privileged minority was necessary and progressive because it had made it possible to set society in motion. Without the division of labour nobody would have understood the value of individuality in any of the possible meanings of this word. The principle of the division of labour still performs a progressive function and will be progressive until critical thought has been made the property of all. And even then— argued Lavrov—the striving for the maximization of equality will not be equivalent to progressiveness. Men are not born absolutely equal and, this being the case, the free and all-round development of the individual must also include the development of what distinguishes him from other people. Equality should be ensured only in those attributes which are common to all men, which constitute the essence of man, and such an equality is not incompatible with a certain differentiation of society.[1]

Lavrov's arguments did not convince Mikhaĭlovskiĭ. On the contrary: in his later works he made his criticism of progress even more radical and he put an even stronger emphasis on the retrospective character of his social ideal. In 'What is Progress?' he had still tried to convince his readers that he placed the 'golden age' in the future, and not in the past, and that he did not accept Rousseau's criticism of civilization.[2] A few years later, however, he withdrew these qualifications. In one of his articles ('On Schiller and on Many Other Things', 1876) he stated explicitly that Rousseau and Schiller had been right in claiming that the 'golden age' was not before us, but behind us.[3] He even confessed that his own interpretation of the legend of the 'golden age' was much more literal than that of Schiller: the 'golden age' is not a hypothesis but something very real, in many countries it only recently disappeared and some of its essential features are still to be found in the way of life and in the old customs of the Russian peasantry.

2. *'Sociological Romanticism'*

By analogy with Lenin's category of 'economic romanticism' Mikhaĭlovskiĭ's sociological views could be defined as a kind of 'sociological romanticism'. Mikhaĭlovskiĭ himself —although with a qualification—used this term as a definition of the growing interest in archaic forms of social life, characteristic of the socialist and conservative scholars and reflecting the general disappointment in classical

---

[1] Cf. Lavrov, *Formula progressa N. K. Mikhaĭlovskogo* (quoted edition), pp. 12, 13–14, 16, 31, 35, 39.

[2] Mikhaĭlovskiĭ, op. cit., p. 60.

[3] Mikhaĭlovskiĭ agreed with Schiller that the progresses of society have been achieved at the cost of the individual man, who has been stripped of his *Totalität*. He rejected, however, Schiller's idealization of ancient Greece and his aesthetic utopia, interpreting the 'golden age' in terms of peasant economy, primitive equality, and simple co-operation.

bourgeois liberalism. In his series of articles entitled *The Struggle for Individuality* (1875–6) he wrote about it as follows:

We see today, first, a surprisingly rapid decline of confidence in the principles of formal freedom and individual welfare as a guarantee of public welfare and, secondly, an equally rapid decay of doctrines which used to treat these principles as the foundation of the whole edifice of society. (. . .) The workers, on their own initiative, are reconstructing some purely medieval institutions and voluntarily subjugating themselves to them [Mikhaĭlovskiĭ meant the trade unions, being, in his view, a reconstruction of medieval guilds—A. W.]. In doing this they are accompanied by the social sciences, which accompanied earlier the rise of bourgeois ideas. This looking backward, towards the Middle Ages and even to the more remote past, is an interesting aspect of contemporary scholarship. Both Marx and the representatives of the ethical orientation (Kathedersozialismus) display a great tolerance in their attitude toward some medieval forms of social life, such a tolerance as would, until recently, have been absolutely impossible. And it is not a mere tolerance. In the dusty archives documents on old, outlived forms of social life are being discovered, and social forms which are outliving their time are recommended to be preserved, at least in order to be studied and described. In other words, extolling of the present begins to give way to a new attitude, an attitude which could be defined as sociological romanticism if the interest in the old were not combined with an interest in some new forms of social relations, if it were a mere idealization of the past and not an effort to study it and to apply its teachings to new needs. This enlargement of the field of study has proved already to be surprisingly stimulating and inspiring for scholars. Maurer, Nasse, Maine, Brentano, Laveleye have harvested a rich crop.[1]

[1] Mikhaĭlovskiĭ, *Polnoe sobranie sochineniĭ*, vol. i, Spb. 1911, p. 432. Mikhaĭlovskiĭ referred to the following scholarly works: G. L. Maurer, *Einleitung zur Geschichte der Mark-, Hof-, Dorf-, und Stadtverfassung und der öffentlichen Gehalt*, 1854 (Russian trans., 1880); idem, *Geschichte der Markenverfassung in Deutschland*, 1856 (Maurer's works were highly regarded by Marx and exerted an influence on his attitude towards the Russian peasant commune); E. Nasse, *Über die mittelalterliche Feldgemeinschaft in England*, 1869 (Russian trans., 1878); H. S. Maine, *Ancient Law, Its Connection With the Early History and Its Relation to Modern Ideas*, 1861, and *Village Community in the East and West*, 1871 (both translated into Russian); L. Brentano, *Die Arbeitergilden der Gegenwart*, 2 vols., 1871–2; E. L. Laveleye, *De la propriété et de ses formes primitives*, 1874 (Russian trans., 1885).

Positive appraisal of the 'looking backward to the Middle Ages' was something new in Mikhaĭlovskiĭ's world outlook. In *What is Progress?* retrospection was directed to the life of primitive man; the Middle Ages, as the epoch of the maximum development of hierarchical order of society, were seen as the culmination of the 'eccentric period'. The peculiar quality of Mikhaĭlovskiĭ's 'formula of progress' consisted in the fact that it could be set against both feudalism and capitalism, or, to be precise, against some aspects of both of them. The ideal of social homogeneity could be levelled against the division of society into separated and closed estates, which had reached an extreme in the Middle Ages, and, at the same time, against the division of labour, increasing with the capitalist development of society; bourgeois progress was accepted by Mikhaĭlovskiĭ as a process destroying the barriers of estates, but, at the same time, it was rejected by him as a process depriving small, independent producers of their economic 'self-sufficiency'. Already in 1869 Mikhaĭlovskiĭ, in fact, was concerned mainly with the criticism of the *new*, capitalist structure of society, but then he saw it as a mere continuation of the 'eccentric' tendencies of feudalism and did not see in the feudal society anything worth 'looking backward to' (with the exception of such enclaves of equality and 'simple co-operation' as, for instance, the military communes of the Cossacks). Later, in the seventies, the rapid growth of Russian capitalism increased his sensitiveness to the specific and (from his point of view) negative traits of the emerging bourgeois order and, at the same time, enabled him to appreciate some aspects of medieval society, to which he had not paid much attention before. First of all

It should be added that Mikhaĭlovskiĭ's objection to the term 'sociological romanticism' can be easily countered. It was in the very essence of 'economic (sociological) romanticism' that the 'teachings of the past' were applied to meet new needs. Lenin strongly emphasized that 'economic romanticism' did not mean 'a desire simply to restore medieval institutions', that it was rather an attempt 'to measure the new society with the old patriarchal yardstick'. (Lenin, *Collected Works*, vol. ii, p. 241.)

it was the similarity between the peasant commune and the medieval handicraft trades and guilds. Mikhaĭlovskiĭ did not deny that the guilds and the contemporary Russian *artel's*, had limited individual freedom and the possibilities of individual development; he thought, however, that the negative consequences of this limitation had been less dangerous than the negative results of the development of capitalism. Using the terminology of Marx, it is justified to say that the superiority of the commune and the guild over the capitalist structures was seen by the Populist thinker in the fact that human relations had not been *reified* in them: in the commune and in the guild 'capital was not united with capital but men were united with men, *individuals with individuals*'. For the individual, the consequences of social development were much less disastrous in the Middle Ages than in contemporary capitalist countries. Mikhaĭlovskiĭ concluded from this that it was utterly unjustified to say that capitalism 'had liberated the individual' or that the bourgeois political economy had displayed an even excessive care of the individual's freedom and welfare, falling thus into 'individualism and atomism'. Individualism, in the sense of seeing the central value in the human individual, is in itself the only proper attitude toward the world, but it would be a vain undertaking to look for an expression of it in the liberal economy. The economists have their own phantom (the *Spuk* of Stirner) to which they mercilessly sacrifice the freedom and welfare of men. This new phantom is the 'system of maximum production'. Such a system cannot make happy even the rich, because it sets in motion a frantic race of ambitions and needs without offering any real possibility of satisfying them. True individualism, therefore, must look to the past, to the Middle Ages and to the archaic 'golden age'.[1]

There is no exaggeration in maintaining that among the authors whose books contributed most to Mikhaĭlovskiĭ's

[1] Cf. Mikhaĭlovskiĭ, op. cit., pp. 457–63.

espousal of such a view, the main part has been played by Marx. In *Capital* Mikhaĭlovskiĭ found a dramatic story of how 'great masses of men were suddenly and forcibly torn from their means of subsistence and hurled as free and "unattached" proletarians on the labour market';[1] a story of the 'forcible driving of the peasantry from the land',[2] of divorcing the producer from the means of production, of depriving him (to use Mikhaĭlovskiĭ's language) of his economic 'self-sufficiency' and, by the same token, of his individual 'wholeness'. According to Marx's scheme, capitalism has for its fundamental condition the annihilation of self-earned private property, i.e. the expropriation of the labourer; socialism, in turn, being 'the negation of a negation', will expropriate the expropriators, making the means of production the property of producers (although it will not be a restoration of their *private* property). Mikhaĭlovskiĭ, like other Populists, deduced from this that Russia, in order to avoid the atrocities of primitive accumulation, whose history was 'written in the annals of mankind in letters of blood and fire',[3] should do everything possible to skip 'the capitalist phase', to prevent industrialization on the English model. Moreover, the adaptation of Marx's schema to his own views made it evident to him that socialism and the 'medieval forms of production', especially the common ownership of the land as preserved in the Russian peasant commune, were but different 'levels' of the same type, and, therefore, that the shortest way to socialism in Russia was in the developing of 'the labour and property relations' which already existed, although in a crude form, in the Russian villages and in the *artel's* of the Russian artisans.[4] His final conclusion rang paradoxical:

[1] K. Marx, *Capital*, vol. i, Foreign Languages Publishing House, Moscow 1954, p. 716.
[2] Ibid., p. 718.
[3] Ibid., p. 715.
[4] A similar line of argument, although without reference to Marxism, was evolved by Chernȳshevskiĭ in his *Criticism of Philosophical Prejudices against the*

The worker's question in Europe is a revolutionary question because its solution consists in giving the means of production back to the producers, that is in the expropriation of the present proprietors. The worker's question in Russia is a conservative question because its solution consists merely in keeping the means of production in the hands of the producers, that is, in protecting the present proprietors against expropriation.[1]

These reasonings of Mikhaĭlovskiĭ's make it evident that he misinterpreted Marx by adopting only such aspects of the latter's theories as fitted easily into the general structure of his own Populist views. Nevertheless, Marx's impact on Mikhaĭlovskiĭ should not be reduced to this—it went much deeper, to the very core of Mikhaĭlovskiĭ's thought. Already in 1869, in his article 'The Theory of Darwin and the Social Sciences', Mikhaĭlovskiĭ referred to Marx's views on the division of labour, putting the emphasis, naturally, on its negative effects which, as he admitted, had been fully understood and theoretically explained by the author of *Capital*;[2] he referred also to the views of A. Smith, Ferguson, and others—whom Marx had quoted in this connection. And, indeed, it is not difficult to find in *Capital* many passages which Mikhaĭlovskiĭ could have quoted in support of his views, such as:

The one-sidedness and the deficiencies of the detail labourer become perfections when he is a part of collective labourer. The habit of doing only one thing converts him into a never failing instrument, while his connexion with the whole mechanism compels him to work with the regularity of the parts of a machine. ... In manufacture, in order to make the collective labourer and,

Communal Ownership of the Land. In later years, Marx himself, under the impact of Russian Populism (and, also, under the influence of Chernўshevskiĭ's article), reproduced this line of reasoning in the famous drafts of his letter to Vera Zasulich. Communism, he argued, is the revival in a higher form of the 'archaic property relationship' as represented by the Russian peasant commune; hence the possibility of Russia's direct transition to communism, thus avoiding the painful process of the disintegration of her peasant communes (cf. last chapter of this book, pp. 188–91).

[1] Mikhaĭlovskiĭ, op. cit., p. 703.
[2] Cf. ibid., pp. 170–2.

through him, capital, rich in social productive power, each labourer must be made poor in individual productive powers. . . . Some crippling of body and mind is inseparable even from division of labour in society as a whole. Since, however, manufacture carries this social separation of branches of labour much further, and also, by its peculiar division, attacks the individual at the very roots of his life, it is the first to afford materials for, and to give a start to, industrial pathology.

After this Marx quoted with approval from the *Familiar Words* of D. Urquhart: 'To subdivide a man is to execute him, if he deserves the sentence, to assassinate him if he does not. . . . The subdivision of labour is the assassination of a people.'[1]

It seems to us that Mikhaïlovskiï not only found in these utterances of Marx strong support for his own, already established views; it is much more probable that they were the real starting-point for his own conceptions, that he not only took from Marx what fitted his own theory but, in fact, that the general framework of his views was formed under the strong influence of *Capital*. It seems certain that he first read Marx, and only afterwards found the problem of the division of labour and its destructive effect on individual wholeness in earlier writers, such as Rousseau and Schiller. It seems very likely that his fundamental conception—the assertion of the incompatibility between the progress of society and the progress of individuals—was derived from Marx's conception of the perfection of the 'collective labourer' as being achieved at the cost of, and in inverse ratio to, the development of the individual labourer. It is really amazing how deeply Mikhaïlovskiï had assimilated this aspect of Marx's thought and how little attention was paid to it by his Marxist opponents in Russia, such as Plekhanov and, especially, the 'legal Marxists' who almost completely overlooked the painful contradictions and the tragic aspect of industrial progress.

[1] K. Marx, *Capital* (quoted ed.), pp. 349, 361, 363 (all quotations from chap. xiv: 'Division of Labour and Manufacture').

The conclusions of Mikhaïlovskiĭ and Marx were, of course, quite different. For the author of *Capital* the division of labour, culminating in modern capitalism, was a tremendous progress since it had enabled the labourer to 'strip off the fetters of his individuality' and to 'develop the capacities of his species'.[1] From Mikhaïlovskiĭ's point of view the reverse was true. Having found in Marx the corroboration of Chernȳshevskiĭ's view that 'national wealth' is identical with the poverty of the people,[2] he proclaimed that the welfare of the people, i.e the welfare of individual labourers, should have been treated as the only measure of progress. Having learned from Marx about the high price of capitalist development he refused to pay this price, and set his hopes on the alleged possibility of restoring the archaic forms of social life and adapting them to fit the new conditions. Thus, from the Marxist point of view, he became a 'sociological romanticist', i.e. a reactionary in the 'historico-philosophical' sense of the word. For—as it was put by Lenin—

it is this mistake that quite justly earns for the romanticist the designation of *reactionary*, although this term is not used to indicate a desire simply to restore medieval institutions, but the attempt to measure the new society with the old patriarchal yardstick, the desire to find a model in the old order and traditions, which are totally unsuited to the changed economic conditions.[3]

The sociological content of Mikhaïlovskiĭ's 'reactionary' utopia will become even clearer if we compare it with another 'reactionary' doctrine which emerged in Russia at the same time and which represented, to some extent, a quasi-religious counterpart to Russian Populism—the teaching of Lev Tolstoĭ. Mikhaïlovskiĭ often referred to it, he even wrote an article in which he drew a parallel between it

---

[1] Ibid., p. 329.

[2] Cf., for instance, the following quotation from *Capital*: 'The 18th century, however, did not yet recognize as fully as the 19th, the identity between national wealth and the poverty of the people.' (Ibid., p. 725.)

[3] Lenin, *Collected Works*, vol. ii, p. 241.

and his own views.[1] He was repelled by Tolstoï's dogma of 'non-violence' and by his idealization of patriarchal family relations, but, in spite of this, he found in Tolstoïanism many elements which made it congenial to his own outlook. Some of these similarities were quite striking. Like Mikhaïlovskiï, Tolstoï questioned and rejected the current conception of progress, asserting flatly that 'the golden age is behind us'. In accordance with 'subjective sociology' he vindicated the primacy of the ethical point of view and condemned theories of the inexorable laws of history, accusing them of immorality and blind optimism. Like the Populist thinker, he thought that perfection consisted in a harmony of development rather than in a high level of it; peasant children—he proclaimed—should not learn from us, from 'enlightened' people, but, on the contrary— we should learn from them. Mikhaïlovskiï accepted this assertion interpreting it in the light of his theory of 'types' and 'levels' of development: from the point of view of the *level* of development Fed'ka, a country lad, cannot equal, of course, an internally divided Faust or Hamlet; he represents, however, a more harmonious and (therefore) superior type, and had he been able to write he would have written better things than Goethe.[2]

Mikhaïlovskiï's article on Tolstoï was written in the middle of the seventies, that is, at the time when Tolstoï's doctrine existed only in its germinal state, as formulated in his pedagogical articles of 1862. In his later writings the similarities between his views and Mikhaïlovskiï's are, perhaps, even more salient. This was due to the fact that there appeared in them the central theme of Mikhaïlovskiï's thought: the criticism of 'organic' sociological theories (especially that of Spencer)[3] and of the bourgeois apologists of the division of labour. The theory of a 'social organism',

---

[1] 'Desnitsa i shuĭtsa L'va Tolstogo', 1875 (in Mikhaĭlovskiĭ, *Literaturno-kriticheskie stat'i*, Moscow 1957).

[2] Cf. Mikhaĭlovskiĭ, *Literaturno-kriticheskie stat'i*, pp. 156–8.

[3] Cf. chap. xxx of Tolstoĭ's treatise *Tak chto zhe nam delat'?*

presupposing the division of labour, was, in Tolstoĭ's eyes, but a 'shameless excuse of idlers'. He thought, like Mikhaĭlovskiĭ, that the division of labour was detrimental even to the privileged minority which had 'liberated' itself from physical labour. Diversity in the daily round is the precondition of happiness:

The bird has such a nature that it must fly, walk, peck and calculate, and only when it can do all this, only then it is glad and happy, only then it feels itself a bird. The same holds true in the case of man: he is happy, he feels himself a man only when he walks, bustles about, heaves and carries, when he is able to use in his work his fingers, eyes, ears, tongue and head.[1]

From this assumption Tolstoĭ drew the conclusion that the principle of the division of labour in society should be replaced with the principle of the division of each individual's daily work into different 'harnesses': each man should occupy himself, successively, with all kinds of labour, thus exercising all his capacities.[2] It is easy to see that this was exactly the same ideal which Mikhaĭlovskiĭ had expressed in his 'formula of progress'.

There can be no doubt that these similarities were significant and, therefore, that the social utopias of Mikhaĭlovskiĭ and Tolstoĭ were meaningfully related to each other. Both of them expressed the point of view of the peasantry as a class of pre-capitalist society; both of them protested against social inequality, rejected bourgeois progress, and looked backward to the archaic past. Nevertheless their forms of expression—in the case of Mikhaĭlovskiĭ a quasi-scientific, in the case of Tolstoĭ a quasi-religious form—were entirely different and the meanings they conveyed were also far from being the same. Apart from the obvious disagreement in the matter of non-violence, Mikhaĭlovskiĭ did not share Tolstoĭ's attitude toward science and

---

[1] L. N. Tolstoĭ, *Polnoe sobranie sochineniĭ*, vol. xxv, Moscow 1937, p. 390 (*Tak chto zhe nam delat'?*).
[2] Ibid., p. 389.

art, nor his enthusiasm for patriarchalism: in this respect he was, conventionally speaking, more 'on the left', but, on the other hand, his radicalism could not match that of Tolstoĭ, who was a real 'nihilist' in his criticism of society and state. Tolstoĭ—a patriarchal aristocrat, firmly rooted in country life—was apparently more easily able to identify himself with the world outlook of the primitive, patriarchal villagers. Mikhaĭlovskiĭ, in contradistinction to the count from Yasnaya Polyana, was, and remained, an intellectual, a product of Westernization, and it was only natural for him to try to adapt his peasant Utopia to the tradition of the Russian 'Enlighteners' and to the generally accepted values of the progressive intelligentsia. That is why the Utopia of Tolstoĭ was genuinely archaic, whereas the Utopia of Mikhaĭlovskiĭ reflected rather a romantic longing for the lost harmony of the archaic world.

Mikhaĭlovskiĭ himself was keenly aware that he belonged to the intelligentsia, but he made a distinction between the genuine intellectuals and the narrow specialists in this or that branch of intellectual labour. His ideal of the intellectual was a 'layman'—a man who refuses to subordinate himself to the demands of the division of labour, who consciously defends his many-sidedness, who does not restrict his responsibility within the narrow limits of a specialized job, who is interested in the fate of all his brethren and actively engaged in the struggle for a better future.[1] The 'layman' in the domain of intellectual labour was thus a counterpart of the peasant in the domain of physical labour; the combination of the many-sidedness of the 'layman' with the many-sidedness of the peasant on the basis of a highly developed 'simple co-operation' was conceived as the social ideal, the realization of which would bring about the fullest possible development of the human being. The 'layman' and the peasant were thus, according to Mikhaĭlovskiĭ, natural

[1] Cf. Mikhaĭlovskiĭ's 'Notes of a layman', 1875-7 (*Polnoe sobranie sochineniĭ*, vol. iii).

allies in their common fight against the capitalist system, which maximized 'complex co-operation' and, thereby, threatened the individual with the total subordination to a supra-human 'social organism'.

Mikhaĭlovskiĭ did not deny that, in spite of this alleged community of interests, the gulf between the peasant and the 'layman' was not at all easy to bridge. Moreover, he even admitted the possibility of a conflict between the intelligentsia and the peasantry, arising from the obscurantism of the latter, and for this reason he was always careful to distinguish between the 'interests' and the 'opinions' of the people. At a time when the 'opinions' of the 'common people' were often being quoted by the most notorious reactionaries, who were fond of opposing them to the opinions of progressive intellectuals, and who praised the peasants for their faithfulness to the Russian autocracy, his awareness of the possibility of such a conflict sometimes attained to tragic keenness.

I am a layman . . . [wrote Mikhaĭlovskiĭ]. Upon my desk stands a bust of Belinskiĭ which is very dear to me, and also a chest with books by which I have spent many nights. If Russian life with all its ordinary practices breaks into my room, destroys my bust of Belinskiĭ, and burns my books, I will not submit to the people from the village; I will fight. . . . And even if I should be overcome with the greatest feeling of humility and self-abnegation, I should still say at least: 'Forgive them God of verity and justice; they know not what they do.' For all that, I should still protest.[1]

And here is another, equally expressive quotation:

What matters is the exchange of values between us and the people, an honest exchange, without cheating and hidden thoughts. Oh, if I could drown in that grey rough mass of people, dissolve irrevocably, preserving only that spark of truth and idealism which I succeeded in acquiring at the cost of that same

[1] Mikhaĭlovskiĭ, *Polnoe sobranie sochineniĭ*, vol. iii Spb. (1909), p. 692. Quoted, in the translation by J. H. Billington in his book: *Mikhailovsky and Russian Populism*, Oxford 1958, p. 95.

people. Oh, if only all of you readers were to come to the same decision, especially those whose light burned brighter than mine and without soot. What a great illumination there would be, and what a great historical occasion it would make! unparalleled in history![1]

The same idea, the same longing for being drowned in the grey mass of the people, was expressed later by Dostoev-skiĭ, who, in his famous *Speech on Pushkin* (1880), summoned the Russian 'wanderers'—the alienated, Westernized intelli-gentsia—to humble themselves before the people, to merge into it, while preserving at the same time the universally human quality of their ideals and enriching thereby the people's scale of values. Many other analogies could easily be found, since such ideas and emotions were indeed very characteristic of many currents of nineteenth-century Russian thought. It seems, however, that Dostoevskiĭ and Mikhaĭlovskiĭ—a visionary conservative and a Populist from the 'conscience-stricken' gentry—were certainly among those who gave to these ideas and emotions the best and the most touching expression.

The above quotations from Mikhaĭlovskiĭ's *Notes of a Layman* throw light on a peculiar contradiction in his thought. Unlike Tkachëv, he tried to combine an espousal of the egalitarian ideal of social homogeneity with a firm clinging to the values which—according to his own statement—had been acquired *at the cost of the people*, i.e. due to the process of social differentiation, so severely condemned in his socio-logical theory. Conceding that the 'spark of truth and idealism' has been acquired in such a way, and that it might even be endangered by crude villagers, he returned in fact to Lavrov's theory of 'critically thinking individuals'. It was tantamount, essentially, to the recognition that the Russian Westernized intellectual élite represented some values which—in accordance with Herzen's doctrine of 'Russian Socialism'—should be introduced *from outside* into

[1] Mikhaĭlovskiĭ, op. cit., p. 707.

the communal archaic world of the Russian peasantry. By the same token, Mikhaĭlovskiĭ, although involuntarily and only partially, rehabilitated Western 'bourgeois' progress. This is what Lenin meant when he wrote:

> When Mr. Mikhaĭlovskiĭ begins his 'sociology' with the 'individual' who protests against Russian capitalism as an accidental and temporary deviation from the right path, he defeats his own purpose because he does not realize that it was capitalism alone that created the conditions which made possible this protest of the individual.[1]

There was, of course, a certain polemical oversimplification in this statement but, nevertheless, it rightly pointed out a contradiction which Mikhaĭlovskiĭ could not escape. It would be stupid to look for a direct causal relation between the values of the Russian intelligentsia and the rise of Russian capitalism, but it would be difficult to deny that these were born in Europe as a result of anti-feudal, 'bourgeois' progress, and that the Russian intelligentsia owed its existence to the process of Westernization. Its values were not 'bourgeois' in the narrow sense of this word but they were bound up with 'bourgeois progress' in the sense of the totality of economic and social processes whose function, as seen in the perspective of the historical development of Europe, consisted in destroying the precapitalist structures and thus paving the way for the modern 'bourgeois' type of society. The values and ideas created by these processes showed a marked tendency to become autonomous and to transcend the framework of bourgeois societies, which proved unable to realize them. This accounts for the fact that the Russian Populists could so easily combine them with their utterly negative attitude toward Russian capitalism. But it proved impossible, in fact, to adjust them to the archaic institutions and the archaic world outlook of the peasants, whom the Populists wished to defend against capitalist exploitation. Hence the fundamental contradiction which can be found

[1] Lenin, *Collected Works*, vol. i, p. 415.

in almost all variants of Populism. The archaic world of the Russian peasantry and the ideological heritage of the Russian intelligentsia were heterogeneous, and Mikhaĭlovskiĭ's attempt to prove their essential homogeneity, its ingenuity notwithstanding, was doomed to failure.

In the middle of the seventies Mikhaĭlovskiĭ evolved a more comprehensive theory, claiming to throw a new light not only on progress and regress in human history but also on the most general problems of evolution in the organic world. He called it the theory of 'the struggle for individuality'. In point of fact, the scientific character of this theory was from the beginning rather doubtful: in this respect Mikhaĭlovskiĭ, being truly a 'layman', was much inferior to Lavrov, who was certainly more successful in contributing to the development of sociology as a science, and whose scientific interests were more autonomous, more independent of Populist ideology. But as historical documents revealing the specific quality, the inner contradictions and predicaments of Populist thought, Mikhaĭlovskiĭ's works are unsurpassed, and for that reason they deserve a more detailed treatment in this book.

One of the most characteristic features of Mikhaĭlovskiĭ's quasi-scientific speculations was an odd theoretical inconsistency, illustrating, after all, the well-known phenomenon of being mesmerized by the ideas of one's own enemy. In spite of his acute criticism of biological 'organicism' in social theory, Mikhaĭlovskiĭ yielded to it in his own theoretical constructions.[1] In spite of his criticism of the 'method of analogy', his theory of the struggle for individuality was based on an analogy.[2] In spite of his charges against the social Darwinists in whom he saw apologists of bourgeois

---

[1] Cf. J. F. Hecker, op. cit., p. 134.

[2] Cf. Mikhaĭlovskiĭ's article 'Analogicheskiĭ metod v obshchestvennoĭ nauke', 1869, and a series of his articles entitled 'Teoriya Darvina i obshchestvennaya nauka', 1870–3 (*Polnoe sobranie sochineniĭ*, vol. i).

society,[1] he himself remained within the confines of naturalism and evolutionism. The difference between him and the 'organicists', ideologically very important, consisted in the fact that he challenged their optimistic belief in automatic progress being achieved through the survival of the fittest. In opposition to this complacent optimism he set forth a pessimistic theory which proclaimed that 'natural evolution', both in the organic world and in human society, is always being accomplished at the cost of the constant gradual lowering of the quality (type) of development and that from the point of view of the individual it represents a regressive process.

Mikhaïlovskiï's theory begins with the assertion that there are different stages of individuality which fight against each other and try to dominate each other. This assertion was based upon Haeckel's classification of biological organism and upon his thesis that the more perfect is the whole, the more imperfect must be its parts, and conversely. The relationship between the whole and its parts is always antagonistic: the organ subordinates to itself the 'individuality' of the cells and, at the same time, defends itself against subordination to the higher 'individuality' of the organism; the individual organism, in its turn, wages a struggle for its 'individuality' against the higher 'individuality' of the colony. Man represents one of the stages of individuality (the sixth stage in Haeckel's classification) and as such he must struggle for his own individuality against both lower 'individualities' (the individualities of his organs which he must 'despotically subordinate' to himself) and the higher ones. There is a whole hierarchy of these higher suprahuman 'individualities' (factories as units of 'complex co-operation',

[1] Mikhaïlovskiï's criticism of Darwin, although ridiculed by Plekhanov, was in fact very similar to Marx's view of Darwin, as expressed in his letter to Engels of 18 June 1862. The widespread opinion which implied an essential agreement and a close parallel between Darwin and Marx, was based, in fact, on a misinterpretation. Cf. the excellent comment on it by Shlomo Avineri, 'From Hoax to Dogma. A Footnote on Marx and Darwin', *Encounter*, March 1967.

estates, classes, nations, states, etc.), all of them also fighting against each other and trying to dominate each other. From the point of view of the individual man, they are but different '*social* individualities' which can develop only at the cost of his freedom and wholeness. Therefore—concluded Mikhaĭlovskiĭ—'society is the main, the nearest and the worst enemy of man, an enemy against whom man must always guard himself and keep watch'.[1] In the *Notes of a Layman* he expressed this idea in even stronger words: 'I proclaim that I shall fight this higher individuality which creates a danger of absorbing me. I don't care about its perfection, I wish to perfect myself. Let us fight, I shall try to win, and we shall see to whom the victory falls.'[2]

These words—we must not forget—referred to such a society as develops 'organically', in accordance with the laws of 'natural evolution', i.e. above all, to capitalist society, representing, according to Mikhaĭlovskiĭ, the fullest victory of the social whole over individual men. Men, however, are not doomed to yield to such an evolution, they can and should struggle to prevent it by creating a non-organic society, based upon 'simple co-operation'. Such a society, Mikhaĭlovskiĭ believed, would not grow into a suprahuman 'individuality', its welfare would coincide largely, if not completely, with the welfare of its members. Needless to say, this was the content of his ideal of true socialism. Mikhaĭlovskiĭ conceived of socialism as a society which reduces to the necessary minimum the 'socialization' of men (in the sense of subordinating them to impersonal and supra-individual social mechanisms) and, at the same time, maximizes conscious human solidarity and community of

---

[1] Mikhaĭlovskiĭ, op. cit., vol. i, p. 474.

[2] Ibid., vol. iii, p. 423. In spite of appearances, Mikhaĭlovskiĭ's words should not be interpreted as a declaration of an extreme anarchism. He did not sympathize with the centralized state but his 'enemy number one' was not the State but capitalism, as the most developed and most dangerous form of 'complex co-operation'. Like many other Populists, he thought even that State interference could be utilized to prevent capitalist development, thus defending the interests of human individuality.

interests. It is important to stress this point because the theory of the struggle for individuality leaves the impression that his ideal consisted in the self-sufficient and lonely existence of a monad—an interpretation utterly incompatible with his longing for being drowned and dissolved in the mass of the people. In actual fact Mikhaĭlovskiĭ did not underestimate the significance of social solidarity, although a fascination with the struggle for individual independence overshadowed this problem in his theoretical treaties. Nevertheless he had evolved some thoughts on this subject in *What is Progress?* and he returned to them in the nineties, in connection with Durkheim's famous book *De la division du travail social* (1893).[1]

Although Durkheim, in contrast with Mikhaĭlovskiĭ, was an apologist of the division of labour, his general framework of thought was strikingly similar to that of his Russian reviewer. Like Mikhaĭlovskiĭ, he assumed that the principle of the division of labour applies to the development of both the human society and organic world, and, having accepted the 'law of Baer', saw the essence of developmental processes in the transition from simplicity (homogeneity) to complexity (heterogeneity). Unlike the vulgar organicists he conceded that the advantages of divided labour are bound up with some losses, and posed before his readers the following dilemma: 'Is it our duty to seek to become a thorough and complete human being, one quite sufficient unto oneself; or, on the contrary, to be only a part of a whole, the organ of an organism?'[2] In contradistinction to Mikhaĭlovskiĭ, he voted for the second solution and justified this choice not only by reference to economic necessities but also on ethical grounds: the ideal of individual many-sidedness and autarkic self-sufficiency seemed to him egoistic, antisocial; the new type of social solidarity, created by the division of labour, was in his estimation much superior to the older one,

---

[1] Cf. Mikhaĭlovskiĭ, *Otkliki*, Spb. 1904, vol. ii, pp. 64–99.
[2] E. Durkheim, *The Division of Labour in Society*, Glencoe, Illinois 1960, p. 41.

existing in its purest form in archaic societies and gradually disappearing with their economic development. The old type was defined by him as 'mechanical solidarity' through likeness, the new one as 'organic solidarity' through the differentiation of society. The first—argued Durkheim—binds the individual directly to society, without any intermediary; in the second, he depends upon society because he depends upon the parts of which it is composed; in the first, the individual personality is totally absorbed into the collective personality, in the second, owing to specialization, men become individualized and the social bond, although otherwise tighter, leaves them more freedom of individual choice.

Mikhaĭlovskiĭ's reaction to this line of argument was very interesting. He repeated his thesis that the value of individuality consists not in one-sided distinctiveness but in many-sidedness and wholeness; he declared himself for 'mechanical solidarity', claiming that only a 'solidarity through likeness' binds men as *moral* beings and that it was the gradual dissolution of moral solidarity which made men isolated and lonely, a fact which Durkheim himself has pointed out in his explanation of the growing number of suicides;[1] he stressed once more that the older social ties, in contrast with the new 'organic' ones, were simple, direct, non-reified, and intelligible, that they united men by means of common feelings, thoughts, and aims, without increasing their dependence on each other. In spite of that, however, his idealization of archaic social bonds had little in common with the conservative romanticism of the Russian Slavophiles.[2] He never

---

[1] Mikhaĭlovskiĭ, *Otkliki*, vol. ii, pp. 66–7.

[2] Russian Slavophilism of the forties was, in many respects, a conservative-romantic reaction to the alienating processes connected with the disintegration of the traditional, communal social bonds. Like Mikhaĭlovskiĭ, the Slavophiles espoused the ideal of personal 'integrality' and set a high value on the peasant commune in which they saw a germ of a higher type of social development. However, in sharp contrast to the Populist thinker, they used to set the 'integral personality' in opposition to the 'autonomous individuality', condemned all rationalism, seeing in it a 'disease of the West', and called for

abandoned the ideal of the intellectual and moral autonomy of the individual and, therefore, he could not idealize the unreflective acceptance of tradition and the absorption of the individual consciousness into the collective consciousness of a social group. He dreamed of a community which would be based upon *conscious consent, upon free and rational choice of common values,* and by the same token, although unconsciously, accepted the model of individuality which had been formed due to the 'bourgeois' progress, as a result of the dissolution of archaic social bonds. Once more his ideal turned out to be a double-faced one, and once more it was revealed that the Populist *Weltanschauung,* as expressed in his thought, owed its unity and structure not so much to its homogeneity but rather to its peculiar pattern of contradictions, to the peculiar tension between two sets of historically heterogeneous values.

Let us return, however, to the theory of the struggle for individuality. It was subdivided into many special theories, explaining, more or less ingeniously, different aspects of biological and social evolution. Since lack of space makes it impossible to deal with all of them, we shall confine ourselves to a brief summary of two theories: the theory of 'the heroes and the mob' and the theory of love.

The first of these theories, presented by Mikhaĭlovskiĭ in the treatise *The Heroes and the Mob* (1882), became the

a return to the unreflective acceptance of the internalized tradition. Religious faith, they claimed, is the only guarantee of 'integrality', autonomy is its worst enemy. The autonomy of individuals causes a disintegration of society and dooms the individuals to isolation and loneliness, to the 'freedom of homeless strangers'. The autonomy of reason destroys faith, thus fragmentizing human personality. An individual should become a part of the collective, his consciousness and reason should be subordinated entirely to the supra-individual consciousness of the collective. The 'ecclesiology' of the Slavophiles—the conception of 'sobornost'' (free unity and conciliarism)—was in fact a theory of supra-individual community of tradition excluding any possibility of alienation. The Slavophiles' concept of an 'immediate' synthetic knowledge ('faith') was directed against the rational 'reflection' of the 'uprooted intellectuals'. Their ideal of society can be described in terms of Tönnies's *Gemeinschaft* whereas Mikhaĭlovskiĭ's ideal presents a combination of some aspects of *Gemeinschaft* and *Gesellschaft*. See A. Walicki, 'Personality and Society in the Ideology of Russian Slavophiles: A Study in the Sociology of Knowledge', *California Slavic Studies,* vol. ii, Berkeley and Los Angeles 1963.

subject of strange misunderstandings, stemming mostly from a simple ignorance of its content. The precedent was established by Plekhanov who, judging from the title of Mikhaĭlovskiĭ's treatise, saw it as an expression of the 'subjectivist' belief in the omnipotence of 'heroes' (i.e. the Populist intelligentsia) who could stir up and lead 'the mob' (i.e. the peasant masses).[1] In fact, however, Mikhaĭlovskiĭ's views had nothing in common with hero-worship, and the subject of his treatise was not at all the problem of the 'subjective factor' in history: the theory of 'the heroes and the mob' dealt with the problems of the social psychology and the irrational behaviour of 'the mob', anticipating to some extent Tarde's theory of imitation. Mikhaĭlovskiĭ did not attempt to justify the 'subjectivist' tactics of the terrorist party, the 'Will of the People'; in the social phenomenon of the imitation of 'heroes' by the 'mob' he saw nothing valuable and encouraging—on the contrary, he interpreted it as a symptom of social pathology and degeneration. His interest in this problem was not connected with the traditional Populist question of the mutual relationship between the intelligentsia and the masses; it arose from the wave of anti-Jewish pogroms which had spread over Russia at the beginning of the eighties. He tried to answer the question: what are the social conditions which create such 'heroes' as 'the drunken beast, Vas'ka Andreev', who are able to gather around them 'the mob' and to lead it on to a shameful 'down with the Jews' action.

Mikhaĭlovskiĭ's answer to this question was based upon the sound observation that a connection existed between the growing anti-semitism and the irruption of capitalism into peasant society. His explanation of this connection was, however, rather unconvincing, derived simply from his general historico-sociological theories. The blind imitation

---

[1] Cf. G. V. Plekhanov, *Izbrannȳe filosofskie proizvedeniya*, Moscow 1956, vol. i, p. 735. For Mikhaĭlovskiĭ's polemic against Plekhanov's interpretation (or, rather, misinterpretation) of his views, see Mikhaĭlovskiĭ, *Otkliki*, Spb. 1904, vol. i, pp. 15–33.

of a 'hero'—he asserted—is bound up with the humdrum quality of life in conditions created by the division of labour. A hero, emerging all of a sudden amidst people who are deprived of their many-sidedness and live a meaningless, routine life, easily becomes for them an experience of irresistible force, stifling their critical faculties and arousing them, instead, to irrational imitation. In short, Mikhaĭlovskiĭ's theory accused the capitalistic division of labour of creating the conditions in which people, robbed of their individuality and transformed into a faceless 'mob', become particularly receptive to different social psychoses, with all the dangers resulting from this.

The second theory—the theory of love—was an odd combination of a quasi-scientific form with a speculative and essentially romantic content. It seems significant that it was greatly influenced by Schopenhauer. The author of *The World as Will and Idea* had combined in his philosophy a speculative anti-rationalistic idealism with a kind of pre-positivistic naturalism, and this last feature accounted partially for his great popularity in the second half of the nineteenth century.

Love—argued Mikhaĭlovskiĭ—is a force of nature which deceives individuals by showing them mirages of happiness but, in fact, sacrifices them for its own sake. Lovers are seduced by illusions of self-fulfilment, of overcoming their painful separateness; in fact, however, their love is but a means for the preservation of the species. Mikhaĭlovskiĭ was deeply impressed by Schopenhauer's idea—an idea which he could have found also in Schelling and many other romantic thinkers—that the essence of love consists in the longing for the lost 'totality' and 'completeness' of man. He went so far as to proclaim the superiority of hermaphroditism as a type of individuality.[1] Like every division, the division of human beings into two different sexes deprives

[1] Cf. Mikhaĭlovskiĭ, *Polnoe sobranie sochinenii*, vol. ii, Spb. 1907, pp. 342–3.

the individual of the all-embracing wholeness in which individual perfection consists. To illustrate this idea Mikhaĭlovskiĭ quoted an ancient myth which Plato in his 'Feast' had put into the mouth of Aristophanes. Once upon a time people were hermaphrodites. They were real giants, much superior, incomparably more powerful, both physically and intellectually, than the people of today. Feeling themselves so powerful, they made an audacious attempt to invade Olympus and were punished for it by the gods who cut each of them into two halves. These two halves, however, embraced each other and refused to part, so that many of them died from hunger. Seeing this, Zeus had mercy upon them and gave them the shape of separate beings—men and women. Although these beings were able to live separately, they preserved a dim remembrance of their former state, and thus, from their longing for their lost unity, love was born.

This splendid, wise and poetic myth [concluded Mikhaĭlovskiĭ] is dear to us for two reasons. Firstly, because it clearly points out the superiority of hermophroditism (as a physiological *type*) over a sexually dimorphic organism; secondly, because it is equally clear in indicating that sexual love is a kind of illness.[1]

This conclusion, although formulated in such naturalistic language, shows an aspect of Mikhaĭlovskiĭ's thought which places him surprisingly close to the German romanticists and to the neoromantic idealism of Vladimir Solov'ëv. The romantic philosopher and theosophist, Franz von Baader, gave essentially the same definition of love, although his language, of course, differed considerably from that of Mikhaĭlovskiĭ: he saw love as a striving for the restoration of the primitive androgyny, as 'a means which helps man and woman to supplement each other (both in soul and in spirit) and thus to restore the image of integral man, the image of his primitive godliness'.[2] In contradistinction to Baader, Mikhaĭlovskiĭ did not believe in the *real* existence

[1] Cf. Mikhaĭlovskiĭ, *Polnoe sobranie sochineniĭ*, vol. i, p. 509.

[2] Cf. E. Susini, *Franz von Baader et le romantisme mystique*, vol. iii, Paris 1942, pp. 569–72.

of the primitive androgyny. Solov'ëv, however, also did not share his belief, but it did not prevent him from making androgyny an inseparable part of the ideal of man's 'totality', from proclaiming that the division into sexes was tantamount to the state of disintegration or from creating an appropriate theory of sexual love.[1]

The most peculiar feature of Mikhaĭlovskiĭ's theory was, however, its direct connection with the idealization of the 'self-sufficiency' of the primitive peasant economy. 'Self-sufficiency' with a corresponding 'many-sidedness' and 'wholeness' was in his eyes a common characteristic of hermaphroditism and economic autarky. People, he maintained, were never hermaphrodites, but, none the less, the distinction between the two sexes was, in the past, less marked than today, and among the peasants it is still less marked than among the upper classes of society; analogically, the importance of love has been increasing in direct ratio to the progress of civilization (a similar thought was expressed by Rousseau, who claimed that 'the moral part of love is a factitious sentiment', that only in society has love acquired 'that glowing impetuosity, which makes it often fatal to mankind').[2] The explanation for this was seen by Mikhaĭloskiĭ (as always!) in the development of the division of labour: the more people are 'divided', the more they need love, because they hope that the unitive experience of love will help them to regain their primitive wholeness.

This curious theory seems to us to be a most significant document, revealing the inner substance of Mikhaĭlovskiĭ's vision of the world. Under the cover of scientific naturalism, prevailing in the second half of the century, we find in it romantic, emotive strains and a romantic structure of thought. It was romantic in the historical sense of the word, and not only in the sense of a conventional label for 'looking backward

[1] Cf. K. Mochulskiĭ, *Vladimir Solov'ëv: zhizn' i uchenie*, Paris 1951, pp. 203–7.

[2] J. J. Rousseau, 'On the Origin and Foundation of the Inequality of Mankind', *Works*, vol. vii, Edinburgh 1774, pp. 192–3.

to the past', as in the case of 'economic romanticism'. We find in it—and, through it, in the whole of Mikhaĭlovskiĭ's thought—the typically romantic problem of reconciling individuality with universalism (in the sense of totality, of all-inclusiveness of content); the problem of how to overcome separateness while preserving individual existence, how to be oneself and, at the same time, feel oneself 'at one' with the infinite variety of the world. Mikhaĭlovskiĭ's solution to this problem was in fact one of the most characteristic romantic solutions: the individual should not merge into the pantheistically conceived world but he should strive to embrace the whole world in himself. Such was the romantic longing which underlay Mikhaĭlovskiĭ's ideal of 'heterogeneity' of individual existence, of the all-embracing totality of individual life.

Romantic patterns can easily be found in the vision of the world and, above all, in the emotional attitudes of some of the other Populists, at least those of them who romantically idealized the 'plain folk' and who espoused the romantic ideals of individual heroism. However, it seems that in the writings of Mikhaĭlovskiĭ we have the best material for a study of this romantic admixture to Populist thought.

3. *Socialism and Political Struggle*

The turn from the sixties to the seventies—the years when Lavrov, Mikhaĭlovskiĭ, and Tkachëv disputed over progress —marked the beginning of the distinctively Populist revolutionary movement in Russia.[1] The distinction between the pre-Populist revolutionary movement of the sixties and

---

[1] It seems proper to remind the reader that the subject of this book is Populism as an ideology, and not the Populist revolutionary movement. Therefore, we shall not discuss in detail the activities, political programmes, and organizational principles of all the revolutionary organizations which had espoused the Populist ideas. We confine ourselves to the discussion of those aspects of revolutionary Populism which seem to be the most essential for the understanding of the general structure of the Populist thought and of the pattern of tensions between the different positions within it.

the full-fledged revolutionary Populism of the seventies consisted in a characteristic shift of emphasis—in the shift from
anti-feudal democratic radicalism to anti-capitalist agrarian
socialism. The continuity of the revolutionary tradition
could have been preserved, since some elements of agrarian
socialism were part and parcel of the revolutionary ideology
already in the sixties. Nevertheless, the shift of emphasis
was clear and significant. In contradistinction to the revolutionaries of the first 'Land and Freedom', whose aims
were democratic rather than socialist, the revolutionaries of
the seventies thought it necessary to cut themselves off from
'bourgeois' democracy in order to emphasize the socialist
character of the movement and to make sure that it would
not pave the way for capitalist development. This new
attitude found expression in the theory of the top priority of
'social' revolution over a 'merely political' one—a theory
which became a hallmark of classical revolutionary Populism.
The 'social' revolution—the revolutionary transformation
of the economic basis of society—was identified with the
'socialist' revolution; the 'political' revolution, i.e. the
revolutionary transformation of the existing political structure, was conceived as being merely a 'bourgeois' revolution
from which true socialists should keep themselves away.
In a word, Russian revolutionaries, having realized that
political democracy could not solve the most painful social
problems, took care to ensure that they were not 'bourgeois
revolutionaries', that their revolution, in contrast with
political revolutions in the West, would not further the
interests of the bourgeoisie. Their preoccupation with
manifesting the anti-bourgeois character of their movement
became for them a real obsession. This is what accounts for
the curious fact that the revolutionaries in Russia—a
country which had suffered so much from its autocratic
political structure—became so intransigent and stubborn
in depreciating the 'bourgeois', 'fraudulent' political freedom
of the West.

In this manner the Russian revolutionary Populism of the seventies became bound up with the deepest distrust of liberal constitutionalism and with an ostentatious indifference towards 'political forms'. Western parliamentarianism was seen by the Populists as an instrument of the bourgeoisie and as a token of its final victory. Socialism was set in opposition to 'political struggle'. The latter was not merely neglected but even flatly rejected as 'bourgeois' in its content and detrimental to the revolutionary cause; liberal constitutionalism, it was argued, would make the possessing classes stronger and thus ruin for a long time the chances of the socialists. Although it seems to us today to be a curious paradox, the revolutionaries of the seventies considered themselves to be 'apolitical' and treated this strange 'indifference towards politics' as a pledge that their socialism had been purified from bourgeois contamination.

It is argued sometimes that the disillusionment with political freedom, especially with parliamentarianism, was a common feature of European revolutionaries after the events of 1848–51 in France. This is perfectly true and should be taken into account as one of the factors which made it easier for the Russian Populists to adopt their particular viewpoint; nevertheless, it is not a sufficient explanation of their political indifferentism. Western revolutionaries never became indifferent to such questions as republicanism versus monarchism, let alone autocracy; on the contrary, they became disillusioned with the mechanism of general elections because it had helped the restoration of the empire in France. The case of the Russian Populists was rather different: the peculiar and distinctive feature of Russian classical Populism consisted precisely in the conviction that from the point of view of socialist goals, autocracy was *better* than constitutional monarchy or a bourgeois republic. Sometimes it was connected with a readiness to co-operate with the Tsar if he should decide to push through the necessary social reforms; Russian autocracy was contrasted with constitutionalism as being a political power not bound up with the vested interests of the privileged classes and, therefore, more likely to protect the interests of the people. (We must remember that the advocates of Russian autocracy were always fond of representing constitutionalism as the oligarchical rule of the privileged.) This attitude towards autocracy was very characteristic of the so-called 'legal' Populists, but it was not completely alien to the revolutionary milieu. In the case of the latter, however, much more typical was the view which could be formulated as follows: autocracy as such is certainly bad, but, nevertheless, it should be given preference over constitutional forms since it hinders the development of capitalism and makes impossible the transformation of the Russian bourgeoisie into an independent and powerful political force. It is interesting that a classical formulation of this view may be found in the *Diary* of young Chernȳshevskiĭ. He wrote: 'It does not matter whether there is a Tsar, or not, whether there is a constitution, or not; what really matter are the social relations, that is how to prevent the situation in which one class sucks the blood of another.'[1] And he concluded: 'It would be best if absolutism could retain its rule over us until we are sufficiently permeated with democratic spirit, so that, when a popular form of government comes to replace it, political power could be handed over—*de jure* and *de facto*—to the most numerous and the most unhappy class (peasants+hirelings+workers) and, thus, we could skip all the transitional stages.'[2]

---

[1] Chernȳshevskiĭ, *Polnoe sobranie sochineniĭ*, vol. i, Moscow 1939, p. 110.

[2] Ibid. It is worth noting that these views of the young Chernȳshevskiĭ were combined with a belief that anti-aristocratic absolute monarchy can further the interests of democracy. Such a monarchy, he wrote in his *Diary*, 'must stand above all classes, and is specially created to protect the oppressed, i.e. the lower classes, the peasants and the workmen. The monarchy must be sincerely on their side, must be at their head and protect their interests. Its duty is to use all its energies to work for future equality—not a formal equality but real equality. . . . To my way of thinking this is what Peter the Great did.' (Ibid., p. 122. Quoted in Venturi, op. cit., English ed., p. 139.)

The Populists of the seventies did not know Cherný-shevskiǐ's *Diary*, but they read his articles on the political history of France and learned from them how to distinguish between liberalism, which aims at 'merely political' reforms, and democracy, whose only aim is the real welfare of the people. In his article 'The Struggle Between Parties in France' (1858) their teacher went so far as to proclaim that Siberia, whose population was relatively well off, was a more 'democratic' country than England, stricken with the plague of 'pauperism'. This non-political conception of democracy exerted a profound influence on Populist thought, but, ironically, it was not Chernýshevskiǐ's final word. In his *Letters without Addressee* (whose addressee was in fact Alexander II) he drew the conclusion that *political* democratization was a necessary condition—a *sine qua non*—of true social progress in Russia; for that reason he sided with the gentry liberals of Tver' who demanded for Russia a liberal constitution. Tsarist censors, however, did not permit the publication of the *Letters* and Chernýshevskiǐ himself, from his Siberian exile, could not continue to influence the ideology of the Russian revolutionary movement. According to the memoirs of Stakhevich, who had met Chernýshevskiǐ in the penal settlement of Alexandrovsk, the fellow prisoners of Cherný-shevskiǐ, including the author of the memoirs, were taken by surprise when they heard from him the following statement:

You repeat that political freedom cannot feed a hungry man. But let's take, for example, the air, and let's ask: can it feed a man? Of course not. And yet, without food man can survive a few days, whereas without air he cannot live more than ten minutes. As the air is necessary for the life of human organism, so political freedom is necessary for the normal functioning of society.[1]

The evolution of Chernýshevskiǐ's political views antici-pated, as it were, the evolution of the revolutionary Populism

---

[1] Quoted in Steklov, op. cit., pp. 448-9.

of the seventies. We shall see how the Populists, under the pressure of their own revolutionary experience, were forced at last to recognize the priority of political change over the social tasks of the movement.

The problem of the relationship between 'the political' and 'the social' was, as we can see, not a new one. The generation of the sixties also paid attention to it; what was really new was the conviction that 'political' and 'social' goals were, in the Russian conditions, not only different from, but also *opposed* to, each other. The revolutionaries of the first 'Land and Freedom'—an organization inspired by Chernȳshevskiĭ, Herzen, and Ogarëv—set themselves *political* goals, such as, for instance, the convocation of the Assembly of the Land, and did not see in this a defection from, or a betrayal of, the *social* goals of revolution. The rejection of the 'political struggle' and the negative attitude towards political freedom became prevalent in the Russian revolutionary movement not earlier than at the beginning of the seventies.

Their prevalence was a result of many causes. Of these the most immediately obvious was the influence of Bakunin who had become by then the leader and chief theorist of international anarchism. He opposed Marx and the German Social-Democratic Party on the grounds that socialists should not have participated in any political struggle; they should not have fought for seats in a bourgeois parliament, but should have aimed, instead, at the complete overthrow of all forms of political power. Any importance attached to 'merely political' problems was, in his eyes, a kind of apostasy, a capitulation before trivial bourgeois radicalism. Russian autocracy was preferable, from his point of view, to an orderly bourgeois republic: under an autocratic ruler people are not involved in politics, the State is for them but an external force, whereas in a republic the idea of the State and the desire to participate in political life deeply permeates their consciousness, thus making them less receptive to anarchism. We should add, however, that although the

Populists accepted Bakunin's 'apoliticism', their motives were rather different, since it was not so much the problem of State but the problem of capitalism which was for them of paramount importance.[1]

Another factor was the peculiar psychology of the 'conscience-stricken gentry', so excellently expressed in Lavrov's *Historical Letters*. The members of the circle of 'Chaĭkovskists'—the biggest Populist organization at the beginning of the seventies—were characterized by an extreme intensity of ethical spirit;[2] their longing for purity and total sacrifice was sometimes expressed in religious terms and, finally, found an outlet in the religious teaching of 'deo-humanism'.[3] A similar spirit of quasi-religious apostleship characterized the members of the circle of Dolgushin; Flerovskiĭ, with whom they had got into contact, compared them to the early Christians and wrote for them a manifesto of a new religion—a religion of equality.[4] The rejection of the 'political struggle' was for these young men a form of discharging their debt to the people. It was an act of self-abnegation, an act of self-renunciation in favour of the people for whom, as it was thought, 'political freedom' was something completely meaningless and worthless. Mikhaĭlovskiĭ, who had so often succeeded in formulating in his legally published articles the actual problems and dilemmas of the revolutionary movement, defined it as a victory of 'conscience' (the

---

[1] Although there were many populistic elements in Bakunin's thinking, we must be careful to distinguish between Anarchism and Populism. Anarchism is by definition incompatible with 'Statism' whereas Populism is perfectly compatible both with anarchic tendencies and with the most outspoken 'Statism'. The 'legal Populists' represented a kind of 'State socialism', Tkachëv proclaimed that the victory of his ideals could be achieved only by means of a totalitarian revolutionary State. The anarchists believed in the desirability of a completely spontaneous development of society; in contrast with this, Lavrov's and Mikhaĭlovskiĭ's 'subjective sociology' proclaimed that spontaneous tendencies of social development should be subject to a conscious, rational control.

[2] Cf. Venturi, op. cit., pp. 471–2.

[3] Cf. T. I. Polner, 'N. V. Chaĭkovskiĭ i "bogochelovechestvo"', in *N. V. Chaĭkovskiĭ: religioznye i obshchestvenno-politicheskie iskaniya*, Paris 1929.

[4] Cf. Venturi, op. cit., p. 498.

feeling of moral duty) over 'honour' (the feeling of one's own rights). In his excellent article on Dostoevskiĭ's novel *The Possessed* he expressed this attitude as follows:

> For a man who has tasted the fruit of the general-human tree of knowledge nothing is more attractive than political freedom, freedom of conscience, freedom of speech and freedom of the press, free exchange of ideas, free political meetings and so on. And, naturally, we want all this. But if the rights, which this freedom will give us, are to prolong for us the role of a coloured, fragrant flower—in such a case we reject these rights and this freedom! Curse upon them, if they only increase our debt to the people, instead of enabling us to discharge it! . . . By recognizing the top priority of the *social* reform we renounce the increasing of our rights and freedom, since we see these rights as instruments of the exploitation of the people and of the multiplying of our sins.[1]

The sad conviction that the increasing of the political and civil rights of intelligentsia would result in the increase of their debt to the people was based upon a keen awareness of the fact that political freedom of the English type had been bound up with the development of capitalism. An important part in creating the Populist image of capitalism and of bourgeois political freedom was played by the books of Flerovskiĭ (*The Situation of the Working Class in Russia*, 1869, and *The Alphabet of the Social Sciences*, 1871), who was in contact with what were then the two main centres of the Populist movement—with the circle of the 'Chaĭkovskists' and that of the 'Dolgushinists'. The Populist youth were greatly impressed by the articles published in the journal, *Annals of the Fatherland*: by Mikhaĭlovskiĭ's article 'What is Progress?' and, also, by the articles of Eliseev who vehemently attacked 'plutocracy' and interpreted the parliamentary system as the most convenient tool for brutal class domination by the bourgeoisie.[2] And—last but not least—the

---

[1] Mikhaĭlovskiĭ, *Polnoe sobranie sochineniĭ*, vol. i, pp. 870–2.

[2] Cf. Eliseev's article 'Plutocracy and its Social Base', published in *Otechestvennȳe Zapiski*, 2, 1872. Reprinted in N. K. Karataev, *Narodnicheskaya ėkonomicheskaya literatura*, Moscow 1958, pp. 125–59.

influence of Marx whose *Capital* (vol. i) had been widely known in the Populist circles even before the publication of its Russian edition (1872) was especially important. Marx himself (in contrast with Bakunin) never neglected the 'political struggle'; the Russian Populists, however, could easily interpret him after their own manner: Marx's thesis that the 'political superstructure' always serves the interests of the ruling class, his denunciations of liberal hypocrisy, his acute criticism of the 'formal' bourgeois democracy— all these could be interpreted as powerful arguments for the priority of social (economic) changes over political ones.

The ideological evolution of the revolutionary movement ran parallel with the new processes in the economy and the social relationships of the Russian countryside. A few years after the abolition of serfdom, Russian peasants began to suffer from the new, capitalist forms of exploitation which, in conjunction with the remnants of the *corvée* system and with increased financial burdens, made their situation even worse than before. In addition to intensified exploitation by the landlords, there emerged a new, insatiable class of exploiters—the so-called *kulaks* or *miroeds*, village capitalists and usurers, vividly described in Flerovskiĭ's book. It is quite understandable that the democratic revolutionary movement reacted to these processes by bringing into the foreground the anti-capitalist aspect of its ideology and by an increased idealization of the allegedly socialist quality of the peasant *mir*.

The real explosion of this romantic faith in the socialist instincts of the Russian peasantry was the great 'go to the people movement' in 1873–4. Venturi has called it 'a collective act of Rousseauism'.[1] Following the example of the 'Chaĭkovskists' and the 'Dolgushinists', hundreds and thousands of young men and women, clad in peasant clothes,

---

[1] Venturi, op. cit., p. 503.

without any prearrangement, very often without even having consulted each other, went to the villages in order to taste the authentic, healthy, and simple life. The desire of being merged with the people was so strong that some of them had made a sincere attempt to become converted to Orthodox Christianity. Thus, for instance, Aptekman, a Jew, decided to become Orthodox and after baptism felt himself 'literally renewed'.[1]

The enthusiasm which accompanied the 'go to the people' movement was—according to the unanimous testimony of its participants—something unique, unprecedented, and unrepeatable. Sergeĭ Kravchinskiĭ described it as follows:

Nothing similar had been seen before, or since. It was a revelation, rather than a propaganda. At first the book, or the individual, could be traced out, that had impelled such or such person to join the movement; but after some time this became impossible. It was a powerful cry which arose no one knew where, and summoned the ardent to the great work of the redemption of the country and of humanity. And the ardent, hearing this cry, arose, overflowing with sorrow and indignation for their past life, and abandoning home, wealth, honours, family, threw themselves into the movement with a joy, an enthusiasm, a faith, such as one experienced only once in a life, and when lost one never found again. . . . It was not a political movement. It rather resembled a religious movement, and had all the contagious and absorbing character of one. People not only sought to attain a distinct practical object, but also to satisfy an inward sentiment of duty, an aspiration towards their own moral perfection.[2]

Among the participants of the movement two groups are usually distinguished: the Bakuninists and the Lavrovists. The origins of this differentiation should be traced back to the late sixties—to the years of an interesting controversy over the value of education and science from the point of view of the revolutionary cause. Bakunin, in the *émigré*

[1] Cf. O. V. Aptekman, *Obshchestvo 'Zemlya i Volya' 70-kh godov po lichnȳm vospominaniyam*, 2nd ed., Petrograd 1924, p. 168.

[2] Stepniak [S. Kravchinskiĭ], *Underground Russia: Revolutionary Profiles and Sketches from Life.* With a preface by P. Lavrov, 2nd ed., London 1883, pp. 25–6.

journal *The People's Cause*, 1868, had summoned the Russian youth to give up their schools and universities, since these were merely a form of the exploitation of the masses. In a revolutionary epoch, he argued, learning is an untimely occupation; revolutionaries have no need of the official science which serves the interests of the ruling classes and deepens social inequality. The same views were shared by Nechaev and Tkachëv;[1] among the 'Chaïkovskists' they were upheld by the young prince, Peter Kropotkin, who in his programmatic paper on 'the ideal of future society' postulated a total liquidation of the existing institutions of higher education, and proposed instead to open 'school-workshops', which would combine learning with work and thus prevent the separation of intellectual labour from physical labour; he believed that such schools would be able to develop very quickly and to attain even better results in education than the best of the existing universities.[2] This excessive contempt for 'official science' sometimes passed into a contemptuous attitude towards education and science as such. No wonder that Lavrov, who was a revolutionary and a scholar in one, thought it necessary to cut himself off from Bakunin's views on this question and to oppose them. The best expression of his standpoint is found in his 'Knowledge and Revolution', an article published in the first number of his *émigré* journal *Forward!* (1873).

At the beginning of the 'go to the people' movement, the differences between the Bakuninists and the Lavrovists became, as it were, effaced, overshadowed by the lofty enthusiasm of both; later, however, during daily work among the peasants, they re-emerged and became even more salient.

---

[1] Nechaev, who collaborated with both Tkachëv and Bakunin, formulated their standpoint as follows: 'It's a real nonsense to go to school, because all the educated people inevitably become exploiters and the process of learning is in itself a form of exploitation.' (Quoted in B. P. Koz'min, *P. N. Tkachev i revolyutsionnoe dvizhenie 1860–kh godov*, pp. 193–4).

[2] Cf. P. A. Kropotkin, 'Dolzhný-li mý zanyat'sya rassmotreniem ideala budushchego obshchestvennogo stroya?' (reprinted in *Revolyutsionnoe narodnichestvo 70–kh godov XIX veka*, vol. i, ed. B. S. Itenberg, Moscow 1964).

The Bakuninists, who were in the majority, represented the 'romantic' side of the movement; the Lavrovists, although sharing the general enthusiasm, were much closer to the rationalistic heritage of the 'enlighteners' of the sixties. The first appealed to the *emotions* and *instincts* of the peasants; the second wished to *teach* them to mould their *consciousness*. The Bakuninists were rightly called 'the rebels'; having espoused Bakunin's view that the Russian peasants were always ready to rise in rebellion, they went to the villages not to teach their inhabitants but to stir up revolt; they went particularly to the Ukraine and to the Volga region, hoping to resuscitate the rebellious traditions of Sten'ka Razin and Pugachëv. The Lavrovists were given the name of the 'propagandists'; they went to the people with a peaceful propaganda of socialist ideas, hoping to enlighten the peasants and thus to prepare them for a future consciously socialist revolution. Both the Bakuninists and the Lavrovists highly appreciated the peasant commune, the latter, however, were much less inclined to idealize its archaic 'antediluvian' features; like Chernȳshevskiĭ and Lavrov, they appreciated not so much the existing forms of communal life, but, rather, the socialist potentialities which they ascribed to it. Both currents rejected the struggle for 'political freedom', the Lavrovists, however, in contrast to Bakuninists, were very sympathetic to the German Social-Democratic Party, in spite of its obviously 'political' character. Plekhanov, who had begun his revolutionary career as a convinced Bakuninist, reflected later: '*Their* propaganda [i.e. the propaganda of the Lavrovists] was probably more reasonable than ours.'[1]

Speaking about the Bakuninists Plekhanov has rightly noticed that they preached Bakuninism 'moulded after the Russian fashion'.[2] The word 'anarchism' is not an adequate definition of the ideology of the Russian followers of Bakunin.

[1] G. V. Plekhanov, *Sochineniya*, edited by D. Ryazanov (2nd ed.), Moscow–Petrograd, vol. iii, p. 140.
[2] Ibid., p. 139.

They took from Bakunin what they needed, first of all his high appraisal of the archaic forms of social protest, such as peasant rebellions and banditry.[1] They were greatly impressed by Bakunin's assessment of the Russian 'popular ideal', but their attitude towards the peasant commune obviously tended to be even less critical than that of their teacher.[2] The anarchic ideal of 'statelessness' was in fact abandoned by them and replaced with a postulate of decentralization and self-government; Kravchinskiĭ, for instance, stated explicitly that 'anarchism' meant for him 'federalism' and nothing more.[3] Bakunin's anti-intellectualism and hostility towards bourgeois civilization fused in their ideology with a distinctively Populist criticism of capitalist development and with the 'federalistic' ideals of Shchapov.[4]

[1] According to E. J. Hobsbawm, 'no political movement has reflected the spontaneous aspirations of backward peasants more sensitively and accurately in modern times than Bakuninism, which deliberately subordinated to them'. (E. J. Hobsbawm, *Primitive Rebels: Studies in Archaic Forms of Social Movement in the 19th and 20th Centuries*, 2nd ed., Manchester 1963, pp. 82–3.)

[2] The best exposition of Bakunin's views of the peasant commune is the famous 'Annexe A' to his book *Statism and Anarchism* (reprinted in *Revolyutsionnoe narodnichestvo 70-kh godov XIX veka*). He saw in the commune three positive elements: (1) the conviction that all the land should belong to the people, (2) the communal ownership of the land, (3) self-administration, combined with the obviously hostile attitude towards the State. However, these three positive elements of the commune were, according to Bakunin, linked to the three negative ones: (1) patriarchalism, (2) the absorption of the individual into the community, and (3) faith in the Tsar. Bakunin hoped that these negative features of the Russian peasantry would be eradicated by social revolution.

[3] Cf. *Revolyutsionnoe narodnichestvo 70-kh godov XIX veka*, vol. ii, ed. by S. S. Volk, Moscow–Leningrad 1965, p. 339.

[4] Afanasiĭ Shchapov (1830–76)—son of a poor Siberian deacon, lecturer in Russian history at the University of Kazan', dismissed for political reasons in 1860 and exiled to Siberia in 1864 (cf. Venturi, op. cit., pp. 196–203)—was unquestionably one of the most interesting figures in the history of the early Populism. In his works on the history of Old Believers and on the colonization of new territories by the Russian people, he interpreted Russian history in terms of an unceasing struggle between 'the people' and 'the State', between free federalism and compulsory centralism. He extolled the peasant *mir* in which he saw the 'archetype' of the 'free, popular self-government of the land', and was enthusiastic about the Old Believers who were in his eyes the embodiment of the true spirit of orthodox Christianity, unspoiled by the destructive influence of the State. Like the Slavophiles, he romantically idealized the pre-Petrine Russian past and, to some extent, was directly influenced by them (especially by Constantine Aksakov, who saw the Russian history as a struggle

The results of the 'go to the people' movement were very disappointing. Very often young enthusiasts were arrested by the police with the active collaboration of those whom they wished to 'prepare' for the future revolution, or to rise in an immediate revolt. Russian peasants turned out to be less receptive to socialist ideas than had been believed by revolutionary intellectuals. The Populist movement had undergone an important experience; it remained to think it over and to draw conclusions.

Very characteristic and far-reaching conclusions were drawn by some Lavrovists, first of all by their Petersburg group which was the most coherent and, at the same time, the most inclined to a stubborn and doctrinaire sectarianism. Having lost their faith in the peasantry, they turned to propagandist activity among the industrial workers. They carried it on very cautiously, putting emphasis on long-term educational work, cutting themselves off from direct revolutionary action and condemning not only disturbances and riots, but even strikes, since they thought them to be 'premature'. Soon, in the second half of the seventies they began to justify their standpoint by appealing to the authority of Marx: since the peasant commune, they argued, is

between 'the people' and 'the State') Like other thinkers of the sixties, he was not a fully fledged Populist: capitalism was not the central problem for him, the spirit of the commune was opposed by him not so much to the spirit of capitalism as to the spirit of the centralized State, which had destroyed ancient Russian freedom. His philosophy of Russian history was similar in this respect to the ideas of the Decembrists who had defined their task as a *restoration* of freedom in Russia. Like the Decembrists, he idealized the Old Russian 'republics' of Pskov and Novgorod, and believed that the ancient 'spirit of freedom' was still alive in the hearts of the Russian people. It remains to say that—in contrast to the Populists of the seventies—he was a convinced constitutionalist and a passionate advocate of political freedom. Nevertheless, in spite of all the differences, Shchapov exerted a considerable influence on the Populist revolutionary movement. His ideas became interwoven with anarchic motifs and gave a singular, archaic twist to the Populists' conception of a free federation of self-governing communes. The young Plekhanov, the leader of the Populist organization 'Black Repartition', followed Shchapov in defining Russian history as 'a tragic story of the life-and-death struggle between two diametrically opposed principles of living: the communal principle of the people and the individualistic principle of the State' (*Sochineniya*, vol. i, p. 111).

reactionary and doomed to a natural dissolution, socialist revolution in Russia must be postponed until Russian capitalism and the Russian industrial proletariat have achieved a sufficient level of development.[1] It should be stressed that this theory was combined by them with a strong admixture of the traditional Populist attitude towards the 'political struggle': political freedom was recognized as a necessary stage of development but it was emphasized, at the same time, that the struggle for it belonged to the historical tasks of bourgeoisie and that socialists should keep themselves away from it in order to protect their ideology from being contaminated by bourgeois illusions. This conviction led them, naturally enough, to a wait-and-see attitude, to a peculiar 'philosophy of inactivity'.[2]

This characterization must not be applied to all Lavrovists—not all former 'propagandists' found themselves in such a blind alley; many of them, together with the 'rebels', joined the ranks of the revolutionary organization 'Land and Freedom', created at the end of 1876. As for Lavrov himself, from the very beginning he presented in his journal *Forward* a more revolutionary line than that of his followers in Russia; this brought about a serious dissatisfaction which finally—at the end of 1876, after the meeting of the Lavrovists in Paris—led to a split and to the liquidation of Lavrov's journal. The quasi-Marxist standpoint at which some of his followers arrived by the end of the seventies remained alien to the author of *Historical Letters*. Although he was convinced that revolution must be carefully prepared, he never reduced the 'preparatory' work to mere propaganda; he supported and stimulated revolutionary work among the

[1] Cf. Sh. M. Levin, *Obshchestvennoe dvizhenie v Rossii v 60–70–e gody XIX veka*, Moscow 1958, pp. 378–83. It is interesting and characteristic that these late Lavrovists considered themselves to be social-democrats and after the split in the 'Land and Freedom' group sympathized with Plekhanov's 'Black Repartition' organization.

[2] The expression of Plekhanov (cf. Plekhanov, *Sochineniya*, vol. xxiv, pp. 87–8.

urban workers, but he had not lost hope in the socialist potentialities of the peasant communes. He wished for Russia an agrarian socialism, the precondition of which he saw in the development of peasant communes from the stage of collective *ownership* of the land to the stage of collective *cultivation* of it; at the same time he understood the necessity of modern large-scale industrial production and believed in the possibility of a non-capitalist industrialization of Russia. His arguments for such a possibility anticipated to some extent the theory of Vorontsov, but there was also an important difference: in contrast with the 'legal' Populists, the editor of *Forward* conceived of the possibility of a non-capitalist industrialization as wholly dependent on the previous success of socialist revolution.[1]

The programme of 'Land and Freedom', elaborated by the former 'Chaïkovskists' who had managed to escape imprisonment, was based upon the experience of both the 'rebels' and the 'propagandists'. Their common platform was the conviction that revolutionaries should act only among the people and through the people. The main reasons for their lack of success were seen in the Bakuninist exaggeration of the peasants' rebelliousness and in the too abstract, excessively theoretical forms of socialist propaganda; this latter reproach was directed mainly against the Lavrovists but it also recapitulated the experience of the Bakuninists who had arrived at the conclusion that it was erroneous to begin revolutionary agitation among the peasants by a general attack on the very foundations of the existing social order. To avoid these errors in the future, the programme of 'Land and Freedom' postulated a reduction of the actual tasks of the movement to such as harmonized with the immediate needs and desires of the people. It is not sufficient—proclaimed Kravchinskii—to give up German dress and to go to villages in peasant clothes; not the socialists only, but

[1] Cf. M. M. Karpovich, 'P. L. Lavrov and Russian Socialism', *California Slavic Studies*, vol. ii, Berkeley and Los Angeles 1963.

socialism itself should be clad in the russet coat of the Russian peasant.[1] The new programme was thus an attempt to eliminate abstract intellectualism and utopianism by adjusting socialist ideals to the views of the peasants and to the reality behind them. This was the origin of *narodnichestvo* in the narrow historical sense of this word. Zhelyabov afterwards wrote about it as follows:

Having come to the conclusion that the difficulties which the government created made it impossible to imbue the conscience of the people entirely with socialism, the socialists became transformed into populists. . . . We decided to act in the name of the interests of which the people had already become aware—no longer in the name of pure doctrine, but on the basis of interests rooted in the life of the people, interests of which it was conscious. This was the characteristic quality of *narodnichestvo*. From dreams and metaphysics it made the transition to positivism, and came to adhere to the soil (*pochva*). This is the basic quality of *narodnichestvo*.[2]

The new 'go to the people' movement, started by the revolutionaries of the 'Land and Freedom', was much better organized than the first one. According to Vera Figner the new organization tended from the very beginning to replace 'federalist' principles by centralism and effective leadership.[3] The conditions of underground activity made this tendency stronger and stronger until, finally, 'Land and Freedom' became transformed into a 'militant, centralized organization'. Lenin in *What is to be Done?* praised this achievement highly and set it up as an example for the Russian revolutionary Marxists to follow.[4]

The postulate of a strongly centralized organization had been put forward long ago by Tkachëv. His ideas, however, especially his revolutionary elitism, known under the name

[1] Cf. B. P. Koz'min, *Iz istorii revolyutsionnoĭ mysli v Rossii*, p. 642.
[2] 'Iz recheĭ na sude A. I. Zhelyabova, N. I. Kibalchicha i S. L. Perovskoĭ', *Bĭloe*, no. 3, 1906, p. 64.
[3] Cf. V. Figner, *Polnoe sobranie sochineniĭ*, Moscow 1932, vol. i, p.105.
[4] Cf. Lenin, *Collected Works*, vol. v, p. 474.

of 'Jacobinism' or 'Blanquism', were otherwise incompatible with the generally accepted principle of action *through* the people, let alone the *narodnichestvo* of 'Land and Freedom'. He wished the revolutionary movement to embark on the way of a conspiracy of professional revolutionaries who would strive, first of all, for the seizure of political power. In the 'movements to the people' he saw only a tremendous waste of energy and he set against them the idea of a return to the methods of Nechaev, with whom he had collaborated in the late sixties.[1] His journal *The Tocsin* (*Nabat*) summoned Russian revolutionaries to learn from the experience of the revolutionary conspiracies of the first half of the century, recommending to them, above all, the tradition of Babeuf and Buonarroti. He also highly appreciated the revolutionary experience and conspiratorial skill of the Poles: in the first three numbers of *The Tocsin* he published a long article on the patriotic conspiracy which had given rise to the Polish

[1] Sergeï Nechaev (1847–82), the founder of the utterly centralized clandestine revolutionary organization 'The People's Vengeance', resorted in his revolutionary activities to a mystification, presenting himself as a representative of the International and a member of an All-Russian Revolutionary Committee; he was helped in this by Bakunin who gave him a special warrant with the stamp of a non-existent 'Alliance Révolutionnaire Européenne, Comité Général'. Nechaev's *Revolutionary Catechism* recommended extremely ruthless and immoral methods of struggle: the revolutionary, according to Nechaev, despises and hates the existing social ethic; 'for him, everything that allows the triumph of the revolution is moral, and everything that stands in its way is immoral' (quoted in Venturi, op. cit., p. 366). This rule was applied in the case of Ivan Ivanov, a member of Nechaev's organization, who, because of his protest against Nechaev's methods, was 'sentenced to death' and killed (1869). His assassination enabled the police to pick up the trail of 'The People's Vengeance' and to arrest its members. Nechaev's trial (in St. Petersburg in 1871) aroused great interest both in Russia and in the West. The reactionary press (and, also, Dostoevskiï in *The Possessed*) utilized it to discredit the Russian revolutionary movement as a whole.

For Russian revolutionary youth the 'Nechaev affair' was a tremendous moral shock which contributed greatly to a wholesale condemnation of revolutionary conspiracies of the 'Blanquist' type (from Tkachëv's point of view, this was, of course, a long step backward). However, after the bitter experience of the 'movements to the people', the attitude towards Nechaev underwent a considerable change. The members of the 'Will of the People' seriously thought about organizing his escape from imprisonment in the St. Peter and St. Paul fortress in St. Petersburg.

insurrection of 1830.[1] It seems significant in this context that his closest collaborators (in the *émigré* period of his life) were Poles: Karol Janicki and Kacper Turski.[2]

The people—maintained Tkachëv—cannot liberate itself by its own efforts. The people's support is necessary for the victory of the revolution but most important is strong leadership and well-organized action by the revolutionary vanguard. 'Preparatory' work among the people makes no sense; it is merely a way of shirking genuine revolutionary action, a convenient dodge of 'reactionary revolutionaries'. Revolution in Russia cannot be postponed since its chances are *decreasing* with the passing of time. Today the Russian State is 'absolutely absurd and absurdly absolute', having no roots in society and lacking any genuine support, 'hanging in the air';[3] tomorrow, having become 'constitutional and moderate', it will be able to gain a strong social basis; today the Russian bourgeoisie is weak and Russian capitalism is still in its initial stage; tomorrow it might be too difficult to eradicate bourgeois weed from the Russian soil.

This diagnosis fitted the mood of the impatient Bakuninists, always eager to engage in a direct revolutionary action; on the other hand, however, Tkachëv's view of the people and his vision of the society of the future, moulded by the totalitarian revolutionary State, were diametrically opposed to their belief in spontaneity and to their ideal of a free federation of self-governing communes. The peasant commune—argued Tkachëv—cannot beget socialism; autarkic, self-contained rural communities belong to the most conservative, stationary forms of social life and no germ of progressive

---

[1] Cf. *Nabat*, nos. 1–3, 1875–6.

[2] In Venturi's book their names are spelled 'Yanitsky' and 'Tursky'; similarly the name of the assassin of Alexander II, Hryniewiecki, is spelled 'Grinevitsky'. Such twisting of Polish names (if they appear in a Russian context) is a common practice in many Western books—a fact, however, which does not justify it. It does not matter that Hryniewiecki (in contradistinction to Janicki and Turski) was a *russified* Pole: nobody denies that Herzen was a Russian but nobody spells his name as 'Gertsen'.

[3] An expression used by Tkachëv in his *Open Letter to Engels*.

development can be found in them. The collectivism, the 'innate communism' of the Russian peasantry, can greatly facilitate the revolutionary transformation of society, but does not constitute an adequate basis for socialism. The people alone would not be able to create a dynamic, progressive society; it would not even be able to remain true to its old ideals and to defend them against hostile social forces.[1] The task of the revolutionary vanguard cannot, therefore, be confined to the overthrow of absolutism. The revolutionary party should take over and strengthen the absolute power of the Russian State in order to make of it a powerful instrument of revolutionary dictatorship and to utilize it for a thorough transformation of the whole of social life. The authority of the revolutionary party running the revolutionary State should replace for the Russian people the authority of its 'mythical Tsar'.

Among the members of 'Land and Freedom' the attitude towards Tkachëv was, as a rule, utterly negative: they often accused him of compromising the Russian revolutionary movement and of betraying the cause of the people for the sake of his own political ambitions.[2] In spite of this, however, some of Tkachëv's ideas accelerated the process of differentiation among the revolutionaries from 'Land and Freedom'. Their influence had been instrumental in the crystallization of a new current within the movement—the current which proclaimed that 'work among the people' should give way to a systematic and well-organized political struggle against autocracy.

This reluctant withdrawal from the purely 'Populist' positions ('Populist' in the narrow, historical sense of the word) was caused by both the partial successes and the over-all failure of the second 'go to the people' movement. The revolutionaries who had settled in remote villages as country doctors, teachers, or artisans in order to help the

---

[1] P. N. Tkachëv, *Izbrannȳe sochineniya*, vol. iv, p. 264.
[2] Cf. B. P. Koz'min, *Iz istorii revolyutsionnoĭ mȳsli v Rossii*, pp. 366–7.

peasants in their daily life and to organize their resistance to the landlords, the *kulaks* and the officials of the local administration, could rightly claim to have achieved many positive results; at the same time, however, they were forced to come to the conclusion that a really effective continuation of their work was impossible in the existing political conditions. Their experience has been recapitulated in the memoirs of Vera Figner:

> We saw that our case in the countryside was lost. In us the revolutionary party had suffered a second defeat. And this time it was not because its members lacked experience; it was not because we had an abstract programme which appealed to the people for purposes which did not concern it or for inaccessible ideals; it was not because we had put excessive hopes in the state of preparation of the masses. No, no, we had to give up the stage, knowing that our programme was vital, that our demands met with a real response in the life of the people. What was lacking was political freedom.[1]

The bitter awareness of the inefficiency of the 'purely Populist' (in the narrowest sense) methods of struggle led the revolutionaries to engage in political terrorism. In January 1878 a young girl, Vera Zasulich, fired at General Trepov, governor of St. Petersburg, in order to avenge a revolutionary who had been flogged in prison; using the terminology of Mikhaïlovskiĭ we may say that with this action the revolutionary movement of the seventies made the shift from a struggle in the name of 'conscience' to a struggle in the name of its own 'honour'. In May a gendarme, Colonel Heyking, was assassinated in Kiev; in August Kravchinskiĭ, helped by Barannikov, killed General Mezentsov, head of the Third Section (i.e. of the secret police), with a dagger; on 2 April 1879 Alexander Solov'ëv, having previously informed the organization 'Land and Freedom' but without being aided by it, attempted to assassinate the

---

[1] V. Figner, op. cit., vol. i, p. 157. (Quoted in the English edition of Venturi's book, p. 577.)

Tsar; a few weeks later an autonomous terrorist organization 'Death or Liberty' had constituted itself within 'Land
and Freedom'. The new current was disapproved of by the
orthodox *narodniki*, who, centred round Plekhanov, accused
the terrorists of abandoning the work among the people and
betraying the traditional principle of the top priority of
the 'social' tasks. Quite different—almost enthusiastic—was
the opinion of the 'Jacobin' journal *The Tocsin*: although
Tkachëv himself was rather sceptical about terrorism, the
majority of his followers—especially Turski—saw in it the
best way to achieve the disorganization and overthrow of
the existing apparatus of the State. But the main advantage of terrorism was—from the 'Jacobin' point of view—
the fact that it led to a considerable reduction of the work
in the countryside and to the concentration of revolutionary
forces in a highly centralized, militant, clandestine organization. Plekhanov has rightly indicated that the editors of *The
Tocsin* had good reason to rejoice over this. In 1879 they were
indeed in a good position to recognize the fiasco of the 'movements to the people' and to make the following statement:

> We were *the first* to point out the inevitability of this failure,
> *we first* besought our youth to abandon this pernicious, anti-
> revolutionary way, to return to the tradition of direct revolu-
> tionary action through a militant, centralized revolutionary
> organization [i.e. to the tradition of Nechaev]. And we were not
> crying in the wilderness.[1]

The transition to terrorism was often accompanied by
hesitation and scruples; many leading members of 'Land and
Freedom' conceded the necessity of terrorism but tried, at
the same time, to remain true to the tenets of *narodnichestvo*.
Very significant in this respect was one of Kravchinskii's
articles published in the first number of the clandestine
journal of the party (autumn 1878).[2] The brave assassin

---

[1] Quoted in Plekhanov's *Our Differences* [Sochineniya, vol. ii, p. 148].
[2] *The Programme of the Journal 'Land and Freedom'*. Reprinted in Karataev,
op. cit., pp. 322–6.

warned his comrades about the danger of an excessive enthusiasm towards terrorism.

We must remember [he wrote] that this is not the proper way to achieve the liberation of the working masses. Terror has nothing in common with the struggle against the very foundations of the existing social order. Against a class only another class can rise; only the people itself can overthrow the (social) system. Therefore the main part of our forces should work among the people. The terrorists are only a defensive detachment whose task consists in protecting the revolutionaries working among the people against the treacherous blows by the enemy.

The concentration of all revolutionary forces on the political struggle against the existing State would entail a serious danger of paving the way for the bourgeoisie, which—as it has been proved by the fate of political revolutions in the West—always displays great skill in utilizing the apparent successes of revolution for its own ends. To prevent this the revolutionary party should secure for itself the active support of the people, creating thereby a force which would be able to utilize the political freedom, gained by the *political revolution*, for engaging in an effective *social struggle* against the bourgeoisie.

However, neither Kravchinskiǐ's article nor the new version of the party programme, worked out in 1878,[1] could save the unity of 'Land and Freedom'. After Solov'ëv's attempt, Plekhanov and Popov, acting on behalf of the orthodox *narodniki*, demanded the immediate convocation of a general meeting of the party. Their demand was accepted and the general meeting, preceded by a gathering of the 'innovators' in Lipetsk, was opened in Voronezh on 24 June 1879. The 'innovators' had expected that the victory might fall to their opponents but it turned out otherwise. A very favourable situation was created for them by the dogmatic stiffness of Plekhanov who, having met no adequate

---

[1] For the programmes of 'Land and Freedom' (and, also, of the other revolutionary organizations of the seventies) see Karataev, op. cit., and *Revolyutsionnoe narodnichestvo 70–kh godov XIX veka.*

response to his attack on terrorism, burst out in anger and left the meeting. It was very distressing for the participants but it enabled them to attain a compromise: both kinds of revolutionary activity were sanctioned by the meeting and the terrorist Executive Committee was granted full autonomy. This was, however, a shaky compromise. By October 1879 the existing split had become formally recognized, and 'Land and Freedom' ceased to exist. The orthodox *narodniki* (joined, to the disappointment of the 'innovators', by Vera Zasulich) created a separate organization under the name of the 'Black Repartition' (*Chërnyĭ peredel*); this name meant, literally, an equal repartition of all the land among the 'black' people, i.e. among the peasants. The 'innovators' adopted the name *Narodnaya volya* which, owing to the ambiguity of the word *volya*, meant at the same time the *will* of the people and the *freedom* of the people. Thus even the name of the former organization had been divided up. Vera Figner, repeating Morozov's observation, wrote about it: '*Chernyĭ peredel* took the "Land", we took the "Freedom", and each faction embarked on its own separate way.'[1]

Thanks to the almost universal feeling that work among the people had failed to bring any lasting results, it was easy for 'The Will of the People' to secure for itself an absolute hegemony in the revolutionary movement. 'Black Repartition' could not stand any comparison with it, the more so since a denunciation by a traitor had forced its leaders to emigrate. The theoretical innovation of the 'Will of the People' consisted in the view that 'political tasks' must be given priority over 'social tasks', and in an attempt to justify this view by reference to some specific features of the Russian State. The chief theorist of the party, Lev Tikhomirov, saw clearly that in the class struggle which was going on the Russian State could not remain neutral, that its interests were closely bound up with the interests of the privileged; on the other hand, he did not wish to abandon

[1] V. Figner, op. cit., p. 157.

the optimistic view that the Russian State lacked a strong social base, that it was, to use Tkachëv's expression, 'hanging in the air'. In a word, he wished to prove that the Russian State strongly supported the possessing classes without being, in return, strongly supported by them. This could be done by utilizing the conception of the so-called 'State school' in Russian historiography (S. Solov'ëv, B. Chicherin) which claimed that in Russian history, in contrast with the history of the West, the State had always been a completely independent force, not a mere instrument of the existing social classes, but the creator of them, the supreme organizer of the whole of social life.[1] Solov'ëv and (especially) Chicherin drew from this a conclusion that the State was, and would remain, the main source of initiative and the prime mover of true progress in Russian life; the theorist of the 'Will of the People' utilized their conception to prove the thesis that in the Russian conditions, the struggle against the possessing classes (including the bourgeoisie) must necessarily turn into a political struggle—it was a logical conclusion from the assumption that the Russian gentry and bourgeoisie had been called into being by the State and remained entirely dependent on it. In a programmatic article 'The Tasks of the "Will of the People"' it was stated as follows: 'Every attempt to do something in the interests of the masses pushes us willy-nilly into collision with the government. Thus our activity assumes a political character.'[2]

The acceptance of the postulate of a 'political struggle' did not exclude, of course, important differences in the interpretation of it. According to Plekhanov two tendencies opposed each other within 'The Will of the People': the 'constitutional tendency', represented by Zhelyabov, and

---

[1] Chicherin went so far as to proclaim that even the peasant commune (in which he saw the greatest hindrance to the normal development of Russia) was only an artificial and relatively modern institution, created by the State in order to impose on peasants the collective responsibility for taxes. His apologia for a centralized bureaucratic State was inspired by the philosophy of Hegel.

[2] Cf. N. K. Karataev, op. cit., pp. 386–7.

the 'Blanquist' ('Jacobin') one, to which Tikhomirov was inclined.[1] It is possible to accept this view. We should add, however, that Tikhomirov was, after all, very far from a consistent 'Blanquism'; much more consistent in this respect was another member of the Executive Committee, Mariya Oshanin, a disciple of the veteran of Russian 'Jacobinism', P. G. Zaĭchnevskiĭ, and an ardent follower of the ideas of Tkachëv.[2]

According to Zhelyabov, to switch the movement to political struggle meant to strive for an alliance with all the social forces which wished the overthrow or the limitation of Russian absolutism, that is, first of all, with the liberals; the aim of this alliance was to be the installation of representative government and the introduction of political freedom which would give the socialists legal ground on which their struggle in the name of the economic interests of the people could be carried on. A theoretical foundation was given to this conception by Mikhaĭlovskiĭ who had evolved it in the series 'Political Letters of a Socialist', published (anonymously, of course) in the journal *Will of the People* in 1879. He opposed the views which until quite lately he himself had preached, arguing that in Russian conditions political freedom could become a weapon of anti-bourgeois forces: the Russian bourgeoisie, in contrast to the French bourgeoisie of the eighteenth century, was, happily, still too weak to install its class rule after the overthrow of Russian absolutism.

The interpretation given by Tikhomirov was less clear. He was torn between 'Populism' (in the narrow historical sense) and 'Blanquism'. In contrast to Zhelyabov he put the emphasis on the *seizure of power*, on a determined action by the revolutionary vanguard, and not on a broad alliance with the liberals; on the other hand, however, he rejected Tkachëv's idea of a long-term post-revolutionary dictatorship.

[1] Plekhanov, *Sochineniya*, vol. xxiv, pp. 104–13.
[2] Cf. V. Figner, op. cit., p. 164. For information about Zaichnevskiĭ see Koz'min's work: 'P. G. Zaĭchnevskiĭ i 'Molodaya Rossiya' (in his *Iz istorii revolyutsionnoĭ mysli v Rossii*, pp. 127–403).

Revolutionaries, according to Tikhomirov, should seize power, but they should keep it only until the moment when a spontaneous popular revolution has broken out. Irrespective of these differences, all the members of the party had agreed that the shortest way to the overthrow of absolutism was the assassination of the Tsar. And, indeed, all possible efforts had been made to achieve this end. The first two attempts—the attempt to blow up the emperor's train and the explosion in the Winter Palace, carefully prepared by Stepan Khalturin—had failed, but the third attempt was successful. On 1 March 1881 Alexander II was killed by a bomb thrown by a member of the 'Will of the People', a russified Pole, Ignacy Hryniewiecki. The hopes of the revolutionaries, however, were bitterly deceived. Their deed brought about not chaos and revolutionary disturbances, but—on the contrary—the consolidation of autocracy; instead of political freedom the rule of the most extreme reaction was installed; instead of the expected tremendous increase in the strength and popularity of the party, the assassination of the Tsar was followed by an effective repressive action which, in practice, put an end to its revolutionary activity inside Russia. The Executive Committee, or, strictly speaking, those members of it who had managed to escape arrest, sent to the new Tsar a letter (written by Tikhomirov, modified in some details by Mikhaïlovskiĭ) in which they exhorted him to summon the representatives of all the Russian people in order to rebuild the existing system of the State, avoiding thereby a bloody revolution in the future. There was in this letter a solemn declaration that the revolutionary party would unconditionally submit to the decisions of a freely elected National Assembly.[1] Alexander III, however, preferred a policy which precluded any hope for the peaceful evolution of the Russian monarchy.

On 3 April 1881 the main organizers and perpetrators

---

[1] Cf. *Literatura partii 'Narodnoĭ voli'*, Moscow 1907, pp. 451 ff. See also Venturi, op. cit., pp. 716–18.

of the assassination—Rȳsakov, Zhelyabov, Mikhaïlov, Kibalchich, and Sof'ya Perovskaya—were hanged (Hryniewiecki
was killed by his own bomb). During the hearing only
Rȳsakov—a youth aged nineteen—broke down. The courageous behaviour of the rest—especially the fortitude of
Zhelyabov and Perovskaya—amazed the judges and gained
the admiration of the entire world.

4. *The Privilege of Backwardness*

'The Will of the People' had been defeated, but for the
Russian revolutionaries there was no return to their former,
always more apparent than real, 'apoliticism'. The last
bulwark of the orthodox 'apolitical' *narodnichestvo*—Plekhanov's organization 'Black Repartition'—had ceased to exist
already in 1881; soon after its former members adopted the
social-democratic standpoint and created in exile, in 1883,
the first Marxist organization in the Russian revolutionary
movement—the 'Emancipation of Labour' group. By the
same year Plekhanov had published his first Marxist book,
entitled *Socialism and Political Struggle*, in which he tried to
prove that social revolution in Russia must and should *be
preceded* by political revolution. Thus, at the beginning of
the eighties the idea of 'political struggle' had been accepted
by all the currents of the Russian revolutionary movement.
Another dispute arose instead: a dispute over the interpretation of 'political struggle' and over the time-table of the
two revolutions—the 'political' and the 'social'. Plekhanov's
group upheld the view that the overthrow of absolutism
would be of necessity a bourgeois revolution and that it should
be separated from the future *social* revolution by a period
of time sufficiently long to ensure the full development of
Russian capitalism. The survivors of the 'Will of the People'
set against this the view that political revolution in Russia

would be the first step of social revolution and that the foundations of socialism could be laid in Russia immediately after the overthrow of Tsarist absolutism.

It does not mean, however, that the old Populist 'apoliticism' completely disappeared from the historical scene. *Revolutionary* Populism had become politically orientated, but apart from it there existed also a *social-reformist* current of Populism, and for this current the eighties were not a period of crisis but, on the contrary, the period of its fullest bloom. The Russian students of Populism used, and still use, to call this current 'the *liberal* Populism', this name, however, is inappropriate both from political and economic points of view; it seems much better to define it as a 'legal', non-revolutionary Populism. The representatives of this current, being 'apolitical' in a much more literal sense than the revolutionaries, were by no means advocates of the liberal parliamentary system; liberalism in political economy was for them a real bugbear, a synonym of the most ruthless capitalist exploitation which they fought in the name of the interest of the people, not differing in this respect from revolutionary Populists.[1] They were 'liberals' only in the very broad and specifically Russian sense of this word—in the sense of hoping for a non-revolutionary progress by means of social reforms from above. In the seventies the most characteristic representative of this current was Grigorii Eliseev who treated Ricardo and Malthus as two main pillars of the new slavery and who saw in Russian autocracy a much superior political form to the parliamentary systems of the West.[2] Russian autocracy, he thought, was not bound up with the class interests of bourgeoisie, its true interests coincided with the interests of the Russian people, what had been proved by the emancipation and

---

[1] This was acknowledged by N. K. Karataev who wrote: 'The liberal Populists also belonged to the democratic camp.' There was a 'class difference' between their economic programme and the programme of the liberals (Karataev, op. cit., p. 10).

[2] Cf. his article 'Plutocracy and its Social Base'. (See p. 87, n. 2.)

enfranchisement of the peasants; in accordance with this view he tried to persuade the Tsarist government that it was necessary to engage the power of the State in the struggle against Russian capitalism, and in doing this he made the fullest possible use of Marx's description of the atrocities of primitive accumulation and industrial revolution in England. Mikhaĭlovskiĭ, who was the closest and lifelong friend of Eliseev, also belonged to this current: in spite of his sympathy and admiration for the revolutionaries, he personally did not believe in the victory of revolution and therefore had to appeal to the Tsarist government, trying in vain to convince the ruling élite of the necessity of defending Russian peasant communes against the inroad of capitalism.[1] He was, however, not a typical representative of legal Populism: his significance was much greater since he was a theoretician who formulated the most general ideals of Populism, a thinker whose ideas could be shared, and were often shared, by revolutionary and non-revolutionary Populists alike. The central figure among the legal, social-reformist Populism was certainly V. P. Vorontsov, who wrote under the initials V. V. His book *The Fates of Capitalism in Russia* (1882) was the most ambitious attempt to analyse the specific features of Russian capitalism and, at the same time, the most elaborated and original theoretical argumentation for the possibility and necessity of a non-capitalist development of Russia.

Vorontsov's theories should be placed, of course, within the context of the economic views of the earlier Populist writers. Strictly speaking it would be proper to begin with Chernȳshevskiĭ's criticism of the epigones of economic liberalism and with the outline of his 'political economy of

---

[1] There was, however, a considerable difference between Eliseev's and Mikhaĭlovskiĭ's views. The former considered autocracy to be much better than a parliamentary system whereas the latter, in his *Political Letters of a Socialist*, espoused the cause of political freedom. Later, in the nineties, Mikhaĭlovskiĭ cut himself off from Vorontsov, thus protesting against the latter's acceptance of Russian absolutism.

the working masses'; such a task, however, would lead us too far beyond the scope of the present study. Therefore, in order to avoid unnecessary digressions, we shall confine ourselves to a short presentation of the views of V. Bervi-Flerovskiĭ, the most important economic publicist among the Populist writers of the seventies.

According to Marx, Flerovskiĭ's book *The Situation of the Working Class in Russia* (1869) was the most important book of this kind since Engels's work on the condition of the working class in England; it was 'the first work to tell the truth about Russian economic conditions'.[1] By 'working class' Flerovskiĭ meant both the urban and the rural workers, both proletarians and small proprietors, in a word 'the working people' as a whole. Unlike many other Populists, he did not idealize the economic conditions of the Russian peasants and artisans; on the contrary, he gave a terrifying picture of their growing destitution, of their increasing dependence on *kulaks* and speculators, and of their inability to cope with the financial burdens imposed on

[1] K. Marx and F. Engels, *Correspondence 1846–1895. A Selection with Commentary and Notes*, trans. by Dona Torr, London 1936, pp. 282–3 (Marx's letter to Engels of 10 February 1870). Marx wrote: 'The man [Flerovskiĭ] is a determined enemy of what he calls "Russian optimism". I never held very rosy views of this communistic Eldorado, but Flerovskiĭ surpasses all expectations. . . . A glowing hatred of landlords, capitalists, and officials. No socialist doctrine, no mysticism about the land (although in favour of the communal form of ownership), no nihilistic extravagance. Here and there a certain amount of well-meaning twaddle, which, however, is suited to the stage of development reached by the people for whom the book is intended. In any case this is the most important book which has appeared since your *Condition of the Working Class*. The family life of the Russian peasants—the awful beating to death of wives, the vodka and the concubines—is also well described. It will therefore come quite opportunely if you would now send me the imaginative lies of Citizen Herzen.'

However, this opinion was expressed by Marx on the basis of the first 150 pages only of Flerovskiĭ's book (cf. ibid.: 'I have read the first 150 pages of Flerovskiĭ's book'). And we should remember that Flerovskiĭ's Populism found its best and most characteristic expression not in the descriptive part of his book but in the last chapter of it (reprinted in Karataev, op. cit., pp. 192–219). If Marx had read this chapter before expressing his above quoted opinion on Flerovskiĭ's book, this opinion, very probably, would have been much less favourable.

them by the State; he went so far as to proclaim that the situation of the 'working class' in Russia was, in fact, much worse than that of the proletariat in the West. Nevertheless, he remained a true Populist, since the main reason of this was seen by him not in the backwardness of Russia but in the defection from her traditional, national principles, in the blind imitation of the Western ways in the economic and social sphere. In the West—he argued—there are two main forms of agricultural production: the large and the middle-size estates, cultivated by tenants or by hirelings, and the small parcels, owned and cultivated by individual peasants. Both forms have their advantages and disadvantages, the latter, however, decisively predominate. The first form—the large and middle-size estates—brings about a low level of productivity and a catastrophic situation of agricultural workers. Small individual parcels are much better since 'the possession of the land by those who cultivate it is the pre-condition of the normal relationship between the workers and the land'.[1] But this form of agriculture, characteristic of France, has also many negative sides. A small individual proprietor is a privileged worker, always ready to exploit others;[2] he is greedy, individualistic, and anti-social, hostile to the spirit of solidarity and co-operation; finally, small landed property entails never-ending subdivisions of land, very detrimental from the point of view of economic efficiency. In the Russian peasant commune Flerovskiĭ saw the third and the best form of agriculture, making possible to combine the advantages and to eliminate the disadvantages of the first two.[3] For the low level of productivity of the communes only the external circumstances account: if the

---

[1] V. Bervi-Flerovskiĭ, *Izbrannye ékonomicheskie proizvedeniya*, Moscow 1958, vol. i, p. 608.

[2] Ibid., p. 593.

[3] It is interesting to observe that the same argument in favour of the peasant commune had been developed as early as 1849 by the Slavophile thinker, A. S. Khomyakov. Cf. A. S. Khomyakov, 'O selskoĭ obshchine. Otvetnoe pis'mo k priyatelyu', *Polnoe sobranie sochineniĭ*, 4th ed., vol. iii, Moscow 1914, pp. 459–68.

State lessened its financial demands, first of all if it cancelled the redemption payments, if the principle of the communal ownership of the land was made universal in Russia, that is if the estates of the gentry became the property of the peasant communes, in a word, if the external obstacles were removed, the productivity of Russian agriculture would rapidly increase and the economic advantages of the peasant commune would become evident. It should be stressed that, in contrast with the conceptions of Lavrov, Flerovskiĭ did not postulate the transition from collective ownership of the land to collective cultivation of it; on the contrary, he highly appreciated the peasant commune on the ground that it allegedly combined the rational, egalitarian distribution of land with the full independence of individual peasants on their temporarily owned plots. The communal principles were sharply contrasted by him with 'communism', which he conceived as tantamount to the total subordination and engulfment of the individual; latifundia, collectively cultivated by hired labour, were, in his eyes, much closer to communism than the peasant communes. In his protest against the 'socialized labour', in his stress on the economic independence of individual peasants, he has come very near to the 'sociological romanticism' of Mikhaĭlovskiĭ.

In contradistinction to Vorontsov, Flerovskiĭ was directly and closely connected with the revolutionary milieu; his book *The Alphabet of Social Science* (1871) was written at the request of the Dolgushinists; his pamphlet *How One Must Live According to the Laws of Nature and Truth* (published secretly in a clandestine press) summoned the peasants to fight against their landlords; during his first exile he did not refrain even from engaging himself in a direct revolutionary activity among the peasants. As we see, he was by no means a 'legal', non-revolutionary Populist. At the same time, however, his Populist indifferentism towards 'political forms' made it possible for him to appeal to the authority of the existing State and to assume that 'political revolution' was unnecessary in Russia; moreover, he appealed even to the landed gentry showing them how to fraternize with, and to work for the benefit of, the people, without giving up their position of landlords.[1] These appeals stemmed from his conviction that embarking on the non-capitalist way of development was desirable for the Russian nation as a whole, that it was, indeed, the only means of avoiding a nation-wide catastrophe. His socialistic programme—peasant communes in agriculture, workers' *artel's* in industry—was bound up with a nationalistic motivation; it was propagated not only in the name of social justice but also, if not first of all, as a means of raising the Russian nation from humiliation (the defeat suffered in the Crimean war) and poverty, as a way to overtake and outstrip the West.

When I think about our political and social situation [wrote Flerovskiĭ] when I observe how we tail away after the European civilization and when I compare us with the Persians who, just as we, had had a great State and nevertheless had perished because of their tailing away after the ancient civilization, it comes to my mind that the only way out for us is the realization of the great idea, an idea which no other nation as yet ever tried to put into practice.[2]

Avoiding the unprintable word 'socialism', Flerovskiĭ defined this 'great idea' as introducing a social system based upon nation-wide solidarity and co-operation, excluding the class war with which the West is being torn. Liquidation of poverty and social antagonisms would give Russia a tremendous advantage over Western Europe; in this way the Russian nation could play 'a great and glorious part' in universal history, 'standing in the van of civilization and being the leader of mankind'.[3]

This characteristic motif of 'overtaking and outstripping the West' is to be found also in the writings of Vorontsov. The main difference between Flerovskiĭ and Vorontsov was

---

[1] Cf. Flerovskiĭ, *Izbrannуe ėkonomicheskie proizvedeniya*, vol. i, pp. 612–13.
[2] Ibid., p. 589. [3] Ibid., p. 566.

I

the latter's much better understanding of the necessity of industrialization. It was by no means something completely new in the Populist thought; thus, for instance, Lavrov's *émigré* journal *Forward* stated explicity that hostility towards capitalism did not amount to hostility towards industrialization: large-scale industry is nowadays a prerequisite of civilization, but it can and should be based upon socialist principles.[1] A. Gerschenkron, a well-known specialist in the field of economic backwardness, described Russian Populism as a manifestation of 'the specific Weltanschauung of Russian intellectuals, with its deep and immediate concern for the welfare of the peasantry and its unwillingness to accept industrialization';[2] the present author feels this generalization to be rather one-sided, fitting very well to the Populist 'economic romanticism' but disregarding the elements of modern socialism which (as, for instance, in Lavrov) were also inherent in the Populist thought. The position of the Populist economists of the eighties was characterized not so much by opposition to industrialization as such, but rather by a search for a distinctive, non-capitalist model of industrialization, a model which would take account of the interests of peasantry and of the specific features of the economic situation of Russia as a backward agrarian country in co-existence with the developed capitalist countries. In this respect the ideas of Vorontsov seem to be of particular interest.

The party of the people [wrote Vorontsov] would have gained a great deal in practical respects if the duality that split its view of the world had been eliminated, if its faith in the viability of popular principles had been united with a conviction of the historical impossibility of the development of capitalist production in Russia. Such a conviction can stem from our generalizations (if only they are true).[3]

[1] Cf. 'Ocherki uspekhov ékonomicheskoĭ éksploatatsii v Rossii za poslednie godỹ', *Vperëd*, no. 5, London 1877. Reprinted in Karataev, op. cit., pp. 284–5.
[2] A. Gerschenkron, *Economic Backwardness in Historical Perspective*, New York–Washington–London 1965, p. 186.
[3] V. V[orontsov], *Sud'bỹ kapitalizma v Rossii*, Spb. 1882, p. 4 (the essential parts of Vorontsov's book are reprinted in Karataev, op. cit.).

This quotation sums up the main ideological intention of *The Fates of Capitalism in Russia*. The Populist thinkers of the seventies were deeply imbued with a pessimistic conviction that time was against them, that the so-called 'objective course of events'—the automatism of economic development —pushed their country to follow the capitalist path. Mikhaĭlovskiĭ, for instance, called in question not the existence of an 'objective course of events' but only its inevitability; he opposed it in the name of his 'subjective', moral postulates, but he conceded that the chances of a successful realization of these postulates were diminishing with the passage of time. Among the revolutionaries this 'duality in the view of the world' was expressed with particular force by Tkachëv who proclaimed that the whole future of Russia depends on what is to come first—the socialist revolution or the formation and stabilization of Russian capitalism. The book of Vorontsov was to provide arguments for a more optimistic conception, claiming that the 'objective course of events' was not at all a sworn ally of Russian bourgeoisie. This optimism, though, was only partial and did not lead to quietism: Vorontsov argued that capitalism as the prevailing *form of production* was impossible in Russia, but he did not forejudge the fate of Russian capitalism as a *form of exploitation* of the masses.

Vorontsov's belief in the ultimate failure of Russian capitalist industrialization was grounded on his analysis of the international conditions in which Russian capitalism was born. He wrote:

The historical peculiarity of our large-scale industry consists in the circumstance that it must grow up when the other countries have already achieved a high level of development. It entails a two-fold result: firstly, our industry can utilize all the forms which have been created in the West, and, therefore, can develop very rapidly, without passing at a snail's pace through all the successive stages; secondly, it must compete with the more experienced, highly industrialized countries, and the competition with such rivals can choke the weak sparks of our scarcely awakening capitalism.[1]

The general conclusion sounded very optimistic:

> The countries which are latecomers to the arena of history have a great privilege in comparison with their foregoers, a privilege consisting in the fact that accumulated historical experience of other countries enables them to work out a relatively true image of their own next step and to strive for what the others have already achieved not instinctively but consciously, not groping in the dark but knowing what should be avoided on the way. To these peculiarly privileged countries belongs also Russia.[2]

The idea that backwardness can be a kind of historical privilege was proclaimed in Russia already by Herzen, himself inspired by Chaadaev,[3] and, also, by Chernyshevskiĭ,

---

[1] V.V.[orontsov], op. cit., p. 14.

[2] Ibid., p. 13.

[3] Chaadaev, as we know, conceived of this 'privilege' in terms of 'freedom from the burden of the past'. The Western nations, he thought, are shackled by their magnificent history; they are straining under the burden of their past and have no freedom in choosing their future. In Russia the situation is quite different and much more advantageous for an enlightened absolute monarch: 'it is sufficient to reveal the imperious sovereign will and all opinions at once give way to it, all convictions humbly yield themselves to it and all minds are ready to accept new ideas.' Thus, Russia is in a position to learn from the experience of the West and create her own future in accordance with 'enlightened reason and conscious will'. This particular privilege of the 'lack of history' justifies the belief that Russia is destined 'to bring solutions to the most important social problems, to accomplish the realization of ideals which had emerged in older societies, and to give the answer to the most important of the questions which are engaging now the attention of mankind'. (P. Chaadaev, 'Apologie d'un fou', in *Sochineniya i pis'ma*, vol. i, Moscow 1913.)

In Herzen's interpretation, 'freedom from the burden of the past' was regarded as being advantageous to the revolutionaries, and not to an enlightened absolutism. It was, according to him, a guarantee that the Russians, in contrast to the Europeans, were able to achieve a real, radical break with the 'old world'. The thinking Russians, he argued, who are forcibly divorced from the Russian past and have received a cosmopolitan humanistic education which has estranged them from the social reality of Russia's present, are the most independent people in the world. Nothing can restrain them: 'We are independent, because we possess nothing. There are literally no demands upon our affections. All our memories are tinged with bitterness and resentment. . . . We bow to brute force: we are slaves because we have no way of freeing ourselves: but whatever happens, we shall accept nothing from the enemy camp.'

who expressed it in the following aphoristic saying: 'History is like a grandmother; it loves the younger grandchildren. To the latecomers (tarde venientibus) it gives not the bones (ossa) but the marrow of the bones (medullam ossium), while Western Europe had hurt her fingers badly in her attempts to break the bones.'[1] We find an extreme formulation of the same idea in the proclamation *To the Young Generation* (1861),[2] written by Shelgunov and Mikhaïlov and being one of the earliest documents of revolutionary Populism: 'We are a belated nation and precisely in this consists our salvation.' Vorontsov, thus, had behind him a certain tradition to lean on. What distinguished him from his predecessors (with the exception, to some extent, of Chernȳshevskiĭ) was the shift of emphasis to the purely economic aspect of the problem, the idea that the 'privilege of backwardness' could be utilized to accelerate the process of industrialization.

The disadvantages of competing with more developed countries were seen by Vorontsov as unremovable obstacles on the way of the *capitalist* development of Russia. Russian capitalism, he argued, has no external markets and, at the same time, cannot produce for internal market since its own development, by bringing to ruin peasants and artisans, restricts more and more the purchasing power of the population. Thus, capitalist large-scale industry in Russia, having a ready-made, modern technology but devoid of markets, can develop *intensively*, i.e. by increasing the productivity and (by the same token) the exploitation of labour, being unable, at the same time, to develop *extensively*, i.e. to give employment to the increasingly growing number of

(A. Herzen, *From the Other Shore and The Russian People and Socialism*, London 1956, pp. 199–200.)
For an analysis of Herzen's ideas from the point of view of economic development, see Gerschenkron, op. cit., pp. 167–71.
[1] Chernȳshevskiĭ, *Polnoe sobranie sochineniĭ*, vol. v, p. 387 (criticism of philosophical prejudices against communal ownership of the land). Quoted in the translation in Gerschenkron, op. cit., p. 173.
[2] Reprinted in Karataev, op. cit., pp. 83–98.

workers; it can create small islands of modern production which would be able to satisfy the wants of the upper classes, but it cannot become a prevailing, nation-wide form of production; it can exploit the masses and bring to ruin many independent small producers, but is unable to give them employment and thus become for them a school of the higher, 'socialized' methods of work. In Western Europe capitalism was historically necessary and progressive as a form of 'socialization of labour'; in Russia, and in the backward countries in general, it can be only a form of exploitation, a 'usurper', an abortive enterprise, an 'illegitimate child of history'. Russian Government, having identified indus-trialization as such with the *capitalist* industrialization, makes every effort to support capitalism artificially, implants and lavishly subsidizes it, treats it with kid gloves—the result of these efforts, however, resembles rather 'a play at capitalism', 'a parody of capitalism'. Russian capitalists themselves feel a need to explain somehow their obvious lack of success; since such an explanation would have been impossible without finding out a scapegoat to be blamed, they found an appro-priate scapegoat in the peasant commune.

Russian agriculture was, in the eyes of Vorontsov, another proof of the general failure of Russian capitalism. Moreover, he claimed even that in all European countries, with the only exception of England, capitalist methods of production were increasingly receding (to understand properly the meaning of this assertion one should realize that the essence of capitalism in agriculture was seen by Vorontsov in the large-scale farming, presupposing the expropriation of the smallholders; if the small agricultural producers have not been divorced from the land, their production, according to this criterion, was not capitalist, even if it was a highly developed commodity production, destined for, and dependent on, the capitalist market).[1] The drop in the productivity of the land

---

[1] Thus, Vorontsov's assertion simply meant that the European peasants had proved capable of defending themselves against the allegedly inevitable process

and the increasing disintegration of the peasant commune were seen by him as a result of the absurd financial policy of the Government, flogging the peasants in order to force them to sell their livestock and seed corn, that is to destroy the productive forces; in such conditions, argued Vorontsov, all the advantages of the village commune disappear and what remains are only the disadvantages of belonging to an 'association' in the administrative sense of this word, among them, first of all, the notorious collective responsibility for the ruthlessly levied taxes and redemption payments. In spite of this, however, the peasants engaged in a fight for the preservation of their economic independence and began even to win it, although at the cost of the maximum restriction of their own consumption; the owners of great estates, being tempted by high rents, bringing more profit than cultivation of manorial land by means of hired labour, become more and more inclined to put their land out to lease and thereby to renounce the reins of agriculture in favour of peasant tenants. Thus—concluded Vorontsov, using the terminology of Mikhaïlovskiï—the Russian peasants have defended the higher *type* of agriculture and it is not their fault that this victory has been won at the cost of a considerable lowering of the *level* of development.[1]

The alternative for capitalism in Russia was seen by Vorontsov in the industrialization initiated and controlled by the State. The Government, according to this conception, should nationalize the large-scale industry and stimulate the gradual transfer of small enterprises to the workers' *artel's*, whose activity could be controlled and directed by means of indirect methods; the handicraftsmen and home-workers should be encouraged to organize themselves into cooperatives, which would be helped by the Government by ensuring the supply of raw materials and the outlets for their

of the concentration of agricultural production and landed property. And we should concede that in claiming this he was essentially right. Cf. D. Mitrany, *Marx against the Peasant*, London 1952, pp. 25–8.

[1] V. V[orontsov], op. cit., p. 290.

products. Similar help should be rendered to the peasant communes. As we see, Vorontsov expected that non-capitalist industrialization would be less painful, more humane than the capitalist variety, that it would save the Russian peasants and handicraftsmen from the atrocities of 'primitive accumulation'. It would be erroneous, however, to conclude from this that he wished to eternalize the existence of small independent producers as such—he wished only to give them the possibility of a smooth and painless transition to the 'socialized form of labour'. He was only partially a disciple of Mikhaïlovskiï—he could not espouse the ideal of non-divided, non-socialized labour since he had learned a great deal from Marx, whom he often quoted in his book. The 'socialization of labour' was for him—in contrast with Mikhaïlovskiï—a mark of progress and a necessity of economic development. In historical development of economic relationships he saw the following three stages: (1) the pre-industrial 'popular production', (2) the 'socialization of labour' in the process of industrialization, and, finally (3) the socialized 'popular production', i.e. socialism (the word 'socialism' was avoided for the sake of Tsarist censorship).[1] Non-capitalist industrialization under the auspices of the State was presented in this conception as the only means of overcoming economic backwardness and, at the same time, as the shortest and, in a sense, 'privileged' way to the highest stage of economic development. The conclusion concerning Russia ran as follows:

Let us hope that it will fall to the lot of Russia to serve them (the Western workers) as an example in their attempts to re-organize the social system; let us hope that the mission of Russia consists in the realization of equality and fraternity, although she is not destined to fight for freedom.[2]

Vorontsov's hope that Russia—the Tsarist Russia—could embark on the socialist road stemmed from his conviction that industrialization was an objective necessity for the

---

[1] V. V[orontsov], op. cit., p. 16.   [2] Ibid., p. 124.

Russian State and that it could not be achieved by means of capitalist methods: 'following the capitalist path', he wrote, 'we will never create a highly developed large-scale industry'.[1] This assertion was deduced by him from a more general thesis, concerning the peculiarity of economic backwardness as such: 'the more belated is the process of industrialization, the more difficult it is to carry it on along the capitalist lines'.[2] Only the State is an institution which can invest capital not for the sake of profit but for the sake of social welfare; only an industrialization by means of socialist planning through the agencies of the Government can ensure the economic independence of Russia and protect her from being exploited by the more developed capitalist countries; only the non-capitalist way of development will enable Russian industry to compete with its Western rivals and to secure necessary outlets for its products—to oust England from Asiatic markets and to defeat America in the corn trade.

Similar conclusions were drawn by N. Danielson (pen-name: Nikolaĭ-on), the translator of Marx's *Capital*, who since 1868 corresponded with Marx and Engels, providing them with the first-hand information about economic development in Russia. He considered himself to be a Marxist and this claim was by no means totally baseless. His main book—*Outlines of our Social Economy after the Enfranchisement of Peasants* (1893)—was written at the suggestion of Marx who had strongly insisted that the data on the development of Russian economy which he had received in Danielson's letters should have been presented and analysed in the press.[3] Having been encouraged by Marx, Danielson published in the Russian periodical *The Word* (1880) a long article, containing all his basic ideas and being the first chapter of his book. It should be noted that this article was highly appreciated by Marx, who saw in it a confirmation of his

[1] Ibid., p. 63.　　　　　　　　　　　　　　[2] Ibid., p. 15.
[3] At the same time Marx authorized Danielson to quote in the press from his correspondence with him. Cf. *Istoriya russkoĭ ékonomicheskoĭ mȳsli*, vol. ii, part 2, edited by A. I. Pashkov and N. A. Tsagolov, Moscow 1960, p. 322.

views of the social effects of the capitalist development. In a letter to Danielson (19 February 1881) he wrote:

I have read with the greatest pleasure your article, which is in the best sense of the word 'original'. Hence the boycotting—if you break through the webs of routine thought, you are always sure to be 'boycotted' in the first instance; it is the only arm of defense which in their perplexity the *routiniers* know how to wield. I have been 'boycotted' in Germany for many, many years, and am still so in England, with that little variation that from time to time something so absurd and asinine is launched against me that I would blush to take any public notice of it. But try on![1]

This appreciation of Danielson's article should not surprise us. Danielson's image of capitalism was moulded under the decisive influence of Marx; the author of *Capital*, for his part, was delighted to see that the growth of Russian capitalism, as described by Danielson, gave lie to petty-bourgeois illusions of a smooth and mild economic development. Not without a certain satisfaction did he predict that things would go from bad to worse, that the economic processes, analysed by his Russian correspondent, were paving the way for a *famine-year* in Russia;[2] he saw in it a corroboration of his theoretical views of the regularities of the capitalist development: 'This is a bleeding process, with a vengeance! The famine years are pressing each other and in dimensions till now not yet suspected in Europe!'[3]

Danielson, who was, of course, deeply impressed by this diagnosis, used it as an argument against the flat optimism of Russian liberals who saw capitalist progress as a panacea for all the social maladies of their country. In the nineties he felt himself confirmed in his views by the fact that Marx's gloomy prediction had materialized in Russia in 1891. The 'legal Marxists' interpreted the great famine of this year as a result of Russian economic backwardness, against which the only remedy was seen by them to be rapid

---

[1] K. Marx and F. Engels, *Correspondence 1846–1895* (cited ed.), p. 383.
[2] Ibid., p. 384.
[3] Ibid., p. 386.

capitalist progress; Danielson saw it as a result of Russia's embarking on the capitalist road and believed that all the thinking Russians should have learned from this that it was necessary to combat capitalism and to find for their country another way of economic development.

Feeling himself a Marxist, Danielson tried to cut himself off from the publicists who represented in their economic views 'a narrowly-peasant point of view'.[1] He deliberately avoided quoting Vorontsov (although in fact he had borrowed a great deal from him), trying instead to utilize every occasion to support his views by reference to the authority of Marx and Engels; his *Outlines* are full of quotation not only from *Capital* (on such topics as the destruction of peasant industries, proletarianization, centralization of capital, the role of public credit and of the development of railways, and so on) but also from his private correspondence with his teachers. In spite of this, however, there can be no possible doubt that he belonged to the 'legal Populists'. In the basic issues he was in agreement with Vorontsov—what distinguished them from each other could be reduced to the difference in emphasis. The translator of Marx's *Capital*, in contradistinction to the author of *The Fates of Capitalism in Russia*, did not assert that it was completely impossible to industrialize Russia along the capitalist way; like Vorontsov, however, he used to play upon the argument of the lack of foreign markets and constantly referred to the catastrophic situation of Russian agriculture in order to persuade the Government that the price of capitalist industrialization was too high and that furthering capitalist development was contrary to the true interests of the Russian State; like Vorontsov, he was a spokesman of the small producers, tried to save them from paying the cost of industrialization, and believed that the 'socialization of labour' could be accomplished in Russia without passing through 'the capitalist stage'. In a word, he shared Vorontsov's conviction that it

---

[1] Cf. *Istoriya russkoĭ ékonomicheskoĭ mȳsli*, vol. ii, part 2, p. 329.

was possible for Russia to embark on a non-capitalist, State-controlled industrialization which would enable to combine the increase of productivity with the increase of the welfare of the people. He wrote:

> It fell to our lot to solve a task which could be formulated as follows: how to raise our industry to the level of the Western industry, in order to prevent Russia from becoming a tributary of more advanced countries, and, at the same time, to increase the welfare of the whole people. But, having identified large-scale modern industry with its capitalistic form, we reduced this problem to the following dilemma: to what should we sacrifice our popular industries—to our own capitalist industry or to English industry? When the problem was set in such a way—and it was set precisely in this manner—our popular industries got a sentence of death and we began to spread out our own large-scale capitalist industry.[1]

The readers of Danielson's *Outlines* did not know that this dilemma, presented by him as false and deserving only ironical treatment, was formulated in fact by Engels. In the letter to Danielson of 22 September 1892 Engels wrote:

> Another thing is certain: if Russia required after the Crimean War a *grande industrie* of her own, she could have it in one form only: the *capitalistic form*. And along with that form, she was obliged to take over all the consequences which accompany capitalistic *grande industrie* in all other countries. . . . As far as this side of the question: the destruction of home industry and the branches of agriculture subservient to it—as far as this is concerned, the real question for you seems to me this: that the Russians had to decide whether *their own grande industrie* was to destroy their domestic manufacture, or whether *the import of English goods* was to accomplish this. *With* protection, the *Russians* effected it, *without* protection, the *English*.[2]

As we see, the above quotation from Danielson contained in fact a direct, although hidden, polemic with Engels.

[1] Nikolaï-on [Danielson], *Ocherki nashego poreformennogo obshchestvennogo khozyaĭstva*, Spb. 1893, pp. 330–1 (the most essential parts of this book are reprinted in Karataev, op. cit.).

[2] K. Marx and F. Engels, *Correspondence 1846–1895*, pp. 499–500.

This was not a unique case: although Danielson considered himself to be a Marxist, he was by no means inclined to give up his own, long-established views of the economic development of his country; he did everything possible to convince Engels of the validity of his ideas but, having failed to achieve this, he stuck even more resolutely to his guns; he used to invoke the authority of Marx and Engels at every appropriate occasion, but wherever he polemized with them, he used to do it without reference to them, trying thus to pass for an orthodox Marxist.

The influence of Marxism found expression in Danielson's attempts to eliminate from his views the backward-looking utopia of 'economic romanticism'. For that reason he rejected the projects of Vorontsov, Krivenko, and other Populist writers who demanded from the State an organized help for homeworkers and peasant handicraftsmen: he motivated this attitude by emphasizing, in accordance with Marx, that it was impossible to preserve the 'patriarchal production', that the real improvement of the situation of the direct producers could be achieved only by means of a structural transformation of the entire economic system.[1] At the end of his *Outlines* he formulated his programme as follows:

. . . The incompatibility of our forms of production with the needs of the majority threatens us with such disasters concerning both the population and the State, that we have no other choice than this: to lean on our historical inheritance and cease to destroy our ancient, historical form of production, a form being based upon the ownership of the means of production by the direct producers. It is necessary to do this in order to avoid the danger which threatens every nation which departs from the age-long foundations of its welfare. All efforts must be directed at a unification of agriculture and manufacturing industry in the hands of the direct producers, but a unification not on the ground of small-scale, fragmented productive units—which

---

[1] Cf. A. P. Mendel, *Dilemmas of Progress in Tsarist Russia. Legal Populism and Legal Marxism*, Cambridge, Mass., 1961, pp. 56–7.

would be tantamount 'to decree universal mediocrity'—but on the ground of the creation of a massive socialized production based on the free development of social productive forces and the application of science and technology, with the aim of satisfying the genuine requirements and well-being of the whole population.[1]

An American student of legal Populism, A. P. Mendel, called this programme 'the maximalist solution' and contrasted it with the 'minimalist' programme of Vorontsov.[2] This distinction can be accepted but it should not overshadow the essential similarity between the two programmes. In point of fact, Vorontsov and Danielson propagated two variants of the same model of industrialization. The author of *The Fates of Capitalism in Russia* was also quite familiar with Marxism and, like Danielson, did not deny the necessity of 'socialization of labour'; Danielson, on his part, could not get rid of the idealization of 'patriarchal production'— contrary to his intentions, 'economic romanticism' conducive to an embellishment of the picture of pre-capitalist economy and to the underestimation of the harmfulness of some remnants of feudalism, was, sometimes, even more conspicuous in his writings than in the writings of Vorontsov. Both Vorontsov and Danielson wished such an industrialization which would enable to prevent the ruination of small producers and the lowering of the level of mass consumption. The difference, which divided them, could be reduced, in practice, to their respective estimation of such means of combatting capitalism as cheap credit for handicraftsmen, lower taxes, free agronomic advice for the peasants, and so on; Vorontsov promoted these means, whereas Danielson was much more sceptical about such half-measures and emphasized the necessity of a global transformation of the economic system, enacted and implemented by the State.

And—last but not least—we should not forget that both

---

[1] Nikolaĭ-on [Danielson], op. cit., p. 375-6.
[2] Cf. A. P. Mendel, op. cit., chap. 2.

Populist writers believed in a possibility of carrying out their economic programmes without any political reform. This characteristic feature of legal Populism aroused a real indignation among the Russian Marxists. Plekhanov wrote about it to Engels:

> Let us suppose that the peasant commune is really our anchor of salvation. But who will carry out the reforms postulated by Nikolaï-on? Tsarist government? Pestilence is better than such reformers and their reforms! Socialism being introduced by Russian policemen—what a chimera![1]

The ideology of the legal Populists, especially that of the professional economists, shows Populism in a different aspect than ideologies of revolutionary Populists. Its connection with international Socialism was much weaker, almost non-existent, but, on the other hand, the interests of peasants and of the pre-capitalist small producers in general were represented by it in a much more direct way. It is by no means accidental that the article 'New Shoots in the People's Fields', analysed and highly appreciated by Lenin as typifying the best sides of Populism,[2] was written by a legal Populist—Eliseyev or Krivenko.[3]

> Populism [writes a Soviet scholar] was a Russian variant of the petty-bourgeois current of social thought, which had come into existence in many countries as a reflection of the ideology of small commodity-producers being ruined by the triumphal march of capitalism. Sismondi and Proudhon also belonged to the representatives of this current. But nowhere, in no other country, the ideology of petty-bourgeois democracy found such a broad popularity and such an acute theoretical expression as it was in the case of Russian liberal Populism of the 1890's. Although the ideology of petty-bourgeoisie had been reflected earlier—long ago Russian Populism—in the respective teachings of Sismondi and Proudhon, it would not be erroneous to state that

---

[1] *Perepiska K. Marksa i F. Engel'sa s russkimi politicheskimi deyatelyami*, 2nd ed., Moscow 1951, p. 334.

[2] Cf. Lenin, *Collected Works*, vol. i, pp. 340–95.

[3] Cf. Karataev, op. cit., p. 660, note 145.

the ideas of the Russian liberal Populists of the 1890's could be treated as an especially distinct and expressive variant of it.[1]

We accept this statement with a qualification. The sociological representativeness and expressiveness of the ideology of Vorontsov and Danielson seems to us to be beyond a doubt, but there is also little doubt that it was not homogeneous, that its petty-bourgeois 'economic romanticism' was very far from being consistent and, in this sense, classical; much more classical expression of it could be found in the utopian historiosophical constructions of Mikhaĭlovskiĭ. The economic views of Vorontsov and Danielson were rather a curious blend of heterogeneous elements: the idealization of the peasant commune and of the archaic 'popular industry' was combined in their ideology with a programme for industrialization, a high appreciation of the 'independence' of small producers went along with the postulate of 'socialization of labour'. This heterogeneity and incongruity of constituent elements was noted by Engels who in a letter to Plekhanov made the following comment on Danielson's views:

. . . in a country like yours, where modern large-scale industry has been grafted on to the primitive peasant commune and where, at the same time, all the intermediate stages of civilization co-exist with each other, in a country which, in addition to this, has been enclosed by despotism with an intellectual Chinese wall, in the case of such a country one should not wonder at the emergence of the most incredible and bizarre combinations of ideas.[2]

This observation seems very much to the point; I should add only that we are more conscious today of the relativity

---

[1] A. I. Pashkov, *Ékonomicheskie raboty V. I. Lenina 90-kh godov*, Moscow 1960, pp. 68–9. In the light of the above statement it is difficult to understand why so many Soviet scholars (including Koz'min) treat the 'legal Populists' of the nineties as the mere epigones of Populism. If their ideology was 'an acute theoretical expression' of what was (according to Lenin) the social content of Populism, it would be more reasonable to place them among the most classical' representatives of Populist thought.

[2] *Perepiska K. Marksa i F. Engel'sa s russkimi politicheskimi deyatelyami*, p. 341 (letter of 26 February 1895).

of such notions as 'bizarreness' in the domain of economic and, respectively, ideological development. What was 'bizarre' from the point of view of the classical Western model of economic development, is seen today as a typical feature of the development of backward countries in conditions of a rapid but uneven growth of the economy of the world. The historical heterogeneity of the constitutive elements of Vorontsov's and Danielson's ideology was in fact a faithful reflection of the peculiar 'coexistence of asynchronisms', typifying all the backward countries in the process of modernization.[1] Russian Populism, therefore, was not only an ideology of small producers but also the first ideological reflection of the specific features of economic and social development of the 'latecomers' of the backward agrarian countries carrying out the process of modernization in conditions created by coexistence with highly industrialized nations. Moreover, it was also the first attempt at theoretical explanation of these specific features and at deducing from it practical conclusions. And *in this sense*, it was a really representative ideology *not in spite of* the heterogeneity of its elements but *because of* it.

The conceptions of the Populist economists are, perhaps, the best exemplification of it. Flerovskiĭ, Vorontsov, and Danielson pointed out a double capitalist threat: the internal danger, threatening the Russian people, and the external danger, threatening the Russian nation as a whole. They were concerned not only with the problem of how to prevent the proletarianization of Russian peasants, but also with the problem of how to avoid the proletarianization of Russia as a nation, how to prevent her from being exploited by more advanced countries and how to secure her an honourable place among the nations of the world. This nation-wide aspect of Populism made its appearance already in the writings of Herzen, especially in his image of Russia as

[1] Cf. W. Kula, *Problemy i metody historii gospodarczej* [*Problems and Methods of Economic History*], Warsaw 1963, p. 189.

proletarian among the bourgeois nations: his saying that Russia is a country which 'has nothing to lose, but everything to gain'[1] ran parallel to Marx's image of proletariat as a class which has nothing to lose except its chains. The idea that backward countries in general were closer to socialism than the developed ones could be traced back at least to Bakunin, and the problem of external factors (diffusion of modern ideas and technology, the necessity of keeping pace with more advanced neighbours, etc.) had been given a thorough treatment already in the works of Chernÿshevskiĭ.[2] Nevertheless, only the 'legal Populists' of the eighties and nineties brought matters to a head by posing the problem of non-capitalist industrialization as a means of 'outstripping and overtaking' economically more advanced nations. From the perspective of our times we see in the theories of Vorontsov and Danielson not only a legitimate attempt to defend the peasants, whom so many socialists of that time too readily proclaimed to be 'doomed', but also the first attempt to pose and to solve some problems of economic backwardness which are still topical in the backward or unevenly developed countries of the world.[3]

To avoid misunderstanding we must make it quite clear that this thesis is by no means bound up with a conviction that their strictly economic views were essentially right— we claim only that they asked the right questions and posed for the first time some new and important problems. There is no doubt that the fate of peasants was for them far more important than the economic development of the country. It seems without doubt that they grossly underestimated the possibilities of Russia's capitalist development because they

---

[1] A. I. Herzen, *Sobranie sochineniĭ*, vol. vii, Moscow 1956, p. 16 ('Nous n'avons qu'à gagner, nous n'avons rien à perdre').

[2] For an interesting analysis of Chernÿshevskiĭ's views on the economic development of backward countries, see *Istoriya russkoĭ ékonomicheskoĭ mÿsli*, vol. i, part 2, pp. 707–19.

[3] Thus, for instance, A. Mendel (op. cit., chap. 2) pointed out that Vorontsov's programme of economic development can be interpreted as an anticipation of the 'Indian' model of industrialization.

were too optimistic about non-capitalist industrialization, and at the same time too uncritical in their belief that under the auspices of the State it would be easy to combine industrialization with a steady increase of the welfare of the people; there is little doubt that they also committed many errors, misinterpreting facts and tendentiously interpreting statistical data, presenting false pictures of trends in the Russian economy, and so on. In the present context, however, more important is the consideration that they were painfully conscious of the fact that economic backwardness creates its own specific problems and that the backward countries not only should not, but also *cannot*, repeat in their development the classical English pattern. Vorontsov's assertion that Russian capitalist industry would never be able to win foreign markets might have been erroneous, but the very problem of the influence of international conditions on the industrialization of the backward countries was, certainly, not a pseudo-problem; his hope that Tsarist government would carry out a non-capitalist industrialization in the interests of the people was, undoubtedly, a reactionary illusion, but this illusion stemmed from correctly grasping the connection between economic backwardness and the role of the State in initiating and planning economic development. Today, nobody is shocked by the thesis that backward countries cannot develop along the lines of the classical Western capitalism; no Marxist claims today, as Plekhanov did, that socialism is possible only in those countries which have passed through the whole cycle of capitalist development. And there is nothing surprising in the fact that it was the Russian Populists who were the first to postulate the non-capitalist industrialization of the backward countries—after all, Russia had embarked on industrialization much later and was more backward than any other of the great European countries and, thus, had to carry it out in conditions strikingly different from the classical pattern.

III

POPULISM AND MARXISM

1. *Russian Populists in confrontation with Marx and Engels*

IN the first chapter of this book we tried to show that the definition of Russian Populism was provided by Marxists; in the next chapter we emphasized the significance of certain Marxist ideas for the Populist ideology and the Populist movement; now we shall try to show that classical Populism was not only defined, and not merely influenced, but, in a sense, called into being by Marxism. Marxism, we think, should be recognized as the main frame of reference for the proper understanding of classical Russian Populism; classical Populism, in its turn, should be recognized as one of the most important chapters in the history of a broadly conceived reception of Marxism.

This was due to the fact that classical Populism was *not only* a reaction to the development of capitalism *in Russia* but also (especially at the beginning) a response of the democratic Russian intelligentsia to capitalism and socialism of the West; after all, it was a traditional preoccupation of the Russian intellectuals to ponder over Russia's future in terms of desirability or undesirability of following the example of Western Europe. From this point of view it becomes highly important to establish what was the Populist *image of Western capitalism*, of its history and its present state. And it is no exaggeration to say that this image was formed under the overwhelming influence of Marx. It may seem paradoxical but it was Marx's *Capital* which caused the Russian democrats to conceive of capitalism as their 'enemy number 1', thus contributing to the intensification of their idealization of the pre-capitalist social relationships and, by the same token, making them full-fledged Populists.

It might be easily demonstrated that in the seventies it was the Populists who played the greatest part in the propagation of Marxism in Russia. To Marx's surprise,[1] the first translation of his *Capital* came out in Russia (it was published in 1872, that is a short five years after the publication of the German original and fifteen years before its English translation). The translation was begun by a close friend of Marx, the revolutionary Populist Herman Lopatin who, however, had to abandon it in connection with his bold but abortive attempt to free Chernÿshevskiĭ from Siberia; it was continued and brought to an end by another Populist, Nicholas Danielson, who, as we know, felt himself to be a convinced Marxist. It was due to the Populists that the ideas of *Capital* began to spread among Russian peasants and workers: an activist of 'Land and Freedom', Y. M. Tishchenko, never parted with Marx's book during his participation in the 'go to the people' movement;[2] another member of 'Land and Freedom', the eminent revolutionary S. Kravchinskiĭ, wrote a tale *Mudritsa Naumovna* in which he tried to illustrate and popularize among the workers the Marxian theory of surplus value. Almost all Populist thinkers—both revolutionaries and reformists, from Tkachëv to Vorontsov—used to refer to Marx and to draw largely from him in their criticism of liberal political economy. Tkachëv already in 1865 called himself (in print) a follower of K. Marx whose ideas 'have now become common to all thinking and honest men'.[3] Eliseev in 1869 called Marx 'the most talented and the most honest man among the contemporary political

---

[1] In a letter to Kugelmann (12 October 1868) Marx wrote: 'A few days ago a Petersburg publisher surprised me with the news that a Russian translation of 'Das Kapital' is now being printed. (. . .) It is an irony of fate that the Russians, whom I have fought for twenty-five years, and not only in German, but in French and English, have always been my "patrons".' (K. Marx, *Letters to Kugelmann*, London, p. 77.)

[2] Cf. O. V. Aptekman, op. cit., p. 246.

[3] Tkachëv, *Izbrannÿe sochineniya*, vol. i, p. 70.

economists';[1] in the same year Mikhaĭlovskiĭ drew from Marx the main arguments for his conception of the negative effects of the social division of labour.[2] Lavrov, having escaped from Russia, almost immediately established relations with Marx and Engels and became a member of the International; later, under Marx's influence, he began to argue for social revolution by referring to the 'objective laws of development' and by quoting in his journal *Forward* from *Capital* and from the *Communist Manifesto*. In a letter to Marx of 25 October 1880 the Executive Committee of the 'Will of the People' informed him that his *Capital* has long since become a book of everyday use for the Russian democratic intelligentsia.[3] This was, perhaps, an exaggeration. Many of the rank-and-file Populists possessed but a second-hand knowledge of *Capital*. Nevertheless, it is justified to assert that the indirect influence of Marx reached even those Populists who never read any of his books. It was so because Marx's description of the atrocities of the primitive accumulation and of the industrial revolution in England, his theory of surplus-value and his criticism of the 'formal' character of the bourgeois 'political democracy' were immediately adapted to Populist thought and made a part and parcel of it.

An instructive example of the influence of *Capital* upon Populist thinking was provided by two articles of the early seventies (both published in 1872). One of them, already mentioned by us in another context, was Eliseev's paper entitled *Plutocracy and its Social Base*.[4] It shows us that the Populist image of capitalist development was shaped entirely and wholly by Marx. Eliseev quoted widely from Marx

---

[1] Quoted in A. L. Reuel, *Russkaya ėkonomicheskaya mÿsl' 60–70-kh gg. XIX veka i marksizm*, Moscow 1956, pp. 219–20.

[2] Cf. Mikhaĭlovskiĭ, *Polnoe sobranie sochineniĭ*, 5th ed., vol. i, Spb. 1911, pp. 170–2 (Teoriya Darvina i obshchestvennaya nauka).

[3] Cf. *Perepiska K. Marksa i F. Engel'sa s russkimi politicheskimi deyatemyai*, p. 251. A similar opinion was expressed by Vera Zasulich in her letter to Marx of 16 February 1881 (ibid., p. 299).

[4] Reprinted in Karataev, op. cit., pp. 125–59.

and, moreover, many pages of his article were simply and solely paraphrases or summaries of the respective pages in *Capital*.[1] The general conclusion was, of course, that everything should be done to prevent the capitalist development of Russia. Strangely enough, Eliseev seemed to have thought that this conclusion was in accordance with Marx's saying (quoted by him at the beginning of his article) that in the process of begetting a new social order the function of midwife is performed by force and that force itself is also an economic power.[2] If force is the midwife, reasoned Eliseev, it means that the role of the State is active, that the State can legitimately interfere with the process of social transformation in order to prevent undesirable results. In this manner Marx's *Capital* was used by the Populist publicist to persuade the Tsarist government that it was its duty to combat Russian capitalism.

Fiercely denouncing the Western parliamentary system as being merely an obedient tool of the egoistic propertied classes, Eliseev contrasted it with the Russian State which, in his view, was not committed to capitalism and thus could protect the general interests of society. We may add to this that a similar view was held by the Tsarist censor, a certain Skuratov, who had permitted the publication of *Capital* on the ground that Marx's denunciations of capitalism were directed only against the social order of the Western countries and did not concern the Russian State which, as he put it, never espoused the principles of *laissez-faire* and 'mindfully protected the welfare of the workers'.[3]

The second article, entitled 'On the Occasion of the Russian Translation of "Capital"',[4] was written by Mikhaïlovskiï. *Capital* was used in it as a powerful argument for the

[1] See the notes to Eliseev's article in the Polish anthology of Populist thought: *Filozofia społeczna narodnictwa rosyjskiego* [*Social Philosophy of Russian Populism*], edited and with an introduction by A. Walicki, 2 vols., Warsaw 1965.

[2] Cf. K. Marx, *Capital*, quoted ed., p. 751.

[3] Cf. Reuel, op. cit., pp. 234–5.

[4] Reprinted in Karataev, op. cit., pp. 160–9.

Populist conception of the absolute primacy of 'social' over 'merely political' questions. The Populist 'grudge' against political liberals was justified by reference to the very foundations of historical materialism—by indicating that political systems are mere reflections of economic relations and, therefore, that the changes in the economic (i.e. 'social') sphere are the only things which really matter. Moreover, the Marxian criticism of the 'illusory and formal character' of bourgeois democracy supported the Populist conviction that 'political freedom' was bound up with capitalism and devoid of any autonomous value of its own; that, therefore, a constitutional government in Russia could only serve the interests of the bourgeoisie and make the situation of the people even worse.[1]

We may safely say that in the seventies such an interpretation of Marxism was very widespread, even prevalent among the Russian Populists. The fact that Marx himself never neglected the so-called 'political struggle' was considered as a sheer inconsistency deriving from his political opportunism; such was the view of Bakunin, and he undoubtedly succeeded in diffusing among the Russian revolutionaries the opinion that Marx, as the leader of the International, was an advocate of moderation and a spokesman of the semi-bourgeois workers' aristocracy. But it should be remembered that Bakunin also highly appreciated the

---

[1] The fact that Populist 'apoliticism' had usually been justified by reference to Marxism was confirmed ex post facto in an important article 'The Political Revolution and the Economic Problem', published by N. Kibalchich in the clandestine journal of the 'Will of the People'. The commitment to 'political struggle', we are told in the article, was usually countered with the theories of Marx 'who in his "Kapital" has shown that the economic relationships of any country are the basis of all its other social, political, and legal institutions. This has led some people to deduce that any transformation in the economic system can only be the result of a struggle in the economic sphere, and that therefore no political revolution can either delay or start an economic revolution.' (*Narodnaya volya*, no. v; quoted in Venturi's translation, op. cit., p. 679.)

We should note that as regards one point Kibalchich's testimony is not accurate: in fact the opponents of 'political struggle' usually thought that political revolution *would delay* the socialist solution of the economic and social question.

scholarly production of his great adversary, subscribed in a sense to historical materialism, and offered even to translate Marx's *Capital* into Russian. The combination of a rather negative attitude towards Marx as a politician with a deep reverence for him as a theorist was, indeed, very typical of the Russian Populists. Stefanovich, one of the most representative Populist followers of Bakunin, expressed this dual attitude as follows: 'Marxism as a theory—not as a membership in the Western Socialist party and espousal of its practical policy—does not exclude Populism.'[1]

As we see, the Populists' reception of Marxism was a very peculiar one. They readily accepted Marx's criticism of 'political democracy' but refused to espouse his firm conviction that it was, nevertheless, a long step forward in comparison with autocracy. They were deeply impressed by his exposition of the cruelties of the capitalist development— so deeply, that they could not accept his thesis that the rise of capitalism was, all the cruelties none the less, the greatest progress in human history. Their image of capitalism was, on the whole, non-Marxist since they saw capitalist development as an essentially retrogressive process, but, none the less, this image would have been impossible without the mesmerizing influence of Marx. Their practical conclusions were often incompatible with Marxism but, none the less, they were supported by theoretical argumentation which had been either borrowed from Marx or derived from a particular interpretation of his views.

A particularly striking example of the 'hidden' influence of Marx may be found even in Mikhaĭlovskiĭ's theory of progress, that is, in the most articulate and extreme expression of the Populist economic (sociological) 'romanticism'. As we have shown elsewhere in this book,[2] it was based upon Marxian analysis of the division of labour and its destructive effect on individual wholeness, especially upon Marx's

[1] Quoted in Sh. M. Levin, op. cit., p. 334.
[2] See above, pp. 59–63.

thesis that the perfection of the 'collective labourer' was achieved at the cost of, and in inverse ratio to, the development of the individual labourer. Mikhaïlovskiĭ brought this thesis into the foreground and, having decided that the development of the individual is the only acceptable criterion of progress, deduced from it that the so-called social progress was in fact a retrogression. No doubt, this conclusion ran counter to Marxism, but, none the less, it was derived from Marxian analysis of the painful contradictions of progress.

Engels wrote once in a letter to Marx that even Maurer —the scholar who had so greatly contributed to the understanding of pre-capitalist economic formations—was not free from the 'enlightened prejudice that since the dark Middle Ages a steady progress to better things *must* surely have taken place'. This prejudice, continued Engels, prevents Maurer from 'seeing not only the antagonistic character of real progress, but also the individual retrogressions'.[1] In Mikhaïlovskiĭ's case the reverse was true: he was so eager to free himself from the bourgeois 'enlightened prejudices', so upset by the 'individual retrogressions', that he refused to recognize the progressive character of social evolution and fell into a backward-looking romantic utopianism.

No wonder that the 'economic romanticism' of the Populists fitted so well the Marxist categories in which it was interpreted by Lenin. It reflected, certainly, the petty-bourgeois reaction to capitalist progress, but it expressed also the reaction of the Russian intellectuals to the Marxian *analysis* of the tragic contradictoriness of capitalist development. We may say that it was based upon an absolutization of the 'negative side' of this development, as described by Marx. It was non-Marxist in its conclusions, but, nevertheless, bound up with the classical Marxist description of the

---

[1] Cf. K. Marx, *Pre-capitalist Economic Formations*, edited and with an Introduction by E. J. Hobsbawm, London 1964, p. 146 (Engels's letter to Marx, 15 December 1882).

development of capitalism. Very often it was even formulated in Marxist language: in the nineties not only Lenin but the Populists themselves (Vorontsov, Danielson) defined their views as an ideological expression of the interests of the 'immediate producers' being endangered by the development of capitalism and trying to avoid proletarianization.

Nevertheless, it is quite understandable that, in spite of their great indebtedness to Marx, it was very difficult for the Populists to call themselves 'Marxists'—the case of Danielson was rather exceptional. The main obstacle was for them Marxian determinism and naturalistic evolutionism, as expressed in the preface to the first German edition of *Capital*. It implied that the tormenting process of capitalist development cannot be avoided in Russia. This implication was made explicit by the 'Russian disciples' of Marx, which, not unnaturally, contributed to bring about a significant shift in the Populists' attitude towards Marxism. It was most radical in Mikhaĭlovskiĭ's case. The feeling of indebtedness to Marx gave way to the awareness of the incompatibility with, and opposition to, his theories. Opposition, however, is also a meaningful relationship, sometimes the closest and most significant.

The full story of the changing attitudes towards Marxism in the Populist milieu is long and truly fascinating. However, for the sake of concision, we shall confine ourselves to a brief discussion of those Populist reinterpretations of Marxism which seem to be most relevant to the theoretical problem of social evolution and economic backwardness, of the possibility and desirability of a non-capitalist way of development for Russia and for the backward countries in general.

The first important attempt on the part of the Russian revolutionaries to assimilate some elements of Marxism had taken place already in the first half of the sixties, *before* the publication of the first volume of *Capital*. It was done by Peter Tkachëv who formulated his views as follows:

Social life with all its manifestations, including literature, science, religion and political and juridical forms, is but a result of definite economic principles which lie at the roots of all these social phenomena. The given economic principles, in their gradual and consequent development create an interplay of human relations and beget industry and commerce, science and philosophy, law and political forms; in a word, they call into being the whole of our civilization and of its progress.[1]

This was, of course, a paraphrase from Marx's *Zur Kritik der Politischen Ökonomie*. The idea of economic materialism, maintained Tkachëv in 1865, 'has been transplanted into our press—like everything else worth while in it—from the culture of Western Europe. As early as 1859 the well-known German exile Karl Marx had clearly and exactly expressed it.' 'This idea has now become common to all thinking and honest men, and no intelligent man can find any serious objection to it.'[2]

It should be added that Tkachëv did not content himself with a general declaration of principles—he tried also, more or less successfully, to apply these principles in his interpretation of ideological struggles of the past and present. Thus, for instance, he interpreted the struggle between Catholicism and the Reformation as a struggle between the feudal aristocracy and the rising bourgeoisie;[3] in the emancipation of women he saw a necessary result of the development of capitalism;[4] in his polemic against Lavrov he sharply opposed the exaggeration of the role of 'critical thought' and proclaimed that the decisive part was played in history not by the human intellect and abstract knowledge but by 'affections, deriving from the vital interests of men

---

[1] Tkachëv, *Izbrannye sochineniya*, vol. v, Moscow 1935, p. 93.
[2] Quoted in Venturi's translation, op. cit., p. 395. (Tkachëv, op. cit., vol. i, p. 70.)
[3] See Tkachëv, op. cit., vol. i, pp. 260–2.
[4] See ibid., 'Zhenskiĭ vopros'.

and women and, thus, having their roots in the sphere of economic relations'.[1] This specific 'economic materialism' of Tkachëv did not amount to Marxism; it consisted rather in a peculiar mixture of some elements of Marxism with a rather primitive utilitarianism, grossly exaggerating the role of direct economic motivation in individual behaviour. From the point of view of the history of ideas it is, however, not without interest. In the interpretation of the crude theories of Tkachëv we are faced with an interesting problem: how was it possible that 'economic materialism'—a theory which, as a rule, appears in conjunction with mechanically conceived determinism—coexisted in the ideology of Tkachëv with the extremely 'voluntaristic' conviction that the whole future of Russia depended upon the will and determinate action of the 'revolutionary minority'?

In Marx's *Contribution to the Critique of Political Economy* Tkachëv read that economic formations cannot perish until they have achieved the full development of their productive forces. In the eighties and nineties Russian Marxists used to conclude from this that the socialist revolution in Russia must be preceded by full development of Russian capitalism. Tkachëv, who, naturally, could not espouse such a view, argued, instead, that the socialist revolution in Russia was possible *either after* the termination of the whole cycle of capitalist development, *or before* embarking on the capitalist road. Every economic principle has its own inner logic of development; as in reasoning we cannot jump directly from the first premiss to the conclusion, so in the historical development of an economic principle it is impossible to skip the intermediary phases.[2] It is possible, however, to start a completely *new* cycle of development, provided that the old economic principles have been completely eradicated. Such a possibility of choice is most real in epochs of transition, when the old economic relations have outlived their

---

[1] Ibid., vol. iii, pp. 213–15 ('Rol' mýsli v istorii').
[2] Ibid., vol. i, pp. 260–2.

time and the new ones are not, as yet, firmly established. 'Utopianism', therefore, is not something peculiar to the extreme revolutionaries, who try to replace the existing economic principles by new ones; the true utopians are the 'moderates' who wish to preserve the existing economic system and, at the same time, to skip some of its natural phases of development or to avoid some of its natural and unavoidable results. In Russia the socialist revolution may with *either now*, when the old feudal formation has already exhausted its vitality and the new, capitalist formation has not as yet, taken root, or *in the distant future*, when the country has passed through all the painful phases of capitalist development; today the whole future of the country is still in the hands of revolutionaries, tomorrow it will be too late. Germany faced the same alternative during the time of its great peasant war. In contradistinction to Engels, Tkachëv did not think that the defeat of Müntzer had been caused by historical necessity. On the contrary, he thought that Müntzer had an objective chance to win and that his victory would have saved the German masses from the pains and sufferings of the development of capitalism.[1]

A few years later—in 1874—Tkachëv launched a sharp polemic against Engels. The context of this polemic was international rather than Russian—the controversy arose over the question of the ideological divergencies between Bakunin and Marx and their struggle for leadership in the International. After the affair of Nechaev,[2] in which the International had been involved by Bakunin, a resolution was voted in which the International condemned Nechaev, disapproved of conspiratorial methods, and cut itself off

---

[1] Tkachëv, op. cit., vol. i, pp. 260–2. It seems worth while pointing out that Engels's opinion on the chances of Müntzer's victory (diametrically opposed to that of Tkachëv) was quoted many times by Plekhanov who used it as an argument against the idea of the 'seizure of power'. In *Our Differences* he levelled this argument against Tkachëv; in later years he directed it against Lenin (see Plekhanov, *Izbrannye filosofskie proizvedeniya*, vol. i, Moscow 1956, pp. 473–4; *God na rodine*, Paris 1921, vol. i, p. 28).

[2] See p. 97, n. 7.

from the illegal activities of revolutionary secret societies. Tkachëv, who sympathized with Nechaev and who was, in a sense, his disciple and follower, interpreted this resolution as a radical cutting off from the Russian revolutionary movement as a whole. Bakunin, for his part, accused Marx of betraying the revolution, of giving up the true 'social' struggle for the sake of purely 'political' aspirations; he saw in Marx a spokesman of the skilled, bourgeois-minded proletariat of the rich, highly developed countries, and in himself a spokesman of the 'proletariat of misery', an advocate of the hard-working masses of the poor and backward nations. Oil was added to the flames by the abortive Spanish revolution of 1873, stirred up by the followers of Bakunin. It was condemned and derided by Engels who asserted that Spain, being a backward country, had not matured to a socialist revolution and that the Spanish revolutionaries, instead of committing themselves to anarchic adventures, should rather take part in the elections to the Cortes.[1]

Bakunin's activities split the International and threatened it with collapse (which really took place a little later). Bakunin, like Herzen, had undergone a period in which he had combined revolutionism with a certain Panslavism, an ideology towards which Marx and Engels were always deeply suspicious and hostile. The affair of Nechaev, who recommended and practised an extreme, ruthless immoralism in the choice of the means of struggle, helped to discredit the Russian revolutionary movement in general. All these factors made Marx and Engels, in the first half of the seventies, rather suspicious of Russian revolutionaries, especially those of them who, like Bakunin and Tkachëv, rejected the tactics of the gradual preparation of revolution and claimed that Russia, and the backward countries in general, were more ripe for the great social upheaval than the economically developed bourgeois Western countries.

[1] Cf. K. Marx and F. Engels, *Works* (Russian ed.), vol. xv, Moscow 1933, pp. 105–24.

This was the reason for the offensive tone of Engels's article 'Literature in Emigration': Tkachëv was ridiculed in it as 'a green school-boy' and the Russian revolutionary émigrés were described as 'a group of half-baked students, who, uttering grandiloquent cant-phrases, swell up like frogs and devour one another'.[1]

Tkachëv replied to this article in his famous *Open Letter to Engels* (1874)[2] in which he accused Engels of giving up revolutionary ways and advocating only legal action. Engels, in his turn, polemized with Tkachëv in the next article of the cycle *Literature in Emigration* and in a separate paper entitled *On Social Relations in Russia*. We shall return to Engels's views in the last chapter of this book; in the present context it seems sufficient to state that of the two major accusations, which Tkachëv had levelled against Engels in his *Open Letter*, the first—rejection of illegal forms of struggle— was based, to some extent, upon misunderstanding, but the second—disbelief in Russia's preparedness for socialist revolution—reflected an essential difference of outlook. Contrary to the opinion of Bakunin, Engels was never an apologist of legalism and did not intend to advise the Russian revolutionary movement to reject conspiracy, i.e. to liquidate itself. The difference of opinion on the second question derived, however, from a serious and fundamental theoretical disagreement. For Tkachëv the weakness or, as he put it, the non-existence of the Russian bourgeoisie was an important argument *for* the feasibility of a socialist revolution in Russia: it meant for him that Russian capitalism, being still very weak and artificial, was easy to eradicate, and that the Russian Government, in its struggle against revolutionaries, lacked the support of an important social force which, in Western Europe, became the most powerful antagonist of socialism. Engels thought, of course, that the reverse was true. The necessary condition of socialism is the high level of

---

[1] K. Marx and F. Engels, *Works* (Russian ed.), vol. xv, Moscow 1933, p. 235.
[2] Cf. Tkachëv, *Izbrannye sochineniya*, vol. iii, pp. 88–98.

economic development, being a result of capitalist industrialization.

The Bourgeoisie [wrote Engels] is just as necessary a precondition of the socialist revolution as the proletariat itself. Hence a
man who will say that this revolution can be more easily carried
out in a country, because, *although* it has no proletariat, it has no
bourgeoisie *either*, only proves that he has still to learn the ABC of
socialism.[1]

It could not be denied that this opinion perfectly harmonized with the Preface to the First German Edition of
Capital. The evolution of every economic formation is a
process of natural history, objective and independent of
human will: a society 'can neither clear by bold leaps, nor
remove by legal enactments, the obstacles offered by the
successive phases of its normal development'.[2] The laws of
social development are pushing their way with 'iron necessity', and the underdeveloped countries have to pass through
the same phases of economic development which the developed ones have already completed: 'The country that is
more developed industrially only shows, to the less developed,
the image of its own future.'[3]

For the Russian Populists these generalizations were, indeed, a hard nut to crack. An application of this theoretical
standpoint to Russia led Russian socialists to a dramatic
dilemma, formulated with the greatest force in Mikhaĭlovskiĭ's
article 'Karl Marx before the Tribunal of Mr. Zhukovskiĭ'
(1877). To the Western socialists—argues Mikhaĭlovskiĭ—
the Marxian theory of social development gives a scientific
explanation of the past and a stock of arguments for the
necessity and desirability of socialism; its espousal does not
entail for them a moral split, a divorce between their ideal
and their diagnosis of the existing social reality. A Russian
socialist, espousing the Marxian theory, would find himself

[1] K. Marx and F. Engels, *Selected Works*, London 1950, vol. ii, pp. 46–7.
[2] K. Marx, *Capital*, quoted ed., p. 10.
[3] Ibid., p. 9.

in a different situation: he would be forced to agree that the pre-conditions of socialism are, as yet, non-existent in his country and that the image of the immediate future for Russia is to be found in Marx's description of the development of capitalism in England. Moreover, Marxian historical determinism would force him to accept all the consequences of capitalist progress in spite of the full knowledge of how much harm and pain they would bring to the people.

All this 'maiming of women and children' we have still before us, and, from the point of view of Marx's historical theory, we should not protest against them because it would mean acting to our own detriment; on the contrary, we should welcome them as the steep but necessary steps to the temple of happiness. It would be, indeed, very difficult to bear this inner contradiction, this conflict between theory and values which in many concrete situations would inevitably tear the soul of a Russian disciple of Marx. He must reduce himself to the role of an onlooker, who, with the dispassionate equanimity of a Pimen, writes in the annals of the two-edged progress. He cannot, however, take an active part in this process. He is morally unable to push forward the wicked side of the process and, on the other hand, he believes that activity motivated by his moral feelings would only contribute to make the whole process longer and slower. His ideal, if he is really a disciple of Marx, consists, among other things, in making property inseparable from labour, so that the land, tools and all the means of production belong to the workers. On the other hand, if he really shares Marx's historico-philosophical views, he should be pleased to see the producers being divorced from the means of production, he should treat this divorce as the first phase of the inevitable and, in the final result, beneficial process. He must, in a word, accept the overthrow of the principles inherent in his ideal. This collision between moral feeling and historical inevitability should be resolved, of course, in favour of the latter.[1]

This reasoning was, perhaps, not merely hypothetical: it is quite possible that Mikhaĭlovskiĭ had in mind particular

---

[1] Mikhaĭlovskiĭ, *Polnoe sobranie sochineniĭ*, 4th ed., vol. iv, Spb. 1909, pp. 167–73. Pimen is a character in Pushkin's *Boris Godunov*, a monk and chronicler.

Russian 'disciples of Marx'. Probably they could be found among the later 'Lavrovists', who, having accepted Marx's theory of successive phases of social development, interpreted it in fatalistic terms and so doomed themselves to be passive observers of the allegedly 'objective' and unalterable process. An extreme case of such a 'philosophy of inactivity' was a certain Nasilov, described in the memoirs of Iv. Popov, who was in contact with him in the years 1877–8. This man, considering himself a 'disciple of Marx', deduced from Marxism that events should be left to 'ripen' and that it was equally impossible both to accelerate and to delay their due course. 'Having confirmed himself in this conviction Nasilov relaxed; he talked with friends, played chess and "outlined plans", awaiting the moment when "the event would be ripe".'[1]

Koz'min rightly remarked: 'One must have a fishy temperament, indeed, to feel contented with such a solution.'[2] The revolutionaries from 'Land and Freedom' could not accept it, but this non-acceptance never amounted to outright rejection of Marxism. All of them felt a deep respect for Marx and were deeply troubled when his authority began to be invoked by Russian liberals in support of the thesis that Russia was not ripe, as yet, for socialist transformation. They tried to interpret Marx in their own way and to learn from him as much as possible; thus, for instance, in an anonymous article in their illegal journal they accepted the sociological analysis of the situation in Russia given in Engels's polemic against Tkachëv. But they persisted in considering socialism to be a product of misery and exploitation, and not the corollary of a high level of economic development.[3]

Another solution of the problem was presented by George Plekhanov who was by then the leading theoretician of Populist orthodoxy. His article 'The Law of the Economic

---

[1] I. I. Popov, *Minuvshee i perezhitoe*, Leningrad 1924, i, pp. 42–3. Cf. Koz'min, *Iz istorii revolyutsionnoi mysli v Rossii*, pp. 381–2.

[2] Koz'min, op. cit., p. 382.

[3] See Venturi, op. cit., pp. 622–3.

Development of Society and the Tasks of Socialism in Russia' (1879) is of crucial importance for the proper understanding of both his Populism and his Marxism.

It was very characteristic and significant that Plekhanov began this article with a sally against the followers of Tkachëv and their idea of a 'seizure of power': he remained until the end of his life an intransigent enemy of 'Blanquism' and his rejection of a 'seizure of power' was an important link between his Populist and Marxist period. Equally meaningful was the fact that already then, as an ideologist of 'orthodox' Populism, he tried to criticize 'Blanquism' from the position of the historical determinism of Marx. The time has passed when one could think that in order to change a social structure it suffices 'to make a plot, to seize the state power and, after that, to rain on the heads of the people a number of benevolent decrees'.[1] Such a view was but a reflection of the *theological* phase in the development of social theory; today, however, social science has already entered a new, *positive* phase, represented in the theory of socialism by Marx and Engels. (Together with them young Plekhanov named also Rodbertus and Dühring.) The author of *Capital* had demonstrated that social forms were determined by economic development and that social life was governed by laws which cannot be changed at one's pleasure. But was it necessary to draw from this the conclusion that a struggle for socialism in a backward country, like Russia, was something absurd and doomed to failure? Plekhanov attempted to prove that it was not so, that the socialist tasks of 'Land and Freedom' were in accord with the law of the economic development of society. The laws of development, he argues, are not the same everywhere; history 'is not a uniform nor a mechanical process', 'Marx himself is not a man who would be willing to stretch the whole human race on a Procrustean bed of "universal laws"'. 'To be more precise, we should say that the universal laws of social dynamic do exist but, being inter-

---

[1] Plekhanov, *Sochineniya*, 2nd ed., vol. i, Moscow–Petrograd, p. 56.

related and appearing in different combinations in different societies, they lead sometimes to very different final results. They are like the laws of gravitation which, although always the same everywhere, may result, in one case, in the elliptic orbit of a planet or, in another case, in the parabolic orbit of a comet.'[1]

In evolving his theory Plekhanov, probably without being aware of it, repeated the main idea of Tkachëv: a direct transition to socialism, he claimed, was possible in Russia because she was a country which still had not embarked on the path of capitalist development. According to Marx, 'when a society has got upon the right track of the natural laws of its movement' it can 'neither skip the natural phases of its development nor remove them by legal enactments';[2] Russia, however (argued Plekhanov) had not got, as yet, upon this fatal track. Western Europe developed along the capitalist path because the Western peasant commune had disintegrated in the struggle with feudalism; in Russia, however, the commune had been preserved relatively intact. In the West the objective basis of socialism was provided by the capitalist 'socialization of labour'; in Russia it was provided by the collective possession of land. The socialization of labour in Russia (i.e. transition to the collective cultivation of land) may be brought about without divorcing the producers from the means of production, as a simple corollary of technological progress. The Russian people (at this point the ideas of Plekhanov and Tkachëv begin to diverge)[3] will spontaneously organize the whole of social life upon socialist principles, provided that the external obstacles, created by the constant intervention and the demoralizing influence of the State, are removed. Even if the Government succeeded in destroying the commune, the collectivist ideals and habits of the people would be very slow to change. Therefore the programme of 'Land and

---

[1] Ibid., p. 62. [2] Ibid., p. 59.
[3] Tkachëv, as we know, did not believe in 'spontaneity'.

Freedom' has still a strong base in social reality and does not need any corrections.

There was a weak point in Plekhanov's argumentation: an evident mistake in the interpretation and translation of the phrase quoted from Marx. Properly translated and without abridgement it runs as follows:

> . . . even when a society has got upon the right track for the discovery of the natural laws of its movement—and it is the ultimate aim of this work, to lay bare the economic law of motion of modern society—it can neither clear by bold leaps nor remove by legal enactments, the obstacles offered by the successive phases of its normal development.[1]

It is obvious that 'to get upon the *right track for the discovery of the natural laws*' and 'to get upon the *right track of the natural laws*' (in the sense of entering within the orbit of the operation of these laws) is not the same thing. The correct meaning of the above quotation from *Capital* is that *even the discovery and scientific explanation* of the laws of economic development of a given society does not make it possible to skip the natural phases of this development or to remove them by legal enactments. Plekhanov's interpretation of it was based, therefore, on a simple misunderstanding.

Let us, however, waive this point. More important is the inner logic in Plekhanov's reasoning. There is a hidden pessimism in it: what will happen if Russia gets finally upon the fatal track of the same economic law which governs today the capitalist societies of the West? Tkachëv thought about it in terms of force: who would prove stronger— the spontaneous capitalist tendencies or the conscious and disciplined revolutionary vanguard. For Plekhanov, who rejected 'Blanquism' and disapproved of the very idea of opposing the 'natural' laws, it was a much more difficult problem; the recognition that capitalism was in Russia, like elsewhere, a 'natural' tendency of social development inevitably brought him to a complete break with Populism.

[1] K. Marx, *Capital*, cited ed., p. 10.

It was a peculiar historical paradox: Plekhanov's break with Populism as such was determined by his most 'orthodox' position within the Populist movement. It might be said that he became a Social Democrat because he wished to remain true to the old programme of 'Land and Freedom', which proclaimed: 'Revolutions are made by the masses and prepared by history.'[1]

Plekhanov's way to Marxism was, however, not the only one. In the eighties there existed in Russia—in Petersburg, Kiev, Nizhniï Novgorod, Kazan', and in the other towns on the Volga—a large number of revolutionary circles whose members gradually evolved towards Marxism, very often combining the economic theories of Marx with a cult of the heroic 'Will of the People' and with some elements of 'Blanquism'.[2] An interesting and revealing example of this transitional intellectual formation was Alexander Ul'yanov (1866–87), the older brother of Lenin. He should not be overlooked even in a sketchy review of the Populist adaptations of Marxism.

Ul'yanov was a Populist only in the broadest sense of this word. He considered himself a continuator of the 'Will of the People' but in his *Program of the Terrorist Faction of the Party 'Will of the People'*[3] he dropped the traditional denomination 'Socialists-Populists', calling his followers simply 'socialists'. In his views there was nothing of backward-looking utopianism; the main revolutionary force he saw not in the peasantry but in the working class of the cities, socialism was for him 'a necessary result of capitalist production and of the capitalist class structure'.[4] This, however, he thought, did not exclude 'the possibility of another, more

---

[1] Programme of the journal *Land and Freedom* (written by S. Stepniak-Kravchinskiï). Cf. Karataev, op. cit., p. 322.

[2] Cf. S. V. Utechin, 'The "Preparatory" Trend in the Russian Revolutionary Movement in the 1880's', *Soviet Affairs*, ed. by D. Footman, London 1962, no. 3. See also Y. Z. Polevoï, *Zarozhdenie marksizma v Rossii*, Moscow 1959.

[3] Reprinted in Karataev, op. cit., pp. 631–6.

[4] Ibid., p. 631.

direct transition to socialism, provided that there are special, favourable conditions in the habits of the people and in the character of the intelligentsia and of the government'.[1] The law of economic development through capitalism to socialism was, in his interpretation, not universal but conditional: 'It expresses a historical necessity governing the process of transition to socialism *if* this process is left to develop spontaneously, *if* there is no conscious intervention on the part of a social group.'[1]

To understand the peculiar quality of Ul'yanov's attempt to combine Populism with Marxism we must dwell upon the fact that he had translated an early paper by Marx entitled *Contribution towards the Critique of the Hegelian Philosophy of Law*. This translation was published in Switzerland with an interesting preface by Lavr ov.[2] Criticism of religion, the main content of Marx's paper, was, for Ul'yanov, of secondary importance; he was interested mainly in Marx's thoughts on the possibility of telescoping the historical development of a country by passing through some phases of this development on the ideological plane. According to the young Marx, the political development of Germany got ahead of its historical development, because Germany had experienced *in thought* everything that France had experienced in reality: that was why there existed for Germany the possibility of launching a proletarian revolution although it had not passed through the phase of bourgeois revolution. Ul'yanov quite rightly saw in this an important argument for the thesis that the countries which were historically backward but ideologically developed could skip or telescope some phases of their 'natural' development. A member of the Petersburg group of the resuscitated 'Will of the People', B. Kol'tsov, wrote about it as follows:

We talked very often about this paper of Marx and Ul'yanov always argued that the idea of Germany having experienced in

---

[1] Karataev, op. cit., p. 631.
[2] See Lavrov, *Filosofiya i sotsiologiya*, Moscow 1965, vol. ii, pp. 581–613.

thought everything which other countries have experienced in practice did not contradict the later views of Marx and could be applied also to Russia.... Later it sometimes happened to me to hear from other Social Democrats in Russia that they also had passed through this phase of interpretation of Marxism.[1]

The ideological development of Ul'yanov was cut short by his death—he was executed for his leading role in an attempt on the life of Alexander III (the so-called 'affair of the first March 1887'). 'The fate of his brother', wrote Lenin's wife, N. Krupskaya, 'undoubtedly profoundly influenced Vladimir Il'ich.'[2] The future leader of the Russian revolution was also deeply shocked by the cowardice of the liberals of Simbirsk, who, after the arrest of his brother, became standoffish and broke off relations with his family. According to Krupskaya 'this youthful experience undoubtedly did leave its imprint on Lenin's attitude towards the Liberals'.[3] We may add to this that suspiciousness and hate toward liberals from the very beginning sharply distinguished Lenin from Plekhanov. For the 'father of Russian Marxism' Social Democracy meant precisely a rapprochement and an alliance with the liberals in the common struggle for political freedom.

2. Plekhanov and the 'Rational Reality'

Let us return now to Plekhanov. As we have already noticed, it was not an accident that the most consistent theoretician of 'orthodox' Populism turned out to be the first to break with Populism and to acknowledge the necessity of the capitalist development of Russia. The revolutionaries from the 'Will of the People', having rejected the principle of action *through the people*, became, partially at least, converted to 'Blanquism', whereas Plekhanov, both in his Populist and his Marxist period, was always a stout

---

[1] Quoted in Polevoï, *Zarozhdenie marksizma v Rossii*, p. 315.
[2] N. K. Krupskaya, *Memories of Lenin*, London 1930, p. 5.
[3] Ibid., p. 4.

adversary of 'Blanquism'; his change-over to Social Democracy enabled him to save this 'practical tendency of the old
Populism'. In the preface to his first Marxist book, *Socialism
and the Political Struggle*, he wrote: 'A striving for work
among the people and for the people, a strong conviction that
"the emancipation of the workers should be accomplished by
the workers themselves"—this practical tendency of the old
Populism is no less dear to me than before.'[1] Later—in
the twentieth century—he formulated this idea even more
distinctly:

> ... in theory the Social Democrat has nothing in common with
> the Populist, but from the point of view of his practical activity
> he is much closer to Populism than it once seemed to us in the
> fever of debate. Both of them see all the chances of their success
> in the self-propelled activity of the masses; both are deeply con-
> vinced that their own work makes sense so long as it awakens the
> masses. In this respect a Populist has much more in common
> with a Social Democrat than, for instance, with a member of
> the 'Will of the People'.[2]

The meaning of Plekhanov's conversion to Social Democracy will be even more clear if we recall the current opinion
about the German Social Democracy among the Russian
revolutionaries of that time. A co-founder of the 'Emancipation of Labour Group', L. Deutsch, defined it as follows:
'In the whole civilized world the name "Social Democracy"
was associated then with the concrete, peaceful and parliamentary party whose activity was characterized by almost
complete avoidance of all kind of determined, revolutionary
methods of struggle.'[3] It was very characteristic that the
followers of Plekhanov did not wish to adopt this name:
'If we frankly call ourselves "Social Democrats"—they
argued—all revolutionary elements will become estranged

[1] Plekhanov, *Sochineniya*, vol. ii, p. 27.
[2] Ibid., vol. xxiv, p. 128.
[3] Quoted in V. Vagan'yan, *G. V. Plekhahov. Opÿt kharakteristiki sotsial'nopoliti-
cheskikh vozzreniĭ*, Moscow 1924, pp. 94–5.

from us from the very beginning of our activity.'[1] As for Plekhanov, he wished to adopt the label 'Social Democracy' just because it implied moderation: he aimed at working out a political programme which would be acceptable for liberals, a programme which 'frightening nobody with a distant red phantom' would call forth the sympathy 'of all, except the declared enemies of democracy'.[2]

This programme, presented and justified in *Socialism and Political Struggle*, consisted, to put it briefly, in an emphatic commitment to 'political struggle' combined with a resolute rejection of 'Blanquism'; the main method of struggle was to be agitation among the workers. The dictatorship of a revolutionary class—proclaimed Plekhanov, criticizing the 'Blanquist' tendencies among the members of the 'Will of the People'—differs as day from night from the dictatorship of a group of revolutionaries: 'no executive, administrative or any other committee is entitled to represent the working class *in history*'.[3] The great mission of the Russian working class is to carry to the end the Westernization of Russia, to finish the work of Peter the Great;[4] a seizure of power by revolutionary socialists would only hinder the realization of this end; it would be, indeed, a disaster which, in the final result would bring about a great historical regression. A high level of economic development and a high level of proletarian class consciousness are conditions *sine qua non* of true socialism. A political power trying to organize from above socialist production in a backward country would be forced 'to resort to the ideals of patriarchal and authoritative communism'; the only change would consist in replacement of the Peruvian 'sons of the sun' and their officials by a socialist caste. There was no doubt—Plekhanov added— 'that under such tutelage the people would not only not become educated for socialism but, on the contrary, would

[1] Ibid., p. 86.
[2] Plekhanov, *Sochineniya*, vol. ii, p. 83.
[3] Ibid., p. 166.
[4] Ibid., vol. iii, p. 78.

either lose all their capacity for further progress or retain this capacity at the cost of the re-emergence of the same economic inequality which the revolutionary government had attempted to liquidate'.[1]

To prevent such a result Russian revolutionaries should choose rather 'the long and difficult capitalist way'.[2] The future socialist revolution should be separated from political revolution (i.e. from the overthrow of Tsarist absolutism) by a period of time sufficiently long to enable the fullest capitalist development of the country and to educate the Russian proletariat in the 'political school' of legal activity in a law-observing parliamentary State. This period might be shorter than in the West because in Russia (due to the influence of the West) the socialist movement was organized very early, when Russian capitalism was still in its initial stage. Thanks to their early adoption of Marxism, Russian socialists had a chance of accelerating the development of proletarian class-consciousness among the Russian workers. (In contradistinction to the later 'economists' Plekhanov put strong emphasis on the awareness of the general, historical ends of the movement and rejected any subordination of revolutionary tactics to the demands of the 'immediate', 'trade-unionist' consciousness of the workers.) On the other hand, however, the period of capitalist development should not be *too short*: it is possible to shorten a 'natural' process, but every attempt to shorten it too much, or to replace a 'natural' process by an 'artificial' one, creates the danger of bringing about different and undesirable final results.[3]

In the milieu of revolutionary Populists Plekhanov's book was regarded as amounting in practice to a betrayal of socialism. This was certainly wrong, but not unintelligible.

---

[1] Plekhanov, *Sochinenya*, vol. iii, p. 81.   [2] Ibid., p. 325.

[3] See Plekhanov, *Izbrannÿe filosofskie proizvedeniya*, vol. iv, Moscow 1958, p. 140. Plekhanov referred to Chernÿshevskii's argument that although it is possible to shorten the process of drying cigars, the cigars which have been dried in such a way lose their taste.

The best expression of the reaction to Plekhanov's arguments among the survivors of the 'Will of the People' is to be found in the article 'What Should We Expect from Revolution?' (1884).[1] Its author was Lev Tikhomirov, the leading theoretician of the party and the future renegade. (He was to become not only a convinced enemy of the revolutionary movement but also a staunch supporter of autocracy.) The main line of his reasoning runs as follows: a man who proclaims the inevitability and progressiveness of capitalism is a strange socialist, indeed. According to his own theory the development of capitalism necessarily involves the greatest suffering for the masses but, nevertheless, he accepts these sufferings, comforting himself with the idea that they lead in the final result to a beneficial, although distant, end. To be consistent, such socialists should turn themselves into capitalists, because only capitalists are really able to push forward capitalist progress. It is impossible to raise Russian workers to the level of socialist class consciousness and, at the same time, to prevent them from frightening bourgeois liberals with the 'red phantom'; a socialist trying to do this would resemble a missionary trying to persuade savages that slavery was a necessary stage of historical progress and that, therefore, it would be beneficial for them to become slaves. The real source of Plekhanov's theory is the widespread Russian habit of having one's eyes fixed upon the West and following the example of Western countries, despite the fact that their social history has been completely different from the Russian. As a matter of fact the development of capitalism in Russia is not necessary at all. Arguing for this view Tikhomirov combined some arguments of Tkachëv with the economic theory of Vorontsov. The Russian bourgeoisie—he asserted—is weak, devoid of any social prestige, unable to take over and to keep the state power. Russian capitalism is, indeed, very efficient in its cruel exploitation of the masses, but it cannot perform the great progressive mission of the

---

[1] *Vestnik Narodnoĭ Voli*, Geneva, no. 2, 1884.

'socialization of labour', which had been performed by capitalism in the West.

In Russia [concluded Tikhomirov] socialism is, indeed, an unavoidable necessity, because after the fall of our autocracy nobody else but the Russian working masses will necessarily come into power. . . . No, not by clinging to the bourgeois entrepreneur shall we get anything for our working class. We should not fight for a *bourgeois* constitution and, in general, not a constitution but the sovereignty of the people should be our aim.

The tragedy of a socialist who must accept the capitalist development of his country was, of course, fully realized by Plekhanov himself. This was one of the main reasons for the peculiarly 'necessitarian' quality of his Marxism, his emphatic acceptance of 'rational necessity', and his passionate attacks on 'moralism' and 'subjectivism'. It would be no exaggeration to state that 'necessity' is, indeed, the central category in Plekhanov's model of Marxism. In the writings of Plekhanov we can easily discern two lines of reasoning, based upon different theoretical assumptions. Sometimes he argued that the European capitalist development was *the best* possibility for his country, which implied, at least tacitly, that there existed also some other, worse possibilities, for instance, the possibility of a Peruvian authoritarian communism; at other times he flatly rejected any possibility of choice, claiming that his political programme was based upon the knowledge of the 'objective laws of development', that the validity of his prognosis could be proved 'with mathematical exactness' and that the realization of it was as sure as tomorrow's sunrise.[1] In his first Marxist works— *Socialism and the Political Struggle* and *Our Differences*—the first type of argument was paramount, later, however, the second type prevailed. Against the Populist 'subjective sociology' Plekhanov set his rigid 'objectivism', eliminating and ridiculing all attempts at thinking in terms of 'what

---

[1] Cf. Plekhanov, *Izbrann̄ye filosofskie proizvedeniya*, vol. ii, Moscow 1956, p. 621.

should be'. The scientific socialists—he proclaimed—are struggling for socialism not because it *should be*, but because it is the nearest stage in the magnificent and irresistible march of History.[1] 'The Social Democrat swims with the stream of history'[2] and the causes of historical development 'have nothing to do with human will and consciousness'.[3]

This shift of emphasis—from what is desirable to what is necessary—seems to us quite intelligible. At the beginning of Plekhanov's conversion to Marxism there was an act of choice, determined by his scale of values according to which 'natural' processes were considered better than artificial ones. This choice, however, was open to serious objections from the point of view of the revolutionary socialists. Realizing this, Plekhanov, naturally enough, tried to persuade both himself and his opponents that his choice was the only 'scientific' one, that, strictly speaking, he merely accepted the choice which had already been made by history itself and which could not be changed by any 'subjective' pro-tests. Being convinced that capitalist progress necessarily brought great suffering to the masses, he *had* to put the strongest emphasis on necessity; absolute necessity and a necessity, moreover, which could be believed to be 'rational', was, after all, the only justification for the acceptance of human sufferings. We may say that Plekhanov needed a theodicy and that he found it in the idea of a necessary and rational unfolding of history.

It seems, therefore, that it is not sufficient to explain Plekhanov's 'necessitarianism' by a simple reference to the prevailing spirit of scientific determinism and positivistic evolutionism of his days. Certainly, a positivistic and naturalistic tinge may be found in Plekhanov's Marxism—it was a common feature of the overwhelming majority of Marxist thinkers of that time. In the case of Plekhanov, how-ever—in contradistinction to the naturalistic evolutionism

[1] Ibid., vol. iv, pp. 113–14. [2] Ibid., vol. i, p. 392.
[3] Ibid., vol. iv, p. 86.

of a Kautsky—there was also some influence from Spinoza[1]
and, above all, from Hegel in whom he tried to find arguments against Populist 'subjectivism'. The 'necessity' to
which he appealed could not be a simple necessity of facts—
to adjust oneself to the mere facts would be nothing more than
simple opportunism. Therefore, it had to be conceived as
an ontological necessity, a necessity inherent in the rational
structure of the universe. It was, in a word, the rational
necessity of Spinoza, made dynamic and historical by Hegel
and reinterpreted scientifically by Marx. To become reconciled with such a necessity was, indeed, something inspiring
and lofty; it gave a powerful feeling of historical mission, and
a certainty of final victory.

Especially illuminating, from this point of view, are
Plekhanov's articles on Belinskiĭ. The most important of
them—'Belinskiĭ and the "Rational Reality"'—was written
in the nineties (1897) and referred directly to the controversy
between Russian Populists and Russian Marxists. It is,
therefore, worth while making a digression to examine
Plekhanov's own attitude towards the 'Rational Reality', as
expressed in his articles on Belinskiĭ.

The relevance of Belinskiĭ's philosophical development
to the controversy between Populists and Marxists was
discovered and set forth by N. Mikhaĭlovskiĭ. Polemizing
with Struve (in 1894),[2] whom he accused of an 'aggressive
contempt for the human individual', he drew a comparison
between Struve's Marxism and Belinskiĭ's Hegelianism of
the thirties. Towards the end of 1837 Belinskiĭ, under the
influence of Hegel's famous thesis 'What is real is rational,
what is rational is real', came to the conclusion that it was
necessary to become 'reconciled' with reality, to humble
himself before the Reason of History and to renounce for

[1] Plekhanov saw in Spinoza the greatest predecessor of Marxism. Cf.
Izbrannÿe filosofskie proizvedeniya, vol. ii, p. 360.
[2] See Mikhaĭlovskiĭ, 'O g. P. Struve i jego "Kriticheskikh zametkakh po
voprosu ob ėkonomicheskom razvitii Rossii"', *Polnoe sobranie sochineniĭ*, vol.
vii, Spb. 1909.

ever all 'moralism', 'subjectivism', and 'abstract heroism'.
Quoting some relevant utterances of Belinskiĭ, Mikhaĭlovskiĭ
suggested that there existed an analogy between Belinskiĭ's
'reconciliation' and Russian Marxism: in both cases the
conflict between personality and historical reality was resolved in favour of the latter, and the solution consisted in
the subordination of the individual to an allegedly rational
and beneficial necessity. Belinskiĭ, however, came at last
to himself, cursed his 'base reconciliation with base reality',
revolted against historiosophical theodicy, refusing to accept
its claim that human suffering might be justified. With deep
satisfaction Mikhaĭlovskiĭ quoted the following passage from
Belinskiĭ's letter to Botkin:

> You may laugh if you feel like it, but I still maintain that the
> fate of a subject, the fate of an individual is more important than
> the fate of the whole world and the health of the Chinese Emperor
> [i.e. Hegel's Allgemeinheit]. . . . I thank you humbly, Egor
> Fëdorich [Hegel], and I bow down to your philosophical night-
> cap; but with all due respect to your philosophical philistinism,
> I have the honour to inform you that even if I were to reach the
> highest possible level of development I should ask you for an
> account of all the victims of life and history, of chance, super-
> stition, Inquisitions, Philip II and so forth. Otherwise, I shall
> throw myself down from that highest level. I don't want hap-
> piness, even when it is offered free, if I am not certain about the
> fate of all my brothers, my own flesh and blood. To say that
> disharmony is essential to achieve harmony may sound practical
> and pleasant to music lovers but certainly not to people whose part
> in life happens to be to express by their own fate the idea of
> disharmony.[1]

Plekhanov's article 'Belinskiĭ and the "Rational Reality"'
was in a sense an answer to Mikhaĭlovskiĭ. In contrast to the
Populist publicist, Plekhanov was deeply fascinated not by
Belinskiĭ's 'revolt' against reality but just by his 'reconciliation' with it. In his interpretation the period of 'reconciliation' was a time of Belinskiĭ's most remarkable efforts to

---

[1] Belinskiĭ, *Polnoe sobranie sochineniĭ*, vol. xii, Moscow 1953, pp. 22–3.

overcome idealistic subjectivism, characteristic of Schiller, and 'abstract rationalism' of the Enlightenment; a time when the Russian intelligentsia, in the person of Belinskiĭ, discovered for the first time that ideals, in order to exert a real, positive influence, should have been anchored in social reality, should have reflected its inherent tendencies, and not only the noble but abstract daydreams of idealistic wishful-thinking. Belinskiĭ, according to Plekhanov, was then 'a sociological genius' who 'in the Hegelian doctrine of the rationality of everything real felt instinctively the only possible foundation of social science'.[1] His error consisted not in his general attitude towards reality but only in his too static understanding of it, in the identification of the dynamic 'Reason' of reality (i.e. progressive tendencies inherent in it) with the existing 'empirical' reality of Russia. His 'revolt' against Hegel did not remove this error; on the contrary, it was a return to utopianism, a 'theoretical original sin'.[2] It could not be justified theoretically, although it was fully justified as an outburst of suppressed passions. Plekhanov, however, was very fond of adding to this that Belinskiĭ himself had been aware that a subjective 'revolt' did not amount to a theoretical solution: after all, Belinskiĭ himself expressed the view that there was a sound thought in his 'reconciliation', a thought which needed only to be coupled with the dialectical idea of 'negation'.[3]

It seems very significant that Plekhanov put a strong

---

[1] Plekhanov, *Izbrannÿe filosofskie proizvedeniya*, vol. iv, pp. 542, 271.

[2] Ibid., vol. i, p. 458.

[3] See Belinskiĭ, op. cit., vol. xi, p. 576. In spite of its many advantages, Plekhanov's interpretation is guilty of a certain schematicism. Belinskiĭ's ideological drama was not that of a man unable to solve important *theoretical* problems. His private correspondence proves convincingly that his effort to 'reconcile' himself with 'reality' stemmed from his painful awareness of his personal alienation and 'abstractness'. Not until the 1840s did he start to ponder seriously on the paths of development which lay open to Russia. In the 'reconciliation' period he was mainly a 'superfluous man'; he felt himself to be a mere 'spectre' and tried at all costs to immerse himself in 'real life' and thus become a 'real man'. Cf. A. Walicki, 'Hegel, Feuerbach and the Russian "Philosophical Left"', *Annali dell'Istituto Giangiacomo Feltrinelli*, Anno Sesto, Milano 1963.

emphasis on the tragic aspect of Belinskiĭ's 'reconciliation'. He stresses with great force that 'mad Vissarion' personally never became truly 'reconciled' with 'base reality' of Nicholas's Russia, that his rejection of 'abstract ideals' was an act of self-denial, and not an act of conformity. Intelligent readers of Plekhanov's article were drawn, thus, to the conclusion that there existed a close analogy between Belinskiĭ's rejection of 'abstract heroism' and the Russian Marxists' rejection of the 'abstract ideal' of a 'direct transition to socialism'. In his unfinished *History of the Russian Social Thought* Plekhanov himself intended to draw a parallel between Belinskiĭ's 'reconciliation with reality' and Russian Marxism.[1]

There was yet one more reason why Belinskiĭ's name could be invoked by Plekhanov in his polemics against Russian Populism. Belinskiĭ was a convinced Westernizer and Plekhanov, as we know, inclined to treat Russian Marxism as the final stage in the development of Russian Westernism; the controversy between Populists and Marxists was in his eyes a continuation of the famous controversy between Slavophiles and Westernizers of the forties.[2] An important proof of the consistency of Belinskiĭ's Westernism, and, at the same time, a testimony to the fact that he never ceased to look for an *objective* basis of Russia's progress, was seen by Plekhanov in Belinskiĭ's attitude to Western capitalism. At the end of his life Belinskiĭ went abroad and, unlike Herzen (although not without hesitation), recognized the progressiveness of capitalism, concluding that 'the inner process of civil development will begin in Russia only after the Russian gentry has become transformed into a bourgeoisie'.[3] Plekhanov quoted these words many times, interpreting them as a correct prognosis of Russia's future and as an argument for Belinskiĭ's closeness to historical materialism.[4]

---

[1] Cf. Plekhanov, 'Obshchiĭ plan "Istorii russkoj obshchestvennoj mysli"', *Sochineniya*, vol. xx, p. xxviii.
[2] Cf. ibid., vol. x, p. 162; vol. xxiii, pp. 86–7; vol. xxiv, pp. 43–4.
[3] Belinskiĭ, op. cit., vol. xii, p. 468.
[4] Cf. Plekhanov, *Izbrannye filosofskie proizvedeniya*, vol. iv, pp. 495, 521.

Thus, in the interpretation of Plekhanov, Belinskiĭ was seen as a forerunner of Russian Marxism or rather, strictly speaking, of *Plekhanov's Marxism*. This assertion, however, was not equivalent to a denial of the Populists' share in Belinskiĭ's ideological heritage. According to Plekhanov, social conditions in Nicholas's Russia were not ripe enough for Belinskiĭ to overcome utopianism completely. That was why his heritage was dual, having both a strong and a weak side. Russian Marxists inherited and developed his best theoretical achievements, whereas the origin of the 'subjective sociology' of the Populists could be traced back to his 'theoretical fall'—to his moral revolt against Hegelianism. From this 'theoretical original sin' of the Russian intelligentsia Plekhanov, in later years, tried to derive the tactics of Lenin, accusing him of 'subjectivism' and 'Blanquism'. Even after the October revolution the 'father of Russian Marxism' persistently argued that the Bolsheviks should have learned from Belinskiĭ's fight against utopianism and warned them of the great danger of the 'abstract ideals'.[1] Equally characteristic was his desire to be buried in Petersburg next to the grave of his favourite Russian thinker.

Plekhanov's interpretation of the ideological development of Belinskiĭ throws light on the tragedy of Plekhanov himself. He was familiar with the Hegelian concept of the 'irony of History' but he never expected that he himself would be one of its victims; he firmly believed that his recognition of

[1] This is how he argued—in the revolutionary year 1918— for the necessity of passing through the 'capitalist phase':

'One of the creators of scientific socialism, F. Engels, once expressed a brilliant thought: without ancient slavery modern socialism would have been impossible. Let us reflect on this thought: it is tantamount to a relative justification of slavery, a justification within a certain historical epoch. Is it not a shameful betrayal of the ideal?

'Please, ease your mind: there is no betrayal at all. This is only a rejection of a utopian ideal, born in the vague sphere of abstraction and divorced from concrete conditions of *hic et nunc*. The rejection of such an ideal was Engels's merit and not his fault. An abstract ideal has too long hindered the development of the human mind. And it was not without reason that our Belinskiĭ deplored the period in which he found himself under its detrimental influence.' (Plekhanov, *God na rodine*, vol. ii, Paris 1921, p. 260.)

historical necessity would once and for all save him from utopianism, but his concept of 'rational necessity' turned out to be the very essence of his own utopia. It was, indeed, the utopia of a Russian Westernizer who wished for his country a 'normal', 'European' development, following the rational sequence of 'phases' and always perfectly harmonized with the 'inner', economic and cultural, growth. The ideal of a socialism being built in Russia *after* the final accomplishment of the process of Westernization, on the firm basis of a highly developed and democratic capitalism, proved to be no less 'abstract' than the ideals of the Russian Populists.

3. *Populism and the Russian Marxisms of the Nineties*

The controversy about Russian capitalism achieved its climax in the nineties, when Marxism became in Russia an influential current of thought and part and parcel of the Russian workers' movement. Only then, in the period of Witte's rapid transformation of Russia, the debate between Populists and Marxists focused the attention of the whole Russian intelligentsia on the problems of capitalist industrialization. A strong leaven was added to this debate by the emergence, in the early nineties, of so called 'legal Marxism'. After the publication of Struve's book *Critical Notes Concerning the Economic Development of Russia* (1894) 'legal Marxism' became a powerful stream of thought, having its own periodicals and its representatives among professors of universities and of other institutions of higher education (A. Skvortsov, A. Chuprov, M. Tugan-Baranovskiĭ, and others). Almost all of the many books which glorified the progressiveness of capitalist industrialization and argued for the dissolution of the peasant commune were written by the 'legal Marxists'.[1] For an average Russian intellectual (if he was not directly

[1] 'The most characteristic feature of the Russian bourgeois political economy of the 1890s was the "enthusiastic" attitude of many bourgeois economists towards Marxism, a phenomenon which never appeared in any other country.' (Pashkov, op. cit., pp. 77–8.)

connected with the revolutionary movement) Marxism began in Russia not with Plekhanov but with Struve.

'Legal Marxism' was, in essence, a Russian variant of the 'economic materialism', defined by Gramsci as a blend of bourgeois liberal political economy with the appropriately simplified and castrated Marxism.[1] Lenin, afterwards, defined it as follows:

> Struvism is not merely a Russian, but, as recent events clearly prove, an international striving on the part of the bourgeois theoreticians to kill Marxism with 'kindness', to crush it in their embraces, kill it with a feigned acceptance of 'all' the 'truly scientific' aspects and elements of Marxism *except* its 'agitational', 'demagogic', 'Blanquist-utopian' aspect.[2]

A forerunner of Struve was N. Ziber, professor of the University of Kiev, whose book *David Ricardo and Karl Marx* was highly appreciated by Marx himself.[3] It was published only in 1885 but its parts—the dissertation on Ricardo's theory of value and a cycle of articles entitled 'The Economic Theory of Marx'—had been published earlier, in the seventies, and had greatly contributed to the popularization of Marxism among the members of the 'Land and Freedom'. (It should be noted that they exerted some influence on young Plekhanov who quoted from them in his article 'The Law of the Economic Development of Society and the Tasks of Socialism in Russia'.)[4] Soviet scholars tend to evaluate Ziber much more positively than they estimate Struve, putting an emphasis on his pioneer's role in the propagating of Marxism in Russia. This may be right, but if we are considering the general typology of Russian Marxisms, it cannot be denied that it was Ziber, and nobody else, who initiated the liberal-economic interpretation of Marxism, an interpretation taken up later by the 'legal Marxists'. Marx, in the eyes of Ziber, was, above

---

[1] Cf. A. Gramsci, *The Modern Prince and Other Writings*, London, Lawrence and Wishart 1957, pp. 153–61.

[2] Lenin, *Collected Works*, vol. xxi, p. 222.

[3] In the afterword to the second German edition of *Capital*.

[4] For Ziber's influence on Plekhanov, see Vagan'yan, op. cit., p. 36.

all, a disciple and continuator of Ricardo. ' "Capital" ', wrote Ziber, 'is but a continuation and a development of the same principles upon which the doctrine of Smith and Ricardo has been built.'[1]

According to Ziber, the forms of social life are not to be chosen; they are the inevitable result of a natural development in which the conscious activity of men can play only the role of a midwife who may shorten the birth-pangs but should not interfere too much with the organic process of growth. The necessity of passing through the capitalist phase is implied by a universal law of economic development; it is possible to counteract some socially harmful results of capitalist industrialization (for instance, English factory legislation), but an attempt to liquidate capitalism before it has become ripe for liquidating itself would be equal to the absurd action of a man who grips his own hair and tries to lift himself up.[2] The economic development is evolutionary, its 'natural phases' cannot be skipped or artificially shortened; the institutional structure of the State is a mere reflection of its economy and always automatically adjusts itself to the economic basis of society. Ziber's belief in such an automatic progress was so firm that he did not hesitate to proclaim that even socialism would win its cause without revolution, at the very moment when it became economically justified. The inauguration of socialism will be officially declared by an international congress of economically developed states.[3]

It is obvious that a man like Ziber must have been an intransigent enemy of Populism. He not only proclaimed that the peasant commune was doomed to fall but he was bold enough to add to this that it was necessary for the development of the economy to expropriate and proletarianize the major part of the Russian peasantry. He said once: 'Nothing will come of the Russian peasant if he is not boiled in the

[1] N. I. Ziber, *Izbrannÿe ékonomicheskie proizvedeniya*, Moscow 1959, vol. i, p. 556.
[2] Ibid., vol. ii, p. 673.
[3] Cf. A. L. Reuel, op. cit., pp. 325–6.

industrial boiler.'[1] It is (he thought) a universal law of both industrial and agricultural development that the atomized, scattered production of small, independent producers must be replaced by centralized, capitalist production on a large scale. Aksel'rod was right when he confessed in a letter to Plekhanov that the theory of Ziber led Russian socialists to a sad conclusion: 'The fate of peasantry must be left to the spontaneous process of history and we, ourselves, should become liberals or simply sit down and fold our hands.'[2]

It is interesting to note that Struve set forth a different view: not that socialists should become liberals but that liberals, who wished to act effectively, should, at least for some time, turn themselves into Social Democrats. Thus, the future liberal leader bore witness to the political weakness of the Russian liberal movement.

Struve's *Critical Notes* contained a criticism of Populist doctrine and an apologetic treatment of Russia's capitalist industrialization. In opposition to the Populist 'subjective sociology' Struve proclaimed that in social processes the will of individuals counted for nothing. Our attitude towards capitalism should be, therefore, not 'ideological' but 'objective'; it should be the attitude of a scientist who demonstrates the necessity and inner regularities of a given process. The essence of Struve's book was properly expressed in its final conclusion: 'We must concede that we lack culture and go to the school of capitalism.'[3]

This phrase provoked, naturally, an outburst of indignation among the Populist intelligentsia. Even many Marxists felt themselves obliged to acknowledge that Struve's conclusion had been formulated rather awkwardly. In spite of that, however, for the vast majority of Marxists at that date, Struve, as the author of *Critical Notes*, became a recog-

[1] Quoted in N. K. Mikhaĭlovskiĭ, 'Literaturnȳe vospominaniya', *Polnoe sobranie sochineniĭ*, vol. vii, Spb. 1909, pp. 327–8.

[2] *Perepiska G. V. Plekhanova i P. B. Aksel'roda*, vol. ii, Moscow 1925, p. 197.

[3] P. Struve, *Kriticheskie zametki po voprosu ob ékonomicheskom razvitii Rossii*, Spb. 1894, p. 288.

nized authority. Because of his merits in the struggle against Populism even his open revisionism was viewed with indulgence. His reputation was so high that in 1898 it was he who was commissioned to write the *Manifesto* of the First Congress of Russian Social Democrats. This *Manifesto* (accepted by the Congress) presents a common platform which could be shared in the nineties by both revolutionary and 'legal' Marxists. Nothing was said in it about the hegemony of the proletariat, let alone the seizure of political power; the main task of the Russian working class was defined as the struggle for political freedom, since this struggle could not be waged effectively by the 'weak and cowardly' Russian bourgeoisie. Afterwards Struve confessed that already then political freedom had been for him much more important than the final end, i.e. socialism. He 'passionately loved freedom' and socialism as such never inspired any emotions in him, to say nothing of a passion: 'It was simply by the way of reasoning that I became an adept of socialism, having come to the conclusion that it was a historically inevitable result of the objective process of economic development.'[1]

It is significant and characteristic that already in his *Critical Notes* Struve anticipated some of the crucial ideas of Bernstein's revisionism. He rejected 'Zusammenbruchstheorie' and 'Verelendungstheorie'; although he recognized Marxism as 'the only scientific' theory of social development he stated boldly that as yet it did not have a proper philosophical foundation. No wonder that at the end of the nineties he was fully prepared to link himself up with the German revisionist movement. His paper *Die Marxsche Theorie der Sozialen Entwicklung* (1899)[2] was in some respects much more radical in the criticism of Marx than the theses of Bernstein. Struve accused Marx of being a 'utopianist' (the same charge, as we remember, had been levelled by him—in the name of

---

[1] Cf. P. Struve, 'My Contacts and Conflicts with Lenin', *Slavonic Review*, vol. xii, April 1934, p. 577.

[2] In *Archiv für soziale Gesetzgebung und Statistik*, vol. xiv, Berlin 1899.

Marx—against the Populists); social revolution was described by him as an essentially evolutionary process; in socialism he saw not so much a 'negation' of capitalism but, rather, an inevitable result of the development of capitalism itself.

The fact that Marxist revisionism appeared in Russia so early, earlier even than in Germany, seems to us intelligible and amenable to rational explanation. It was due to peculiar features of the ideological situation in Russia. Plekhanov wrote about it: 'The peculiarity of our history in recent years consisted in the fact that even the Europeanization of our bourgeoisie was being accomplished under the banner of Marxism.'[1] Struve himself expressed a similar thought when he stated that 'legal Marxism' was essentially a 'justification of capitalism' and, thus, that its part in the development of Russian thought could be compared to the part which had been played in the West by liberal political economy.[2] Indeed, 'legal Marxism' was the first pro-capitalist ideology which called forth a response and won a broad popularity among the Russian intelligentsia. It became popular because it was not an *openly* bourgeois ideology, because it seemed to stem from the socialist tradition; on the other hand, it was so deeply engaged in pushing forward the development of capitalism that, from the very beginning, it had to proclaim an appropriate revision of Marxism.

About 1900 the majority of the former 'legal Marxists' finally broke their connections with Russian Social Democracy. They joined the liberal leaders of the zemstro-assemblies, creating thus the nucleus of the future Constitutional Democratic Party. Struve himself became the leader of the right wing of this liberal movement. The diagnosis of the Populist writers, who from the very beginning had seen the 'legal Marxists' as advocates of the bourgeoisie, seemed thus to have proven its validity. For Plekhanov, however, it did not mean that his political alliance with Struve must be

---

[1] Plekhanov, *Sochineniya*, vol. xxiv, p. 181.
[2] Cf. Andreevich (E. Solov'ëv), *Opyt filosofii russkoĭ literaturў*, Spb. 1905, p. 495.

broken: after all, an alliance with the progressive, enlightened bourgeoisie was thought by him to be a pre-condition of bringing to an end the Westernization of Russia. However, let us return to the nineties. The emergence of 'legal Marxism' and its apologetic attitude towards the capitalist industrialization of Russia caused the Populist writers to launch an energetic campaign against Marxism. The leading part in this campaign was played by Mikhaĭlovskiĭ.[1] He attacked the philosophy of Marxism seeing in it an 'inverted Hegelianism', a search for a metaphysical 'essence', a simplifying, reductionist tendency to derive the whole complexity and richness of the world from one, absolutized 'principle of all principles'. Dialectics was in his eyes a kind of sophistry consisting of a peculiar combination of relativism with dogmatism; the concept of 'historical necessity' was treated by him as a mystification, stemming from an unjustified identification of the scientific explanation of historical facts in terms of their *causes* with the metaphysical explanation of them in terms of their alleged *purposes*.[2] It is wholly unjustified, he asserts, to believe that the possibilities which have been realized in history were the only ones or the most 'rational' ones. Naturally enough, Mikhaĭlovskiĭ was particularly indignant about the Marxists' claim to have embodied the Reason of History and understood its 'objective' laws. Engels's saying (quoted by Struve) that ancient slavery was a necessary stage of development because without it modern socialism would have been impossible[3] was, in Mikhaĭlovskiĭ's

---

[1] Cf. especially, the following articles of Mikhaĭlovskiĭ: 'Literaturnye vospominaniya', ix and xx; 'O narodnichestve g-na V. V.' (the ending); 'Iz pisem marksistov', *Russkoe bogatstvo*, January 1894; 'O g. P. Struve i ego "Kriticheskikh zametkakh po voprosu ob ékonomicheskom razvitii Rossii"' (all the above-mentioned articles are collected in the seventh volume of Mikhaĭlovskiĭ's *Polnoe sobranie sochinenii.*

[2] Neither Mikhaĭlovskiĭ nor his Marxist opponents realized that young Marx's criticism of Hegelianism was, in this respect, very similar to Mikhaĭlovskiĭ's criticism of Marxism. See K. Marx and F. Engels, *The German Ideology*, London 1965, pp. 39–64 (especially p. 59).

[3] See Engels, *Anti-Dühring. Herr Eugen Dühring's Revolution in Science*, Moscow 1954, pp. 250–1. Cf. p. 164, n. 7.

estimation, a perfect example of the presumptuous self-aggrandizement, so characteristic of Hegelianism. After all, Hegel also thought that the emergence of his own absolute philosophy was a sufficient justification of all the cruelties of history.

Even more sharp and violent were Mikhaïlovskiĭ's attacks on the Russian Marxists. They claim to have understood the importance of the 'economic factor' but, in actual fact, this has been understood much earlier by the Populists; the only innovation consisted in the conclusion that the 'economic factor' is an autocrat before whom human reason and moral will must bow down. Russian Marxists are very proud of their 'objectivism' but, in fact, they are so 'subjective', so self-centred, that they cannot even follow and understand properly the arguments of their opponents. Their attitude towards the writings of Marx and Engels recalls the attitude of fanatical Moslems towards their Koran (this charge was levelled mainly against Plekhanov); the attitude of rank-and-file Marxists towards their leaders is a living illustration of the theory of 'the hero and the crowd' so much ridiculed by them. They are proud of having liquidated the painful divorce between 'what is' and 'what should be'. No wonder: such a divorce cannot exist in an ideology of capitulation, and it is a real pleasure to ease one's conscience. The roots of Russian Marxism are to be found in the 'dead epoch' of the eighties—in the epoch of 'small deeds' and easy-going philistinism. Marxism, according to Mikhaïlovskiĭ, was invaluable to people who wished to adjust themselves to the ideological climate created by the victory of reaction: whoever was too lazy to think, could live peacefully, in the conviction that all problems had already found their solution in the Marxist doctrine; whoever did not wish to take the risk of action, could convince himself that even without his participation, everything, in due course, would be done by history; whoever was unable to raise himself up to the heights of the ideal could boldly ridicule naïve 'utopians' and take pride in his 'objective', and 'scientific' approach to social reality; whoever was indifferent to human sufferings could rationalize his attitude by saying that they were unavoidable and that the misery of today paved the way for the paradise of the future.[1]

Mikhaïlovskiĭ's bitter diatribes against the Russian Marxists were, thus, a direct continuation of Populist inquiry into the price of progress. To understand them properly we must not forget that the Populists excluded the possibility of a 'mild' capitalism, taking it for granted that capitalist industrialization was of necessity most painful for the masses, and that they were confirmed in this conviction by the Marxists themselves. We must remember that at that time not only Plekhanov and Russian 'legal Marxists' but also German Social Democrats treated peasants as a 'homogeneous reactionary mass' and were quite ready to sacrifice them on the altar of industrial progress: the Erfurt programme of German Social Democracy recognized the ruination of small, independent producers as a 'natural necessity' of economic development.[2] All these factors contributed to the emergence of a peculiar climate of opinion among the Russian Populist intelligentsia: every Russian Marxist was suspected of being an advocate of the expropriation of peasants, or even of furthering the interests of the rising

[1] Cf. Mikhaïlovskiĭ, *Polnoe sobranie sochinenii*, vol. vii, Spb. 1909, pp. 751–8.

[2] Cf. D. Mitrany, *Marx against the Peasant*, London 1952, part 1. It should be noted, however, that the attitude of the *First* International towards the peasants was much more acceptable to the Russian Populists. Thus, for instance, J. P. Becker's *Manifesto to Agricultural Workers*, published in the name of the German section of the International in 1869, suggested that the small agricultural producers could avoid ruin by uniting themselves in co-operatives and introducing communal ownership of the land. This 'manifesto' was translated into Russian by the members of the Russian section of the International and was read, inside Russia, by the members of Chaïkovskiĭ's circle (see B. S. Itenberg, *Pervyĭ Internatsional i revolyutsionnaya Rossiya*, Moscow 1964, pp. 56–9).

We may add to this that Engels as late as 1883 saw the solution of the German peasant question in the restoration and modernization of the ancient German *Mark*. See Engels's article 'The Mark', 1883 (K. Marx and F. Engels, *Works*, Russian ed., vol. xv, Moscow 1933). This article was published also as a separate pamphlet under the title: *The German Peasant: His Present, His Past and His Possible Future.*

bourgeoisie; every individual conversion to Marxism was treated as nothing less than a total betrayal of the progressive tradition of Russia.

The 'legal Marxists' who, as their later ideological positions clearly show, were really moving away from the traditions of Russian socialism, could react to this by shrugging their shoulders, but the *revolutionary* Marxists were, at the beginning at least, painfully sensitive to such accusations. A vivid illustration of this was the case of N. Fedoseev (1871–98), the founder of several Marxist circles in the Volga region. The members of these circles did not consider themselves to be the adversaries of Populism; on the contrary, they wished to continue and adapt to new conditions the still living traditions of revolutionary Populism and, also, the progressive heritage of the Populist thought. Fedoseev was, indeed, very far from thinking about a 'justification of capitalism', let alone proclaiming a necessity of the expropriation of the Russian peasantry; on the contrary, he thought that it was the first task of the Russian revolutionaries to give the peasants more land, at least to give them back the plots which had been taken away from them by the agrarian reform of 1861 and thus to *prevent* their expropriation. His letter to Mikhaïlovskiï—written in September 1893, that is at the very beginning of the latter's campaign against the Russian Marxists—is, from this point of view, a most interesting historical document. He stated that he felt himself personally injured and insulted by Mikhaïlovskiï's allegations and that he could not even understand them: after all, both Populists and Marxists speak in the name of the exploited masses, they both try to counteract the process of pauperization, to defend the peasants and, if possible to transform the rural proletariat into independent, proprietors of the land. He conceded that 'where there's smoke, there's fire', that he himself had heard about some Orenburg Marxists who had proclaimed that to help the starving peasants meant to put an obstacle in the way of

the capitalist development of Russia. A man like Mikhaĭlovskiĭ, however, should not have identified Russian
Marxism with the absurd views of naïve provincial students.[1]

Mikhaĭlovskiĭ's answer appeared in print, in the Populist
journal *The Wealth of Russia*.[2] The severe critic of the Russian
Marxists was pleased to hear that there existed in Russia
different kinds of Marxists and that some of them, like his
correspondent, felt themselves at one with the aspirations
of the suffering Russian peasantry. He added, however,
that, apparently, they were in the minority and that, unfortunately, it was quite different 'disciples of Marx' who
had called the tune.

Fedoseev, in his turn, answered Mikhaĭlovskiĭ in a letter
the size of a rather long article. Up to a point his tone was
conciliatory. He tried to convince Mikhaĭlovskiĭ that the
true Russian Marxists had nothing in common with the
bourgeois economists who, like Skvortsov, Chuprov, and
others, concealed their true essence under the cover of Marxist
language (Struve was not mentioned in this context because
it was before the publication of his *Critical Notes*). He went
even so far as to concede that his previous letter was written
in an inappropriate tone and that he was wrong in feeling
himself personally insulted by Mikhaĭlovskiĭ's views. But
Mikhaĭlovskiĭ, for his part, should have striven for a better
understanding of the new generation of revolutionary intellectuals. Fedoseev's letter was, indeed, a reproach and a
challenge:

Why have you written that we are 'trampling down the ideals
of our fathers'? It isn't so, and it can't be so! We would have been
cretins and moral monsters if we trampled down the ideals of
Belinskiĭ, Chernȳshevskiĭ, Dobrolyubov, Saltȳkov and N. K.
Mikhaĭlovskiĭ!... These names are dear to us as the most precious
treasure of Russian thought. But what should we do if the 'fathers'
either go back or stop dead in their tracks; if they don't like to
hear anything new, if they don't wish to understand the new life

[1] Cf. N. Fedoseev, *Stat'i i pis'ma*, Moscow 1958, pp. 96 ff.
[2] See Mikhaĭlovskiĭ, *Polnoe sobranie sochinenii*, vol. vii, Spb. 1909, pp. 728–33.

with its painful problems, if they only fulminate against those whose duty was to take a step forward in order to keep pace with the changing conditions of life.[1]

A kind of epilogue to this correspondence was provided by the tragic death of Fedoseev. In 1898, deported to forced labour, he committed suicide. One of the main reasons for his decision was moral depression caused by the fact that among his fellow sufferers there were some people who, because of his Marxist views, saw in him an advocate of the class interests of the bourgeoisie. Lenin, who had embarked on his revolutionary career in one of Fedoseev's circles, was deeply shocked by this tragedy.[2]

Mutual understanding and an alliance between Populists and Marxists were thus, indeed, very difficult to achieve. To some extent it was due to the fact that Populism was represented in the nineties almost exclusively by the 'legal Populists' among whom only Mikhaïlovskiĭ had some authority in the revolutionary milieu; Vorontsov, Danielson, and Yuzhakov had been widely discredited because of their attitude towards the autocracy. The ideological situation was such that, on one hand, the 'legal Marxists', like Struve, provoked the Populists into accusing all Marxists of being the 'agents of the bourgeoisie' whereas, on the other hand, the Populists themselves were compromised by people like Vorontsov, who, because of their attitude towards political freedom, had been given by Marxists the nickname of 'police Populists'. The situation greatly contributed, of course, to the polarization of ideological positions and forced the young Lenin to cut himself off from the Populist 'friends of the people'.

The sharpness of Lenin's criticism of the 'friends of the people' should not, however, obscure the fact that his attitude towards Populism was different not only from the position of Struve but also from that of Plekhanov. These

---

[1] Fedoseev, op. cit., p. 120.
[2] See B. Volin's Introduction to Fedoseev, op. cit., pp. 24–8.

differences come out clearly in his work entitled: *The Economic Content of Populism and the Criticism of it in Mr. Struve's Book* (1894–5).

At the very beginning of it we find a statement that Marxism has nothing in common with 'Hegelianism, "faith in the necessity of each country having to pass through the phase of capitalism" and much other nonsense'.[1] Russian Marxism

does not base itself on anything else than the facts of Russian history and reality; it is also [i.e. like Populism—A. W.] the ideology of the labouring class, only it gives a totally different explanation of the generally known facts of the growth and achievements of Russian capitalism, has quite a different understanding of the tasks that reality in this country places before the ideologists of the direct producers.[2]

Lenin did not hesitate to accuse Struve (in whom he still saw an ally) of putting too much stress on what distinguished Populists from Marxists and forgetting that both Populism and Marxism were ideologies of the labouring class.[3] He dissociated himself from Struve's 'narrow objectivism', an objectivism 'which is confined to proving the inevitability and necessity of the process and makes no effort to reveal at each specific stage of this process the form of class contradiction inherent in it';[4] he shrewdly remarked that 'when demonstrating the necessity for a given series of facts, the objectivist always runs the risk of becoming an apologist for these facts' and set against 'objectivism' the method of a 'materialist' who 'discloses the class contradictions and in so doing defines his standpoint'.[5] Capitalism was for Lenin (in contradistinction to both Struve and Plekhanov) not the social system of Russia's future, something which would develop and flourish only after the overthrow of the Russian autocracy, but the social system of Russia's present, 'something already and definitely established'.[6] The conclusion was

---

[1] Lenin, *Collected Works*, vol. i, p. 338.   [2] Ibid., p. 394.
[3] Ibid., p. 500.   [4] Ibid., p. 499.
[5] Ibid., p. 401.   [6] Ibid., p. 495.

obvious: if Russian capitalism was already ripe there was no need for an alliance between Social Democrats and liberals, so much desired by both Plekhanov and Struve. Populists were accused by Lenin not of being too anti-bourgeois but, on the contrary, of being insufficiently conscious of bourgeois tendencies in real life and clinging to bourgeois illusions. In the eighties Plekhanov tried to convince the Populists that they had been too prejudiced against the liberals; a decade later the young Lenin charged the Populists with laying excessive hopes on 'liberal society'. He rejected the apologetic tone of Struve's reasonings about the progressive significance of the destruction of small capital by rationalized, large-scale capitalist production.[1] Moreover, comparing Struve's views with the postulates of the 'legal Populists', who demanded such things as cheap credit for the small producers, technical help, and an organized outlet for their products and so on, he resolutely took the Populists' side.

The Populists [he wrote] *in this respect* understand and represent the interests of the small producers far more correctly, and the Marxists, while rejecting all the reactionary features of their programme, must not only accept the general democratic points, but carry them through more exactly, deeply and further.[2]

The peculiarity of Lenin's position in the debates of the nineties appears even more important if we relate it to some characteristic features of his later political biography: his deep concern with the agrarian question, his refusal to treat peasants as a 'reactionary mass' (an attitude so characteristic of the Mensheviks and of the II International as a whole)[3]

---

[1] Lenin, *Collected Works*, vol. i, p. 501.   [2] Ibid., p. 504.

[3] At the end of 1909 Lenin wrote as follows: 'While fighting Populism as a wrong doctrine of *socialism*, the Mensheviks, in a doctrinaire fashion, overlooked the historically real and progressive historical *content* of Populism as a theory of the mass *petty-bourgeois* struggle of democratic capitalism against liberal-landlord capitalism, of "American" capitalism against "Prussian" capitalism. Hence their monstrous, idiotic, renegade idea that the peasant *movement* is reactionary, that a Cadet is more progressive than a Trudovik.' (Ibid., vol. xvi, pp. 119–20.)

and, finally, his political tactics based upon an alliance not with the *Kadets* (as postulated by Plekhanov) but with the *Trudoviks*, not with the liberal bourgeoisie but with the democratic petit-bourgeoisie and peasantry. We may add that he was aware of this and that in 1912 he himself drew attention to the connection between Bolshevism and the attempt to extract from the Populist utopia its 'valuable democratic kernel'. 'Some day', he wrote, 'historians will study this effort systematically and trace its connection with what in the first decade of the twentieth century came to be called "Bolshevism".'[1]

4. *Marx and Engels in Confrontation with Russian Populism*

We have seen that the impact of Marxism was an important factor in the formation of the full-fledged Russian Populism; on the other hand, we have seen also that in the eighties and nineties Populism was a major frame of reference for the Russian Marxists and that this fact is of paramount importance for the understanding of the reception of Marxism in Russia. Now, let us reflect a while on Marx's and Engels's response to Populism.

The confrontation with Russian Populism raised for them an important theoretical question: was it possible for socialism to win in Russia before Russian capitalism had achieved the Western level of development? Was it possible for socialist revolution to win in a backward country before the victory of socialism in the most developed countries of the West?

Marx and Engels gave an answer to this question in 1882, in the preface to the Russian (Plekhanov's) translation of *The Communist Manifesto*. This pronouncement, widely and differently commented on in Russia, reads as follows:

Now the question is: can the Russian *obshchina* [peasant commune], though greatly undermined, yet a form of the primaeval

[1] Ibid., vol. xviii, p. 359.

common ownership of land, pass directly to the higher form of communist common ownership? Or on the contrary, must it first pass through the same process of dissolution such as constitutes the historical evolution of the West?

The only answer to that possible today is this: If the Russian Revolution becomes the signal for a proletarian revolution in the West, so that both complement each other, the present Russian common ownership of land may serve as the starting point for a communist development.[1]

Seen in the context of the controversy between Plekhanov and the revolutionary Populists from the 'Will of the People', this opinion of Marx and Engels looks rather equivocal, and seems to aim at a theoretical compromise. It does not contain any categorical statements, deduced from a universal 'law' of economic development. It admits the possibility that the capitalist development of Russia may be interrupted and that the existing peasant commune may become the starting-point of a communist development; this possibility, however, is made dependent upon the victory of socialist revolution in the industrially developed, capitalist countries of the West. It reaffirms the thesis that socialism has a better chance in the highly developed countries but at the same time it assumes that the economic development of backward countries may be essentially modified under the influence of international conditions; thus, it implies that the future of backward countries depends not only upon their own inner development but also, and even more, upon cultural contact with their economically developed neighbours.

The political motives of this caution in prognosis are evident: a loss of faith in the socialist potentialities of Russia would bring about a weakening of the energy of the Russian revolutionaries and from the point of view of Marx and Engels such an effect was indeed most undesirable. Since

---

[1] *Communist Manifesto: Socialist Landmark.* A New Appreciation written for the Labour Party by Harold J. Laski together with the original text and prefaces, London 1948, pp. 108–9.

1877 they had been convinced that Russia stood on the threshold of revolution and that this revolution would usher in a new revolutionary era in the whole of Europe. The founders of 'scientific socialism' were enthusiastic supporters of the 'Will of the People' and felt proud of their contacts with it;[1] Plekhanov's party 'Black Repartition' was treated by them ironically, as a party which while preaching the need to work *among the people* went abroad and shirked any real revolutionary activity.[2] Even Plekhanov's conversion to Marxism was, at first, met by Engels (Marx was not alive by then) with a certain reserve and distrust. Plekhanov's criticism of the 'Will of the People' seemed to him premature and too doctrinaire.[3] When Vera Zasulich, in the name of the 'Emancipation of Labour' group, asked Engels to express his opinion about Plekhanov's book *Our Differences* she received from him a rather disappointing answer. Formally Engels neither supported nor rejected Plekhanov's views saying that he knew 'too little about the actual situation in Russia'; by the same token, however, he implied that general theoretical assumptions were not a sufficient basis to give an answer to the 'cursed question' of 'what is to be done'. Moreover, he stated that in Russian conditions a Blanquist conspiracy might become a spark which would cause the genuine revolutionary explosion: 'if ever Blanquism . . . had a certain justification for its existence, that is certainly in Petersburg'.[4] He rejected also Plekhanov's apprehension of the 'seizure of power' by revolutionary socialists saying that even the most ardent revolutionary socialists would not be able to distort the normal development of Russia: post-revolutionary reality always differs from the subjective aims

---

[1] See, for instance, Engels's Letter to Lavrov of 10 April 1882 (*Perepiska K. Marksa i F. Engel'sa s russkimi politicheskimi deyatelyami*, p. 260).
[2] Cf. Vaganian, op. cit., p. 54; Polevoĭ, op. cit., p. 134.
[3] Cf. P. Aksel'rod, 'Gruppa "Osvobozhdenie truda"'. Letopisi marksizma', *Zapiski Instituta K. Marksa i F. Engel'sa*, vol. vi, Moscow–Leningrad 1928, p. 92.
[4] K. Marx and F. Engels, *Correspondence 1876–1895*, p. 437 (Engels to Zasulich, 23 April 1885).

of the revolutionaries and, one way or another, historical necessity always gains the upper hand. 'That is what Hegel calls the irony of history, an irony which few historic personalities escape.'[1] If the members of the 'Will of the People' could have read this letter they would certainly not have liked being treated as unconscious instruments of the ironical Reason of History; on the other hand, Engels's opinion that their 'Blanquism' had some justification and could not do any harm to the development of Russia undermined the central tenet of Plekhanov's political strategy.

Not everything in Engels's attitude can be explained by merely tactical considerations; his disinclination for destroying the illusion which had done so much to strengthen the energy of Russian revolutionaries accounts for it only partially. Russian Populism—a socialist movement in a backward, agrarian country—challenged him with a real problem to be solved: a problem connected with uneven economic development and with the impact on backward countries of capitalist civilization and socialist ideologies of the West.

The opinion expressed by Marx and Engels in their preface to the Russian edition of *The Communist Manifesto* had been formulated by Engels already in 1875, in his polemic against Tkachëv (*On Social Relations in Russia*). That the Western nations were much nearer to socialism than the Russians was for Engels a self-evident truth, a truth which only the utter ignorance of a Tkachëv could afford to doubt. Nevertheless, he conceded that the peasant commune in Russia might survive until the moment when it would be possible to transform it into a higher, communist form of agricultural unit. The realization of this possibility was made dependent by him upon the previous victory of proletarian revolution in the West; only the victory of socialism in the West would create for the Russian peasant the necessary material and political conditions for such a transformation.

---

[1] K. Marx and F. Engels, *Correspondence 1876–1895*, p. 438.

Thus, the Russians were not at all a 'chosen nation of socialism'. Without the help of the socialist West the Russian peasant commune would inevitably disintegrate from within, giving way to the usual capitalist development.

Later, however, Engels modified this view. In 1894, in an 'Afterword' to the re-edition of his article 'On Social Relations in Russia', he proclaimed that the possibility of the 'salvation' of the commune had been already cancelled by the development of Russian capitalism. Moreover, he suggested that this possibility was always rather doubtful, purely theoretical, and that he had indicated its existence mainly for tactical reasons. 'The faith in the miraculous force of the commune' had animated at that time the heroic terrorists whose determination and courage had shaken Russian Tsardom: 'We shall not condemn such men because they thought their people to be a chosen nation of the socialist revolution. But we are not obliged to share their illusions.'[1]

It should be stressed that this view of Engels was based not only on recent data concerning the development of Russian capitalism but also, and above all, upon a certain theoretical assumption: 'A society standing on a lower level of economic development cannot solve the tasks and conflicts which have emerged—and could emerge—only in societies representing a much higher phase of development. It is historically impossible.' It may be possible that the backward countries will find in the relics of the archaic forms of ownership and the corresponding habits of their peoples an effective means of shortening their path to socialism and avoiding many of the sufferings which have fallen to the lot of the Western European nations; this possibility, however, will emerge only after the victory of the socialist revolution in the West.

Only then, when the capitalist economy is overthrown in its fatherland and in the countries where it once flourished, when

[1] Cf. *Perepiska K. Marksa i F. Engel'sa s russkimi politicheskimi deyatelyami*, p. 296.

the backward countries have learned from this example 'how it is to be done', how it is possible to transform the productive forces of modern industry into public property and to make them serve the general interests of society;—only then, and not earlier, will it be possible for these backward countries to take such a short cut in their development. But, on the other hand, their success will be then guaranteed.[1]

An interesting commentary to this article of Engels is provided by his earlier correspondence with N. Danielson. It was an exchange between two men who saw the same facts in completely different perspectives: Danielson's position was that of a man deeply involved in what was going on in his country and anxious to counteract undesirable processes or to prevent them; Engels's standpoint was that of an onlooker who was not directly concerned and who treated the development of Russian capitalism in terms of a 'natural' and inevitable evolution of society. Danielson wished to receive from Engels a confirmation of the Populist belief that there existed in Russia a possibility of non-capitalist industrialization, i.e. of saving the Russian peasant from imminent expropriation and proletarianization; Engels, however, answered him that 'the peasant today appears to be doomed'[2] and that the Russian peasant commune would soon become but 'a dream of the past': 'No doubt a great chance is thus being lost, but against economic facts there is no help.'[3] We may add to this that Engels excluded any possibility of a 'mild' development of Russian capitalism, that the necessity of passing through the 'capitalist phase' was in his interpretation even less acceptable for the Russian Populists than in the interpretation of Struve, who tried at least to prove that the 'evil consequences' of modern capitalism could be softened or avoided in Russian conditions. Struve believed that the development of capitalism in Russia

---

[1] *Perepiska K. Marksa i F. Engel'sa s russkimi politicheskimi deyatelyami*, pp. 290–1.

[2] K. Marx and F. Engels, *Selected Correspondence*, Moscow 1956, p. 525 (Engels to Danielson, 15 March 1892).

[3] Ibid., p. 526.

might be similar to the development of capitalism in the United States; Engels rejected this view arguing that 'it stands to reason that the change, in Russia, must be far more violent, far more incisive, and accompanied by immensely greater sufferings than it can be in America'.[1] He insisted that his Populist correspondent must accept the inevitability of the 'fearful sufferings and convulsions', and reconcile himself with ineluctable destiny: 'Que les destinées s'accomplissent!'[2] The only consolation which he could offer to Danielson consisted in the conviction that the Russian nation would survive the crisis and that 'there is no great historical evil without a compensating historical progress';[2] it was, however, a poor consolation for somebody whose main concern was the fate of those who would fall victim to this general historical progress. 'History', wrote Engels in a letter to Danielson, 'is about the most cruel of all goddesses, and she leads her triumphal car over heaps of corpses, not only in war, but also in "peaceful" economic development.'[3] For Engels it was a theoretical explanation and, in a sense, justification of the cruelties which history had in store for the Russian peasantry; for Danielson (who quoted this statement in his book on Russian economic development)[4] it was a warning against the dangers of the spontaneous, uncontrolled processes of history.

Let us turn now to the utterances of Marx. In 1884 Engels gave to the 'Emancipation of Labour' group a letter of Marx to the editor of *Notes on the Fatherland*, written in 1877 in connection with Mikhaĭlovskiĭ's article 'Karl Marx before the tribunal of Mr. Zhukovskiĭ'[5] (Marx did not send it for fear that its publication would compromise the progressive Russian journal in the eyes of the Russian

[1] Ibid., p. 546 (Letter of 17 October 1893).
[2] Ibid., p. 547.
[3] K. Marx and F. Engels, *Correspondence 1846–1895* (London 1936), p. 510 (Letter of 24 February 1893).
[4] Cf. Nicolai-on [Danielson], *Ocherki*, p. xv (Karataev, op. cit., p. 484).
[5] See above, pp. 145–6.

authorities). Plekhanov's group refrained from publishing this letter; it appeared on the pages of the Populist *Messenger of the 'Will of the People'* (no. 5, Geneva 1886) and, soon after, was reprinted in a legal journal in Russia (*Juridical Messenger*, no. 10, 1888). The Populist writers (Mikhaĭlovskiĭ, Vorontsov, Krivenko) saw in it a proof that Marx himself had not shared the views of his Russian 'disciples' and immediately took advantage of it in their polemics with the Russian Marxists.

Marx pronounced in this letter his judgement on Mikhaĭlovskiĭ's conception of the tragedy of the Russian Marxist. He removed the cornerstone of this conception by stating that his *Capital* did not contain any universal theory of the development of history.

Mikhaĭlovskiĭ [wrote Marx] feels himself obliged to metamorphose my historical sketch of the genesis of capitalism in Western Europe into an historic-philosophic theory of the *marche générale* imposed by fate upon every people, whatever the historic circumstances in which it finds itself, in order that it may ultimately arrive at the form of economy which will ensure, together with the greatest expansion of the productive powers of social labour, the most complete development of man. But I beg his pardon. [He is both honouring and shaming me too much.][1]

The inner regularities of the process of accumulation, as described in *Capital*, apply exclusively to Western Europe and should not be extended mechanically to the other territories of the world, because '. . . events strikingly analogous but taking place in different historic surroundings lead to totally different results'.[2] Each form of evolution should be studied separately and then compared with the others. One will never arrive at scientific explanation of a concrete historical development 'by the universal passport of a general historico-philosophical theory, the supreme virtue of which consists in being super-historical'.[2]

---

[1] K. Marx and F. Engels, *Correspondence 1846–1895*, p. 354.
[2] Ibid., p. 355.

Consequently, Marx rejected Mikhaïlovskiï's suggestion that *Capital* implied a negative attitude towards the efforts of those Russians who tried to find for their country a path of development which would be different from, and better than, that of the West. Being 'not fond of leaving "something to be guessed"' he formulated his view as follows:

In order that I might be qualified to estimate the economic development in Russia today, I learnt Russian and then for many years studied the official publications and others bearing on this subject. I have arrived at this conclusion: If Russia continues to pursue the path she has followed since 1861, she will lose the finest chance ever offered by history to a nation, in order to undergo all the fatal vicissitudes of the capitalist regime.[1]

Naturally enough, the Populists interpreted these words as a confirmation of their belief that there existed in Russia a chance of escaping capitalist development. The eminent Populist writer, Gleb Uspenskiï, saw in Marx's letter a 'bitter reproach' directed against Russian society for its inability to utilize its 'finest chance'.[2] Lenin, polemizing with the Populists, asserted that in fact Marx had avoided giving a definite answer.[3] Plekhanov based his interpretation of Marx's letter upon the fact that Russia since 1877 had continued to pursue the capitalist path and therefore (according to Marx's formula) had now to undergo all the vicissitudes of capitalist development.[4]

[1] Ibid., p. 253.
[2] See Uspenskiï's article 'Gor'kiï uprëk' ['Bitter reproach'], in G. I. Uspenskiï, *Sobranie sochineniï*, vol. ix, Moscow 1957, pp. 166–73. The publication of this article (written at the end of 1888 for the journal *Volzhskiï vestnik*) was not permitted by censorship; in spite of this, however, it was not unknown since its text circulated widely among Russian writers and intellectuals who sympathized with Populism. It was first published by N. K. Piksanov in *Novyĭ mir*, no. 3, 1929.
[3] See Lenin, *Collected Works*, vol. i, p. 266.
[4] See Plekhanov, *Sochineniya*, vol. vii, pp. 263–4; vol. ii, p. 340. It should be noted that in his commentary to Marx's letter Plekhanov had to formulate his view much more cautiously than usual. In other contexts he referred not only to the empirical data on the economic development of Russia but also, and in the first place, to 'general sociological laws' and did not hesitate to state that our knowledge of these laws enables us to foresee 'with mathematical precision' the general direction of social development in the future.

Neither Lenin nor the Populists knew, however, that Plekhanov had in his hands a later document in which Marx's standpoint was still clearer and still more incongruous with Plekhanov's interpretation of Marxism. This was Marx's letter to Vera Zasulich (8 March 1881), found after the revolution in the archive of the 'Emancipation of Labour' group and published in 1924.[1] It was the answer to Zasulich's letter in which she had asked Marx whether it was true that the Russian peasant commune was doomed and that Russia, as the 'Russian Marxists' asserted (she had in mind some of the 'Lavrovists' at the end of the seventies), had no other choice than to pass through all the phases of capitalism.[2] Answering this 'cursed question' of Russian Populism Marx dissociated himself from the 'Russian Marxists' and repeated once more that his *Capital* did not contain a universal theory of economic development. His final conclusion read as follows:

Thus the analysis given in 'Capital' assigns no reason for or against the vitality of the rural community, but the special research into this subject which I conducted, the materials for which I obtained from original sources, has convinced me that this community is the mainspring of Russia's social regeneration, but in order that it might function as such one would first have to eliminate the deleterious influences which assail it from every

[1] It was published by B. Nikolaevskiĭ in *Iz arkhiva P. B. Aksel'roda*, Berlin 1924, and shortly afterwards by D. Ryazanov (*Arkhiv K. Marksa i F. Engels'a*, no. 1).

In 1881 Plekhanov and Zasulich were still Populists; they did not publish Marx's letter (after all, it was a private letter) because they knew that Marx intended to elaborate his views of the possibility of Russia's direct transition to socialism in a pamphlet specially devoted to this subject. Why, however, did they refrain from publishing it later, after Marx's death? Was it a deliberate attempt to conceal certain views of their teacher which did not harmonize with their own interpretation of his theories? Y. Z. Polevoĭ asserts that the publication of Marx's letter was simply unnecessary since his and Engels's views on the subject were expressed in their preface to the Russian edition of *The Communist Manifesto* (op. cit., p. 163, n. 91); this answer, however, does not seem convincing. Cf. the discussion between E. Yurevskiĭ and B. Nikolaevskiĭ in *Sotsyalisticheskij Vestnik*, New York–Paris 1957, nos. 4–5.

[2] See *Perepiska K. Marksa i F. Engel'sa s russkimi politicheskimi deyatelyami*, pp. 299–300.

quarter and then to ensure the conditions normal for spontaneous development.[1]

The task of 'eliminating the deleterious influences' from outside—i.e. the influences of the State, the capitalists, and the landlords—coincided with the tasks of the revolutionary Populists and the successful realization of this task *was not made dependent upon the previous victory of the socialist revolution in the West.* It was not a mere oversight. An additional testimony to this is presented by three drafts of Marx's letter which were found in his archive and which gave an elaborate argument for his general conclusion.[2] If the Russian Populists could have read these twenty pages of Marx they would no doubt have seen in them an invaluable, authoritative justification of their hopes. And—we must add—it would accord with the purpose of these drafts: Marx drafted them not only in connection with Zasulich's letter but also as the first sketch of the brochure which he intended to write at the request of the Executive Committee of the 'Will of the People'.

The reasoning of Marx bears much resemblance to Chernȳshevskiĭ's 'Criticism of Philosophical Prejudices against the Communal Ownership of the Land'—an article which had been carefully read by Marx and which, obviously, had exerted some influence on him.[3] Communism, argues Marx, is the revival in a higher form of the 'archaic property relationship', represented by the Russian peasant commune and, therefore, it might be possible for Russia—provided that the external conditions were favourable—to pass directly from rural communes to modern, large-scale communist production. Primitive communes are extremely hardy, and it is very probable that their decay was not invariably in the natural course of evolution, as bourgeois

[1] K. Marx and F. Engels, *Selected Correspondence*, Moscow 1956, p. 412.

[2] See K. Marx and F. Engels, *Works*, Russian ed., vol. xxviii, Moscow 1935, pp. 677–97.

[3] Cf. V. M. Shtein, *Ocherki razvitiya russkoĭ obshchestvenno-politicheskoĭ mȳsli*, Leningrad 1948, p. 236.

scholars claimed, but sometimes the result of pressure from outside. The Russian peasant commune represents the highest type of archaic collectivism, based not upon ties of blood but upon neighbourly relations, and this fact increases the chances of its progressive evolution. Russia is now in an extremely advantageous situation because Russian primitive communism has survived until the time when the economic, technical, and intellectual preconditions of modern communism have appeared in the West. Russia is neither an isolated country nor, like India, a country under foreign rule; she is connected with the international market and she can avail herself of modern technology and culture, assimilating the fruits of Western capitalism but rejecting its *modus operandi*. In such an exceptional situation there is no necessity of, and no need for, capitalist development. The advocates of Russian capitalism who proclaim the necessity of passing through all the successive phases of development should not forget that capitalist industrialization in Russia also skips some of its 'natural phases', by assimilating the ready-made results of industrial development in the West, such as modern technology, railways, and banking (the same argument had been used in Chernȳshevskiĭ's article). What Russian liberals call 'the natural disintegration of the peasant commune' is in fact the result of a deliberate policy of the State which exerts a heavy financial pressure on the commune in order to subsidize Russian capitalism at the cost of the Russian peasantry. (The same interpretation had been advanced by the Populists.) If the great revenues extracted by the Government from the enfranchised peasants, and used for the stimulation of Russian capitalism, had been utilized for the development of agriculture nobody would have talked about a 'natural disintegration' of the commune, everybody would have recognized in it an important element of Russia's superiority over the capitalist West.

Even from the purely economic point of view only the development of the commune can lead Russia's agriculture out of its blind alley; other means, such as, for instance, the English system of capitalist landholding, would surely prove unsuccessful. The English system is completely incapable of fulfilling the conditions on which the development of Russia's agriculture depends.[1]

The final conclusion was simple and unequivocal. The Russian peasant commune is not menaced by an abstract theory or by an alleged 'historical necessity'. Its real enemy is the Russian autocracy which artificially supports Russian capitalism. What really matters is not a theoretical problem to be solved but a concrete enemy to be destroyed. The Russian commune may be saved by the Russian revolution.[2]

The brochure on the peasant commune which Marx had promised to the Executive Committee of the 'Will of the People' remained unwritten. Was the illness of Marx the only reason for this? It seems rather that Marx himself was not quite sure whether he had thought over this problem to the end and preferred not to utter a premature judgement.

A deeper analysis of the three drafts of Marx's letter to Zasulich lies outside the scope of this study. Such an analysis would be possible only as an integral part of a larger study of Marx's views on primitive communism and of their evolution. It seems proper, however, to indicate in the present context that Marx's sympathetic interest in primitive communities was born rather late in his life and in connection with Russian problems. In the letter to Engels of 25 March 1868, Marx wrote:

Human history is like paleontology. Owing to a certain judicial blindness even the best intelligences absolutely fail to see the things which lie in front of their noses. Later, when the moment has arrived, we are surprised to find traces everywhere of what we failed to see. The first reaction against the French Revolution and the period of Enlightenment bound up with it was naturally to see everything as mediaeval and romantic. . . . The second

[1] K. Marx and F. Engels, *Works*, Russian ed., vol. xxvii, p. 684. One is tempted to note that this thesis of Marx was in fact a precise formulation of the basic assumption of the Populist economists.

[2] Ibid., p. 687.

reaction is to look beyond the Middle Ages into the primitive age of each nation, and that corresponds to the socialist tendency.[1] These words were written in connection with Maurer's books on the rural commune in Germany. Marx considered them to be 'exceptionally important'[1] and he saw their importance in the fact that, among other things, they had deprived the Russians of 'even the last traces of a claim to *originality*, even in this line'.[2] It seems to us that this statement of Marx is a sufficient proof that his interest in Maurer was stimulated to some extent by the early theories of Russian Populism, most probably by the 'Russian Socialism' of Herzen. Later, in turn, the scientific interest in archaic social and economic structures, so much intensified by the fascination which Morgan's *Ancient Society* exercised on his mind, enabled Marx to look afresh at the Russian Populism, which was by then the most significant attempt 'to find what is newest in what is oldest'.[3]

A brief comparison of Marx's views with those of Engels shows that their respective attitudes towards the 'Populist problem' were far from being identical. Engels was, on the whole, more pessimistic about the vistas of socialism in Russia. In contradistinction to the views of Marx (as expressed in the drafts of his letter to Zasulich) he was inclined to interpret the disintegration of the peasant commune in Russia as a 'natural' and inevitable process, and he never ceased to stress that socialist revolution must have won first in the West. He never put any emphasis on the idea that the

[1] K. Marx, *Pre-capitalist Economic Formations*, edited and with an Introduction by E. J. Hobsbawm, London 1964, p. 140.

[2] Ibid., p. 139.

[3] Ibid., p. 140. Hobsbawm correctly pointed out that 'so far as primitive communal society is concerned, Marx's and Engels's historic views were almost certainly transformed by the study of two authors: Georg von Maurer, who attempted to demonstrate the existence of communal property as a stage in German history, and above all Lewis Morgan, whose *Ancient Society* provided the basis of their analysis of primitive communalism' (ibid., p. 24). He has also mentioned the influence of Russian economic and sociological literature which Marx 'devoured' from 1873 onwards (ibid., p. 49). We should add to this that the influence, and the very existence, of Russian Populism were also instrumental in bringing about this 'transformation' in Marx's views on history.

peasant commune was an element of Russia's 'superiority' over the West; on the contrary, in some of his utterances the peasant commune was presented not so much as a mainspring of Russia's social regeneration but, rather, as a traditional foothold of Russian despotism.

We should realize, however, that these differences could be ascribed very often not so much to theoretical divergences but, rather, to immediate political reasons and to the influence of various historical events. Thus, for instance, Engels's polemic against Tkachëv reflected the atmosphere created by the affair of Nechaev and by the sharp conflict in the International between Marxists and Bakuninists; the drafts of Marx's letter to Zasulich reflected the exaggerated hopes which both Marx and Engels at the time placed on imminent revolution in Russia; the more cautious attitude adopted in their preface to the first Russian edition of *Communist Manifesto* may be interpreted as a reaction to the defeat of the 'Will of the People'; and, finally, Engels's correspondence with Danielson and his 'Afterword' to the article 'On Social Relations in Russia' is amenable to explanation by reference to the new perspectives opened by the rapid capitalist industrialization of both Germany and Russia. At the beginning of the eighties not only Marx but also Engels showed a great interest in 'archaic property'. In an article on the German Mark (1883) he advised the German peasants to revive in a new, higher form their old rural commune; such a revival, he thought, would enable the peasants to embark on a noncapitalist way towards modern, large-scale agricultural production.[1] A similar idea of '*grande industrie* being grafted on the peasant commune' was developed later by Danielson.[2] Engels, however, became in the nineties so sceptical about it that he inclined instead to think that 'the peasant today appears to be doomed'.[3] Thus, the relevant views of Marx

---

[1] Cf. K. Marx and F. Engels, *Works*, Russian ed., vol. xv, p. 645.

[2] Cf. Engels's polemic against this view in his letter to Danielson of 24 February 1893 (K. Marx and F. Engels, *Correspondence 1846–1895*, pp. 508–10).

[3] See above, p. 184, n. 2.

and Engels were not unchangeable and cannot be explained without reference to their historical and political context.

Nevertheless, the significance of these views cannot be reduced to their documentary value. Russian Populism set Marx and Engels a real theoretical, and not merely practical, problem, a problem whose importance was to be universally acknowledged only in the twentieth century, and Marx's drafts of his letters to Zasulich were certainly among the first serious attempts to cope with it. The possible role of the peasant commune as a mainspring of Russia's social regeneration was, no doubt, curiously exaggerated in them. It is, perhaps, strange to us, but understandable: it stemmed from nineteenth-century naturalism which, drawing a parallel between the development of society and organic growth, looked always for a 'natural' germ of evolution; it was, also, bound up with the belief in spontaneous development, shared then by liberals and the majority of socialists alike.[1] On the other hand, however, we find in these drafts of Marx many penetrating insights which undermined the nineteenth-century method of interpreting social change in terms of a lawful 'natural' process. We find in them, also, an interesting formulation of a set of new, important problems, such as the problem of an 'asynchronic' development, the peculiar 'privilege of backwardness', the role of cultural contact and demonstration effect in a telescoped, epitomized evolution, in a word, the problem of the non-capitalist way of overcoming economic and social backwardness. The fact that it was the Russian Populists who raised these problems and brought them to the attention of the author of *Capital* is, it seems to us, a sufficient justification for recognizing their ideas as one of the most interesting chapters in the history of nineteenth-century social thought.

[1] This belief in 'natural growth' was a feature which distinguished Marx from the revolutionaries of the 'Blanquist' type. Thus, the exaggerated hopes which Marx placed on the peasant commune were bound up with his attempt to find for Russia such a path to socialism which would be direct and, at the same time, 'natural'.

INDEX

PRINTED IN GREAT BRITAIN
AT THE UNIVERSITY PRESS, OXFORD
BY VIVIAN RIDLER
PRINTER TO THE UNIVERSITY